Penguin Books
The Boat People
An 'Age' Investigation

Bruce Grant, author, diplomat and international affairs writer, was born in Perth, Western Australia, in 1925. He was foreign correspondent in Europe, Asia and America (1954-65), Nieman Fellow at Harvard University (1958), Fellow in Political Science at Melbourne University (1965-68), columnist for the *Age* (1968-72) and Australian High Commissioner in India (1973-76). His publications include *Indonesia*, *The Crisis of Loyalty*, *The Security of South-East Asia*, fiction in leading journals such as the *New Yorker*, and a novel, *Cherry Bloom*, to be published in 1980.

The Boat People draws on the reports of foreign correspondents of the Australian newspaper, the *Age*, which undertook this special international investigation into the events behind the refugee crisis. The boat people's story pivoted on South-East Asia, where correspondent Michael Richardson has been following developments and filing authoritative reports for seven years. He travelled extensively throughout the region to interview, research and report for this book.

Contributors:
Creighton Burns (USA); Jennifer Byrne (Canada); John Slee (Japan); John Hoffman (China); Sunanda Datta-Ray (India); Dev Murarka (USSR); David Mitchell and David Young (New Zealand); Patrick Boyce (London); Christopher Mosey (Sweden); Robin Smyth (France); Colin Smith (USA); Rebecca Batties and Lindsay Murdoch (Australia).

The Boat People

An 'Age' investigation with Bruce Grant

Penguin Books

Penguin Books Ltd,
Harmondsworth, Middlesex, England
Penguin Books,
625 Madison Avenue, New York N.Y. 10022, U.S.A.
Penguin Books Australia Ltd,
487 Maroondah Highway
Ringwood, Victoria, Australia
Penguin Books Canada Ltd,
2801 John Street, Markham, Ontario, Canada
Penguin Books (N.Z.) Ltd,
182-190 Wairau Road, Auckland 10, New Zealand

First published 1979
Copyright © The *Age*, 1979

Made and printed in Australia at
The Dominion Press, Blackburn, Victoria
Set in Plantin by The Dova Type Shop, Melbourne

CIP

Grant, Bruce.
The boat people.

Index
ISBN 0 14 005531 2

1. Refugees — Indochina. I. Title.

361.53'0959

Contents

Preface

When the first wave of boat people sailed quietly over the horizon, out of Vietnam, few observers in the western world realized what those brave and mysterious voyages portended. Since then, as the refugees have been turning up in more or less reluctant host countries from Norway to Australia, it has become gradually apparent that the boat people are not merely another desperate swarm of 'displaced persons', but the victims and indicators of a profound regional instability. With the fall of Saigon in 1975, two centuries of western ascendancy in South-East Asia came abruptly to an end. Thereafter, old nationalisms and new ideologies asserted themselves. Now, the three superpowers – the United States, Russia and China – hover uncertainly on the South-East Asian periphery, their armed forces approaching each other more closely than anywhere else on earth. The boat people are a warning to the rest of us that the whole region, during the next phase of its history, is liable to become increasingly a source of unrest, anxiety, and war.

A newspaper can report the day-to-day manifestations of an international development on this scale, but in the nature of things cannot explore at length its causes and repercussions. When, therefore, Penguin Books approached the *Age* and asked us if we could produce, rapidly, a book that would investigate a phenomenon that, as every week went by, more and more plainly demanded an explanation, we very soon decided, though initially daunted, that we could do it. We asked Bruce Grant, with whom the *Age* has had a long association, if he, with his special Asian experience, would mastermind the book. In the *Age*'s South-East Asian correspondent, Michael Richardson, who had spent seven years in the region, we had a reporter who combined exceptional knowledge and extraordinary stamina; he has supplied the core of the book, and it could not have been written without him.

The other contributors were numerous and international. They included Creighton Burns from Washington, Jennifer Byrne from Canada, John Slee from Tokyo, John Hoffman from China, Sunanda Datta-Ray from India, Dev Murarka from the Soviet Union, David Mitchell and David Young from New Zealand, Patrick Boyce from London, Christopher Mosey from Sweden, and, in Australia, Rebecca Batties and Lindsay Murdoch. The *Age* foreign editor, Cameron Forbes, and assistant editor, Tom Duggan, were actively involved. The London *Observer* allowed two members of their staff to contribute: Robin Smyth sent a report from France, and Colin Smith sent an account of the fall of Saigon. Most of us learned a great deal about the subject as we went along. The book brings together a lot of material that was known but scattered, and a lot besides that was not known of the whole ominous story.

MICHAEL DAVIE
Editor
The *Age*
Melbourne, October 1979

Editorial note

All dollar amounts are in US dollars.

In the case of some refugees interviewed for this book, who believe there may be repercussions on their relatives, pseudonyms have been used.

Introduction

In the last four years, more than a million people are known to have
left the three countries of former Indo-China: Vietnam, Cambodia
and Laos. About half of these have been Vietnamese and, of them,
about half have been 'boat people'. This book is about the boat
people – not because they are more important than other refugees,
but because their dramatic story exemplifies the bitter moral and
political dilemmas posed by all refugees.

Like all refugees, the boat people are testing human reason and
conscience. This is especially so at a time of economic uncertainty
in the industrial democracies and frustration in the developing
world. We have become accustomed to people fleeing from one or
other of the horsemen of the apocalypse. What is ominous about the
boat people is that the forces of politics and history that propelled
them into the sea are not likely suddenly to recede because the flow
of refugees has been turned off. Their personal crisis reflects a
deeper crisis. Like the Balkans before the first world war and the
Middle East today, the Indo-Chinese states are involved with the
major powers in a contest for prestige, influence and mastery that
reverberates far beyond their region.

The twentieth century has been marked by revolution, persecution and war, and its temper shows no sign of moderating. A
recent official estimate is that there are now 13 million refugees in
the world, the highest number since the second world war. In 1945
most of the refugees were in Europe; today they are in Africa, the
Middle East, Latin America and Asia. Their numbers are expected
to increase. Half of them are children. In the case of the Indo-
Chinese refugees, all the traditional ingredients, including natural
disasters, are present, as well as one factor that makes their ordeal
particularly significant. The three major powers, the United States,
the Soviet Union and China, hover over Vietnam in a state of

unresolved rivalry and potential conflict. The story of the boat people cannot be told without taking into account the shifts of power and shaping of new forces in Asia which have followed the emergence of an independent united Vietnam.

A refugee is an unwanted person. He or she makes a claim upon the humanity of others without always having much, or even anything sometimes, to give in return. If, after resettlement, a refugee works hard or is lucky and successful, he may be accused of taking the work or the luck or success from someone else. If he fails or becomes resentful or unhappy, he is thought to be ungrateful and a burden on the community. A refugee is especially unwanted by officials: his papers are rarely in order, his health is often suspect; and sometimes, although he claims to be fleeing from persecution, he is simply trying to get from a poor, overpopulated country to a rich, underpopulated one. Yet it is also true that refugees have contributed richly to their adopted communities. Conspicuous examples are the Jews who left Nazi Germany, and the Huguenots who fled from France in the late seventeenth century to England, Holland, Germany, Switzerland and America.

The distinction between refugee and migrant is not always clear. The pilgrims who became famous as the founders of the colony of Massachusetts left England of their own free will in order to worship in their own way. Early Christians were sometimes exiled by Roman emperors and later recalled. The sack of Carthage produced a flood of refugees, both exiles and fugitives. The Mongol invasions displaced masses of people, while refugee movements caused by western imperialism tended to be, at least initially, local. A refugee is now defined by the 1951 United Nations convention relating to the status of refugees as a person who, owing to 'well-founded fear' of being persecuted for reasons of race, religion, nationality, membership of a particular social group or political opinion, is outside the country of his nationality or habitual residence and is unwilling to return. Even so precisely defined, the problem is as old as man.

The boat people have revived painful memories of the Jewish exodus from Germany. When international pressure was applied on Vietnam to stop the flow in 1979, polemicists used the Jewish refugee of the 1930s as an archetypal figure with which to attack Hanoi for expelling ethnic Chinese from Vietnam. The analogy between

Germany and Vietnam can be misleading, however. Vietnam is a small country and has a long history of conflict with its large neighbour China, whose attitude towards Chinese who live outside its borders has been historically ambiguous. China, now a nuclear power, remains a threat to Vietnam, and it is understandable, if not excusable, that the Vietnamese should both suspect the Chinese in their midst and use them as a political weapon against Peking. The attitude of Germany to the Jews had no such foundation.

The parallel does hold in some respects, however. Jews who left Germany in the early 1930s tended to be those with means or intellectual convictions and being few in number were relatively easy to absorb. This was also true of Vietnamese refugees between 1975 and the middle of 1977, with the exception of the 130 000 who left precipitately with the Americans after the fall of Saigon. These were a special group who in one way or another had come to depend on the American presence to such an extent that they could not remain without its protection; no such group of Jews or such a dramatic foreign presence existed in Germany.

The similarity between the later exodus of Jews and the flood of boat people, mainly ethnic Chinese, in 1978 and 1979 is close. The same kinds of objections were made to accepting both groups. It was said that the Jews/ethnic Chinese would provoke anti-semitism/anti-Chinese sentiment; that they had spies planted among them by the Nazis/Vietnamese; that they were technically German/Vietnamese nationals and therefore the responsibility of the German/Vietnamese government. (This attitude led to Jews being interned sometimes in the same camps as German Nazis.) Much of this, of course, was a veiled version of the same anti-semitism which, in more blatant form in Germany, had caused the exodus, just as the objections in South-East Asia to receiving more Chinese is a mild form of the racism in Vietnam.

Another bitter experience in recent times has been that of the Palestinians. About one million became refugees after the state of Israel was founded and their camps became centres of hopelessness and terrorism. The dispossessed Palestinian has now become entangled in Middle-East politics, increasing the instability of the region and creating a new scourge for the world.

The camps and holding centres of South-East Asia, if not cleared, offer the same danger. This became clear as the trickle of refugees became a flood in 1978 and 1979, not only from Vietnam, but also from Laos and Kampuchea. If the refugees could not be absorbed into neighbouring societies, and if countries beyond the region would not admit them, the camps, if they were not to become centres of discontent, would have to be emptied or at least held to manageable size by moving the boat people on.

Like the Jewish and Palestinian refugees – themselves, of course, tragically connected – the spectre of the boat people haunts us all, for several reasons.

For a start, there is Vietnam itself. It has been at the centre of international controversy almost continuously since the second world war. Of all the countries that have won independence from colonial rule (and the list now numbers over a hundred and stretches back for more than thirty years) Vietnam has had to fight the hardest and longest. Its suffering has been so great that the Vietnamese people have become heroic figures of history, even (perhaps especially) to their adversaries. On no other emerging country has so much diplomatic or military effort been expended. In particular, the war fought in Vietnam by the United States aroused deeper political and intellectual controversy than any since the Spanish civil war in the 1930s. Controversy over the politics of the American war in Vietnam has now been revived in a debate about the politics of the Vietnamese refugees, bringing to the forefront one of the eternal questions about refugees. Do their politics matter? Or is the only issue – whether they are black or white, communist or anti-communist, rich or poor – that of refuge?

The boat people also reflect and create problems of security and stability in their region and beyond. United States policy in Asia lost its certainty after the defeat in Vietnam. This was the first war in which the United States had been defeated and the consequences were not clear, least of all to the Americans themselves. So the uneasy equilibrium of power in Asia between the United States, the Soviet Union and China has not yet resolved itself into a stable system. The Soviet Union's close ties with Vietnam and China's conflict with Vietnam and with the Soviet Union bring out this instability, which, in turn, has exposed political, economic and racial sensitivities in South-East Asia. The non-communist states of

Thailand, Malaysia, Singapore, Indonesia and the Philippines are alarmed by Vietnam's potential as a regional power. Although it is a poor country, it has bigger armed forces than all of them combined; it is nationalistic, ideologically combative and has given notice that it intends to be dominant on the mainland of South-East Asia.

The economies of these states cannot easily absorb large numbers of refugees. When the refugees are ethnic Chinese, an internal racial balance could also be upset. Some leaders have gone so far as to accuse Vietnam of deliberately trying to 'destabilize' South-East Asia by flooding it with refugees. South-East Asia is an international waterway, through which pass the ships of the world's trading nations and the warships of several powers, including those of the United States and the Soviet Union. The region's stability is sensitive to and cannot be isolated from the political forces of the wider world. The disorderly armada of boat people has also revived fears that the waters of the archipelago will become the haunt of pirates and smugglers, harassing shipping and trading illegally between the many islands and remote communities.

The boat people phenomenon reflects, in its most drastic form, the pathos of people fleeing for one reason or another from their country. They are not moving discreetly from one side of a border to the other, waiting to return when conditions become normal or more to their liking. They are leaving without knowing where they are going, without prospect of return, and at the risk of drowning or dying of illness or deprivation at sea. They have little idea what their destiny might be. Whether they leave of their own initiative or as victims of historical events or of the harsh politics of discrimination, they are cutting ties with the land and people of their birth. In the case of an ethnic minority like the Chinese this act may not be as shattering as in the case of refugees fleeing not only from a nation-state but from homeland and people as well. Even so, it is one of the most fateful decisions a human being can take or be forced to make. It means a break with all that one knows about living – how to earn a livelihood, how to fit into a society, how to respond to landscape, how to touch, smell and taste. Every human lives with the images of childhood: for the refugee only memories remain. Sometimes they are replaced by visions of hope for a new world that offers a better way of life. Even if the change to a new way of life is successfully managed, the shock of loss remains. The refugee is thus dispossessed often of material things and always of a personal and social heritage that can never be recaptured.

The boat people challenge in a peculiarly sharp way what we are pleased to call, while scarcely daring to believe in its existence, the international community. As they cast off into the archipelago of South-East Asia in increasing numbers in 1978 and 1979, it became clear that the political interests affected and the range of responsibilities involved were so complex that the problem could not be solved piecemeal. Governments, humanitarian organizations and the United Nations system, especially its high commissioner for refugees (UNHCR), were all concerned. Legal questions had arisen, such as the right to asylum and rescue at sea. A co-ordinated plan was urgently needed to provide money, processing centres and resettlement outside South-East Asia.

In July 1979 in Geneva sixty-five countries took part in the meeting on refugees and displaced persons in South-East Asia, called by the United Nations. The shock of the boat people appeared to have been salutary. For the first time the Soviet Union and countries of eastern Europe attended a major international conference on refugees. A plan that met the immediate needs of the crisis emerged from the meeting, but the source of the problem was untouched and the prospect remained cloudy. Although Vietnam promised to halt the exodus, it was not certain that this could be done indefinitely and, if it were, it would only be by preventing those who might wish to leave from doing so. It is as much a denial of a fundamental right to make people stay as it is to force them to leave. Besides, although the conference concentrated on Vietnam, the refugees from Kampuchea, caught between the traditional rivalry of Thailand and Vietnam, were a serious problem.

This book is partly an anatomy of what has happened since 1975, in the hope of suggesting ways of dealing with refugee crises in the future. Crises in history, although frightening at the time, often produce creative responses. The book is also a case study of a phenomenon. But it is first and foremost a remarkable story, and as much as possible the story is told by the boat people themselves.

Chapter 1
Landfall

The twenty-sixth of April 1976 was a typically hot, northern Australian day as a decrepit wooden fishing boat, with five young men aboard, its three pumps working to keep water in the hull from rising, chugged around the flat, uninviting landscape of Bathurst Island, off Darwin. The boat was the *Kein Giang*, registered in Vietnam as KG 4435.

Several other craft dotted the blue waters off the mainland as the 25-year-old captain, Lam Binh, steered his leaky twenty-metre boat along the coast. Nobody took any notice. At sunset KG 4435 dropped anchor about a kilometre off the Darwin suburb of Night Cliff. Across the still water, the five men could hear the laughter of drinkers and see the lights of the open bar in Lim's Hotel on the foreshore. Lam Binh, who had begun planning to leave South Vietnam after the fall of Saigon a year before, was sure they were off Darwin, but did not know where to land. For the past sixteen days, since leaving Timor, he had navigated from a page torn from a school atlas. The page included Timor but not Darwin. Each day he had taken their bearings from an arrow on the map pointing in Darwin's direction.

His 17-year-old brother, Lan Tac Tam, and their three friends aged 16, 17 and 25, were excited but prepared to wait out the night. They had food, water and fuel to last another four days, and $100. That night the five men slept on the bare boards in the cabin of the boat as they had done every night since they had left South Vietnam two months before.

At first light, Lam Binh decided to head back the way they had come the previous evening, towards a flashing navigation light. But there was nothing but a buoy in the water, so they turned south-east. Thus, without knowing it, they entered the broad expanse of Darwin harbour and followed the coast to the small settlement of Mandorah.

There was no wharf, so Lam Binh turned his boat across the harbour, following the shoreline for a couple of hours. Still no one noticed them. He rounded a point and saw Stokes Hill wharf, the busy centre of the port of Darwin. He brought KG 4435 alongside about midday. Lam Binh then caught the attention of a fisherman working on a boat nearby. 'Where immigration people?' Lam Binh asked. 'We from south Vietnam'. The fisherman told them to stay where they were and drove off. As the wharf was crowded, Lam Binh anchored KG 4435 about fifty metres away. Immigration officials arrived in a pilot boat and stepped on board. Lam Binh, taking a deep breath, made a speech he had rehearsed many times: 'Welcome on my boat. My name is Lam Binh and these are my friends from south Vietnam and we would like permission to stay in Australia.'

These were the first of the boat people to travel through South-East Asia as far as Australia.

*   *   *

On 30 April 1975, Saigon, the capital of the embattled Republic of Vietnam, fell to the Vietnam people's army.

In the last weeks before the surrender the most envied people in the capital were to be found at the airport compound of the US defence attaché's office, which was known as Dodge City. Here the Americans were processing those Vietnamese deemed compromised enough to warrant immediate evacuation to the United States. Officially, only the parents of Vietnamese girls who had married Americans and children born after 1958 were allowed on the flights. But the US immigration officers, sweating men in short-sleeved shirts who had been flown in specially for the job, had long since surrendered to the inevitability of the Vietnamese extended family. Grandparents, uncles, aunts, nephews, nieces and cousins of varying degrees squatted solemnly around the solitary American citizen who was their ticket out of Vietnam. At first glance, it might have been a crowd at a sporting event: the harassed officials calling out names over megaphones; American-Asian children in baseball caps and jeans playing around the suitcases; elderly women, in the peasants' straw hats their daughters so despised, staring at nothing. The sprawl continued to a bowling alley where people were sleeping on the polished lanes under a sign that said, among other things, that profanity was strictly forbidden.

At night, above the distant artillery fire, you could hear the drone of the American evacuation planes coming in and out of Tan Son Nhut airport. Long after curfew, when the streets were deserted except for the lounging adolescents of the militia, the planes' engines would wake you as they went into a steep dive for their final approach – a manoeuvre employed since reports were received that the advancing North Vietnamese were bringing surface-to-air missiles to Saigon.

Delicately built Vietnamese air force pilots, in baseball caps, green flying suits and with low-slung revolvers, stalked about the crowd at the airport, studying faces as if they were making an assessment of the sort of people ahead of their families in the queue. It was common gossip that deals had been made with some Vietnamese officers in the hope that ensuring their own families a place on a plane would persuade them to keep their men under control. There had been instances of abandoned soldiery firing on evacuation flights, hurling grenades at them, even stowing away in the wheel wells and being crushed to death when the landing gear was retracted.

And yet, only three weeks before Saigon fell, the head of the US information service in Vietnam appeared on government-sponsored television to explain that the queues outside the American consulate downtown were merely 'American citizens and their dependants updating their records'. At the same time elements in the Central Intelligence Agency (CIA) were putting out unverified atrocity stories from the areas newly occupied by the North Vietnamese in the hope that a stubborn US congress might be persuaded to release the arms President Ford and Secretary of State Kissinger wanted to send President Thieu. The Vietnamese did not find it difficult to believe these stories. During the 1968 Tet offensive the communists had slaughtered 2000 people and buried them in mass graves in the enclave they held for a few days in Hue. Then the American and Vietnamese marines had defended that city so stoutly that some of the French press had called it the Verdun of Vietnam. Now, when it came to military metaphors, it was the final French defeat in Vietnam at Dien Bien Phu that came most readily to mind.

It is difficult to pinpoint the moment when the general consensus among the South Vietnamese, diplomats and foreign correspondents was that the situation had become what the CIA analysts on the top three floors of the US embassy called 'a worst-case scenario': that this was, indeed, the last communist offensive, that Saigon would fall, that there would no longer be a republic of South Vietnam, that Vietnam might shortly be at peace after thirty years of war. And that anybody who could not come to terms with a communist state might be in for a rough time.

With bewildering speed South Vietnam's dominoes fell as Thieu's strategic withdrawals rapidly became a rout. The South Vietnamese fought their way out of the central highlands, together with thousands of refugees, in what one news agency dubbed 'the convoy of tears'. Hue, Da Nang and Cam Ranh were captured; a coastal town called Nha Trang was bypassed by the communists, offering further proof, if any were needed, that they were no longer interested in small provincial gains. Soldiers and civilians leap-frogged down the coast in a flotilla of unlikely craft that were a harbinger of the boat people. In Da Nang, soldiers who had fled Hue arrived on a barge that was so tightly packed they were standing in terraces, as if some maverick football stadium were adrift down the Cam Le River estuary. Many of the evacuated troops had their families with them. A tough-looking NCO, his flak jacket bedecked with grenades, had a muddy M-16 under one arm and his baby son on the other. A girl aged about ten held her father's rifle by the barrel over her shoulder while he, a gaunt middle-aged man, struggled along behind her with a sack of rice. Boy scouts were often the only people around to offer any assistance at the reception areas.

Yet there were times in those last weeks when Saigon appeared so sanguine, so successfully retained its fragile shell of normality, that it nearly succeeded in camouflaging the essentially surrealistic quality of the place. Almost to the last it remained an unreal world, a fantasy dreamed up as an escape from the chaos and suffering all around it.

The good French restaurants were among the last places to close down before the surrender, although in some you could not get wine, only beer, and in the evening they had special curfew menus with last orders at 8.30 pm. At the tables were the same old faces: the diplomats, the more cosmopolitan of the American contract workers, noisy television journalists, the francophile Vietnamese bourgeoisie and the most adhesive of the old French settlers, one of whom was invariably 'le patron'.

Around the outdoor terrace at the Continental Palace Hotel (where Graham Greene lived when he was researching *The Quiet American*) pedlars, beggars and whores, most of them originally capitalized by the American presence, competed for the attention of the diminishing band of westerners. An army of orphans hung about the 'shelf', as the terrace was known (because an average-sized Vietnamese standing in the street could get his head to the customer's shoe level). There were shoeshine boys with their little wooden boxes, magazine boys in business at both ends of the market with their 'youfiniyour*Newsweek*yougivemeok?' Most of the beggars were amputees in scraps of uniform. The most original line was that of a 19-year-old ex-prostitute, hopelessly addicted to heroin, her arms covered in scabs, who used to say in her GI English: 'I'm not a whore girl, man. I'm a pickpocket. Just come outa jail and no money, but I hurt my leg and can't pick pockets. You give me some bread until my leg gets better and I can get back to work?'

There was a band of coiffured transvestites who were rumoured to be sergeants with grenades in their brassières. Shortly after the surrender the communists rounded them up, only to release them the following day. 'They were very nice boys,' one of the transvestites told a French reporter. 'We explained that we dressed like this for political reasons because we wanted to avoid the draft.'

By day, despite the spiralling petrol prices, the wasp-nest of Hondas still choked the streets. And the élite still read their *Le Monde* and plotted around the swimming pool of the Cercle Sportif, disdainful of all foreigners who weren't French. Just occasionally, a scene illuminated reality in the same way that the parachute flares bursting around the city perimeter at night served as a reminder that the enemy was very nearly at the gate. In one of the bistros an American diplomat's beautiful mistress started publicly berating her lover for not getting her and her family out 'before the VC kill us all'. People at neighbouring tables stared at the red-checked tablecloths and pretended not to notice.

Then the war arrived in Saigon. Rockets began to land for the first time in years. One of the first hit the Majestic Hotel by the waterfront, killing the nightwatchman. They were not dangerous unless you were unlucky enough to have one land close, but the explosions began to make for sleepless nights. Western embassies began to pull out.

For the first time American diplomats began to talk openly about the possibility of an emergency evacuation – 'a bugout' – and the western press corps was let in on the contingency plans. Each of the main hotels was given a secret rendezvous point, where guests would be picked up by buses and taken to the airport. A coded signal for the departure was to be broadcast over the American forces radio. A disc jockey would say 'It's 105 outside and the temperature is rising'. This would be followed by Bing Crosby singing 'I'm dreaming of a White Christmas'.

The Americans, it seemed, were going out not with a bang but a whimper. There was some consternation among the Japanese correspondents who had never heard Crosby's famous song. Floor wardens were appointed in the hotels to ensure that no sleeping colleague was left behind should the evacuation occur, as seemed likely, in the early hours. Everyone was sworn to secrecy, otherwise the pick-up points would be overrun by panic-stricken Vietnamese. It was the worst-kept secret in town. Soon even the shoeshine boys around the Continental Palace were whistling 'White Christmas'.

There was a rumour that the Chinese were trying to persuade the politburo in Hanoi not to capture Saigon because they were worried the North Vietnamese might try to take over the whole of Indo-China, including Cambodia. It was dismissed as the kind of last straw to which the US ambassador, Graham Martin, was clinging. For a while, Jean-Marie Merillon, the French ambassador, also believed in a negotiated settlement that might stop just short of outright surrender. He was said to be looking for a Vietnamese Pétain.

The most bizarre residents of Saigon were the hundred or so North Vietnamese and Vietcong delegates of the joint military commission that came out of the 1973 Paris peace agreement, who had been living at a former US marines' barracks at the airport ever since. They remained in their compound throughout the offensive. Only the Americans, it was thought, had prevented the South Vietnamese from making very short work of them.

Rockets and shells began to fall on Tan Son Nhut despite North Vietnamese assurances that they would not interfere with the American evacuation, and two US marines became the last American servicemen to be killed in Vietnam. An old 'flying boxcar' which was machine-gunning communist troops on the edge of the airfield took a hit and lurched about the sky like a falling leaf until it crashed in flames. One of the 'baby lift' planes taking Vietnamese orphans to the United States developed a mechanical failure and came down in some swampy land at the edge of the airfield shortly after take-off. Helicopters came back from the scene with pathetic little bundles wrapped in green plastic body bags.

A tailor reported that he was getting a lot of orders for red, yellow and blue cloth - the colours of the Vietcong flag (the North Vietnamese flag was a yellow star on a red background). In the classified columns of the *Saigon Post* the list of Vietnamese women wishing to marry foreigners grew longer: 'Guarantee no trouble if something happen later'. Brinks, the US government hostelry for American contractors, where the waitresses wore mini-skirts and white ankle socks just like home, closed down. The bar girls in Tu Do Street began to ask: 'You think VC like bang bang'?

In the early hours of 30 April the US marines were still keeping the crowd at bay outside the US embassy. Frantic Vietnamese, many of them waving legitimate chits entitling them to evacuation, were being beaten back with rifle butts and fists. Some of them had been there for the last twenty-four hours watching the Air America and marine helicopters ferry the lucky ones out to the Sixth Fleet. Marines helped westerners over the embassy wall, stomping on the fingers of Vietnamese who tried to climb after them. A woman who claimed to have worked for the Americans for ten years told a *Chicago Daily News* reporter just before he was pulled over that she was going home to kill herself. The evacuation rapidly became a shambles as mobs gathered around the secret pick-up points. The CIA was unable to rescue hundreds of its Vietnamese agents. As the marine rearguard withdrew to the roof and their getaway helicopter, they dropped tear-gas grenades down the lift shafts, the smell of which lingered in the looted building for days afterwards.

Later that day the BBC reported that a vast flotilla of Vietnamese small craft crammed with refugees had followed the Sixth Fleet out into the South China Sea. That night an Italian reporter remarked at dinner that this panic-stricken flight from their own people was the result of years of American propaganda.

This was how the first 130 000 refugees got out of Vietnam.

*   *   *

Two months after Saigon fell, Lam Binh began to prepare his escape. Food was hard to get and, when you found it, expensive. Prices were between ten and thirty times higher than before the communists took over. The hospitals were run properly but there was a shortage of medicines, which were kept for the army and party members. Ordinary people who went to hospital were told what they needed but had to try to buy the medicine themselves. As a result some people died. The text books being issued to schools all seemed to be written by Ho Chi Minh. More alarmingly, the communists started taking revenge. Prominent people who had worked for the Americans were arrested. People less well known who had not helped the Americans might be left alone, unless they were denounced by someone to the authorities.

With the money saved from the family ice works, Lam Binh bought a boat in July. It cost $10 000 to buy and repair. He registered it as a fishing boat. Then he studied navigation. Only Nguyen Van Chen had had any boating experience. The escape had to be planned in complete secrecy. At that time most people trying to escape were being caught. They were either intercepted by government patrols or betrayed by relatives or neighbours. There had been talk of escapees being blown out of the water by Vietnamese gunboats.

The family, eight in all, decided to leave together, abandoning the ice works. The three friends were later included. They smuggled enough food (mainly dried fish and prawns) on board KG 4435 to last two weeks. Then in daylight they left the port of Rach Gia, four of them hiding on the cabin floor. Rach Gia was a busy port, with 800 large fishing boats like Lam Binh's and probably 3000 small craft. But it was not as easy as it might seem to get away, as about one in ten of the fishing boats acted as security vessels.

It was now February, early in the calm season at sea. They knew, however, that if they headed south there was still a danger of being caught in turbulence from the South China Sea, so, as Rach Gia is on the south-west coast of Vietnam, they steered a course west across the Gulf of Thailand. Even in the relatively closed waters of the gulf, the weather was rougher than expected. Lam Binh's family – his parents, two sisters and two of his brothers – were very seasick and when the boat arrived in Thailand they could not go on. They stayed at Lao refugee camp 14/32 in Ubol. Lam Binh did not like the look of the camp. With his brother Lan Tac Tam and the three friends, none of whom had been seasick, he shoved off in KG 4435 and went looking for something better.

But it took a long time to find it. They were shunted from one port to another by authorities, given food and fuel and told to move on. In Malaysia, Singapore, Sarawak and Sabah (Borneo) it was the same story. The Malaysian government said they would be given anything they wanted as long as they moved on, so they took food and water for three weeks and 4000 litres of fuel and left. The five men spent four weeks in Kuching in Sabah repairing the boat for the long voyage to Darwin. When they reached Darwin their journey had taken them 3500 kilometres. The members of KG 4435, the first of the boat people to reach as far as Darwin, settled in Australia. Had they been refused permission to stay, they intended to try to get to France. By what means is not clear. Presumably not in KG 4435, although a review of the journeys of the boat people would make anyone wary of placing limits upon them.

* * *

From an aircraft, the seas and straits of South-East Asia look sluggish. White caps are unusual, no angry surf pounds the palm-fringed beaches, and the land masses and myriads of islands look flat and at ease with the peaceful sea.

For the kind of small craft of the boat people leaving Vietnam between 1975 and 1977, however, there were hidden dangers, even if they escaped the coastguards and the pirates who began openly to operate in the shallower waters, especially off the coast of Thailand. The waters of the South China Sea and the Java Sea are rarely deeper than forty or fifty metres and shallow seas such as these are subject to currents manipulated by winds. The tides are affected by the rise and fall of the Pacific and Indian Oceans, which converge in parts of South-East Asia. This combination of complicated tidal movements and winds makes the area hazardous for small boats. Even under normal conditions, the journeys taken by refugees in crowded boats, manned by novices and often needing repair, were dangerous.

But what is normal? A build-up of heat over the equator can trigger off violent air movements. Clouds 3000 metres deep can form in as little as half an hour. Within these clouds, vertical movement of air can be as great as 150 kilometres per hour. These conditions are the breeding ground for thunderstorms which can be a daily event near the equator. The violence and power of these storms is such that a small boat would stand little chance of survival.

The typhoon season, from July to November, is perilous for all shipping, not only small craft. Indo-China and the Philippines are especially susceptible to typhoons which usually rise in the South China Sea. From July to September, the maximum danger zone is north of latitude 15 degrees, which affects the Tonkin Gulf and the islands of Hainan and Hong Kong. In October and November the maximum risk is in the southern waters of the South China Sea, including the coastal waters of southern Vietnam. The dark clouds and torrential winds and rains of the typhoons are rightly feared by the people of South-East Asia. Behind and before the eye of the typhoon, which may be five kilometres or more in diameter and calm and clear, winds of up to 150 kilometres per hour blow with devastating violence, and visibility is almost nil. Typhoons have been known to lift trains from their rails and cast steamers hundreds of metres inland.

Typhoons have seldom been recorded between Vietnam and Malaysia or Thailand. There the 'monsoon' rules the waves (the term is derived from an Arabic word for 'season'). The most treacherous time is November/December, when winds blow from the north-west off southern Vietnam and peninsular Malaysia, reaching an average strength of 50 to 70 kilometres per hour, enough to make the sea dangerous for small craft. In December, the roughest month, winds reach gale force of 120 to 130 kilometres per hour. By March, the north-east monsoon dies away only to swing around again in June to start blowing from the south-west. The wind, though, is lighter and more variable. However, off Malaysia, in the south-west monsoon from June to September, the boat people frequently had to face squalls that turned the sea into a frenzy of gale-force winds and driving rain.

Whenever they could, the boat people avoided the bad weather. Even so, for every boatload that made landfall, it is still not known how many set out.

*   *   *

Guests at the Merlin Hotel on Tioman Island, off the east coast of Malaysia, were admiring the tropical sunset one evening in November 1976 when a fishing boat rounded the headland and berthed at the hotel jetty. They strolled down the coral sand beach for a closer look. The deck and the cabin of the thirty-metre trawler were crowded with upturned faces.

Children peeped out from under an awning covering the forward section of the deck. On the roof of the wheelhouse several women squatted over pots of rice cooking on wood and charcoal stoves. The rear of the vessel was festooned with sun-dried fish and clothing strung on poles. The chatter was that of Vietnamese voices. This was fishing boat PK 504.

On the deck was a large sign: 'Please help us. We want freedom'.

Fifty-six people were on board: nineteen men, ten women and twenty-seven children. After ten minutes at the hotel jetty they were moved to another pier about two kilometres away, close to the police station in the main village on the island. Two Malay policemen came on board and a crowd of locals gathered around.

The Vietnamese were not in distress. Unlike some of the frail craft that left Vietnam, their boat looked solid and seaworthy. Its engine ran smoothly and they had 150 litres of diesel fuel left. Those on board appeared healthy, but they were confused and demoralized. Tran Binh Minh, a 25-year-old teacher, said they had slipped out of Cam Ranh Bay on the central coast of Vietnam on 28 October. Of the eighteen other men on board, fifteen were former soldiers, two were policemen and one an old man. 'We didn't like living under the communists,' he said. Fifty more people had been scheduled to come, but they had been stopped at a roadblock on the night of the escape. There almost all the group's savings (gold valued at $500 000) had been found in one of the trucks. The captain's entire family were among those who were caught in the roadblock and had to be left behind.

Their boat, PK 504, had left Vietnam during the typhoon season, choosing that time deliberately because the authorities did not expect escape attempts then. The refugees intended to head for the open sea, hoping to be picked up by a friendly vessel. But after being deliberately ignored by several passing ships, they realized that they would have to find their own way. They headed south-west and arrived on the east coast of Malaysia, where they were noticed by the guests at the Merlin Hotel.

In the crowded wheelhouse cabin a spokesman for the group, Ton Hong Duc, admitted that they had had no clear idea of where they wanted to go when they left Vietnam. If they could find work in Thailand they would stay there; otherwise they would go to any 'free' country prepared to accept them. They had a good compass but no map or chart. Mr Duc asked to which country Tioman Island belonged. He said that their first landing had been at the Malaysian east-coast port of Mersing, sixty-seven kilometres west of Tioman, on 4 November. There they were given fuel and food and asked to leave. So they sailed south to Singapore but were turned away. He said they now wanted more fuel to reach Thailand, several hundred kilometres to the north. The Malay policeman said they could get fuel in Mersing, and must leave Tioman immediately. Soon PK 504 was nothing but a receding pinpoint of light in the darkness, the throb of its engine lost in the calm of the night. That was one of the first reports of PK 504. It was not the end of its story, however, merely a fragment of a voyage that became one of the most remarkable of all those of the boat people.

It was later learned that PK 504 arrived offshore from a Thai village called Songkhla. Although they did not know it, this was the location of a large refugee camp. Before they had a chance to moor, their boat was boarded by a group of men brandishing guns. They were not in uniform but identified themselves as policemen. The refugees, who had heard of plundering and rape by pirates, defended themselves with the only ammunition available to them: the pirates got the last of the gold, worth $20 000.

PK 504 turned south, heading for Singapore, and ran into the edge of a cyclone. For three days and nights they battled against huge seas, barely making any headway. The children vomited continuously; no food could be cooked; the toilet was unusable. By the time the storm subsided some on board were ready to give up, but the thought of reaching Singapore kept them going. In Singapore, however, they were stopped by police boats in the harbour and ordered not to land. They were advised to tell other refugee boats not to bother coming to Singapore. Their boat was turned around and once more pointed out to sea.

Somewhere in the sea off Singapore, they decided to try to get to Australia. It would be a long journey, further than they had already travelled. Much would depend on getting fuel and supplies in Indonesia. They moved slowly down the coast of Sumatra and reached Jakarta. They were met by Indonesian navy patrols, but by now they had learned how to answer questions. They said they were going to Australia and were given fuel and food, as well as advice on the safest route. They were then escorted out to sea.

Hugging the north coast of Java, they eventually found themselves among the islands between the Flores and Timor Seas. They took on fresh water at Bali, then navigated the shallows and reefs of the waters between the islands of Sumbawa and Flores and finally reached Timor, where they were given fuel by the Indonesian navy. Then it was the calm, open sea and Australia. They arrived at a deserted beach between Wyndham and Darwin. Like the seventeenth-century Dutch and Portuguese sailors, who were blown off-course on their way to the East Indies and bumped into the west coast of the Australian continent, they saw no sign of civilization and were disheartened; unlike the traders, however, the refugees persisted. They turned north-east, pushed up the coast and found Darwin. When their journey ended, they had travelled 8000 kilometres.

In 1789 Captain William Bligh, cast adrift in a ship's launch with eighteen of his crew by the *Bounty* mutineers, performed what is considered one of the greatest feats of navigation: he brought his boat safely from the Pacific to Timor – a distance of about 6000 kilometres.

*　　　*　　　*

With the fall of Saigon the victory of the Vietnamese communists was triumphal, but also illusory. The image of almost superhuman tenacity and almost juggernaut military prowess belied a grim reality. Vietnam was – and is – a poor, developing country with disproportionately powerful armed forces, ravaged by thirty years of war.

The north had been more seriously damaged by American bombs than Hanoi had been prepared to admit during the war. Three of six major cities had been virtually destroyed. An extensive civil defence had saved lives, but some 2 million people had been displaced by the bombing and had not been resettled when the war ended. The road and rail system had been broken, industrial and agricultural production was down to 1950s' levels. Hanoi had almost no foreign reserves and a huge trade deficit (1976 exports were $170 million and imports nearly $1000 million), so its ability to import urgently needed technology and food was limited. It depended on aid, mostly from the Soviet Union, eastern Europe and China. Visitors to the north in 1976-77 noticed the shortages (even ballpoint pens were rationed), the desperate housing situation (official allotment: three square metres a person), the way men and women were engaged by hand (not machine) in rebuilding the roads and dikes and repairing erosion from bomb-damaged fields. Thousands of unexploded bombs were embedded in the countryside.

But the morale of the north was high. The machinery of government was intact and the political leadership remained unified. The north had been under a communist regime for twenty years and had survived crises of its own, such as the savage collectivization of 1956. Times had been hard for so long that, now the country was reunified under northern leadership and the war ended, the people looked forward to a better life.

The south, however, was chaotic. Physically, it was in better shape in some respects than the north. The Americans left behind an efficient road system; light industry survived and an effective irrigation system functioned. But agriculture, the mainstay of the economy, was severely disrupted. According to communist assessments, 9000 out of a total of 15 000 hamlets were damaged or destroyed, and 1.7 million tonnes of American defoliants had been dropped on 20 million hectares – about 20 per cent of Vietnam's arable land. Years of war had produced a distorted economy, the taste of a consumer society; cities were bloated with refugees from the rural areas

– about 1.2 million former members of the armed services, as well as civilians closely associated with the Saigon régime, attendant bar girls and other fringe-dwellers. Most of the economy, particularly the rice markets, was in the hands of Chinese, concentrated in the Cholon district adjacent to Saigon.

The long war in the jungles, rice fields and villages had created successive waves of refugees in the south, reaching a total of 10 million by 1975. Some were displaced several times after being resettled in rural areas by the Saigon authorities. Even so, at the end of the war, more than one-third of the southern population lived in cities, compared with only one-tenth in the north. In the early 1960s, when US military intervention in Vietnam began in earnest, the south had 15 per cent of its people living in urban areas and the remaining 85 per cent in the country. In 1975 only 35 per cent of the population was in rural areas; the other 65 per cent was concentrated in cities and towns.

The end of the war brought American aid to Saigon to a halt. During the war communist aid to Hanoi had been channelled primarily into the war effort and essential economic activities, but in the south, foreign aid and trade helped create and sustain a large entrepreneurial-professional class – a highly developed services sector including banks, insurance companies, travel agencies, import-export firms, wholesale and retail outlets, petty traders, cafés, bars, hotels and brothels – and rampant corruption in government, the armed forces, the police, the administration and the private sector. There was also corruption in the communist north, but opportunities for big-scale graft were much more limited there than in the south. American aid to the Saigon government averaged about $2000 million a year in the late 1960s and early 1970s, before a disenchanted congress pruned it in the last few critical years.

At the same time as American aid ceased, South Vietnam's armed forces and its top-heavy services sector – built up in the towns to serve wartime needs – suddenly became superfluous. Hanoi inherited about 3 million unemployed, concentrated in Saigon and other big centres. In Saigon, hundreds of thousands of people – many of them from the military and police – lost their jobs overnight and had to face the prospect of a permanent drop in income and declining material standards. The city – indeed the whole of South

Vietnam – lived beyond its means during the war. While some refugees who flooded into Saigon lived in dire poverty, others found themselves earning more than in their wildest dreams – a young girl working in the American post exchange (PX), or as cook for a foreign agency, might find herself earning more than well-educated civil servants from established middle-class families.

The communists quickly catalogued some of the social problems bequeathed to them. While the figures may be exaggerated, they can be taken as rough indicators. There were 800 000 orphans and abandoned children, many fathered by American, Australian, South Korean and Filipino military and civilian personnel in Vietnam; a million war widows; several hundred thousand prostitutes, heroin addicts and other drug abusers; more than 360 000 war wounded; 'several dozen thousand gangsters and other criminals whose numbers later increased with the release of the former [government's] police, paratroops and rangers'; and four million illiterates.

Two reports prepared by senior officers of the World Health Organization who visited Vietnam late in 1975 chronicled the state of public health. Malaria was endemic throughout much of the south. Tuberculosis was rated as the most serious occurrence in the western Pacific. The reports estimated that there were between 80 000 and 160 000 leprosy cases. Dengue haemorrhagic fever, trachoma and plague were all described as major problems. At the root of southern Vietnam's public health ills were an extremely high birth rate (4.1 per cent a year), a shattered health-care program that never reached out into adequate coverage of the countryside, where much of the fighting had taken place, and an acute shortage of trained medical staff, most of whom were concentrated in the cities.

While Hanoi wanted to transform the whole of Vietnam into a modern, socialist state, it recognized that the south had to be absorbed slowly. A policy of 'gradualism' was adopted. A foreign investment code was prepared to attract western capital and skills to develop Vietnam's potential in manufacturing industry and off-shore petroleum production.

Underlying this relatively flexible line was a desire to foster trade with, and acquire technology from, the non-communist world; to boost food and consumer goods production to satisfy the demands of an expectant peacetime population; to avoid the excesses of the collectivization of agriculture in the north; to allow time for a revolutionary administration to take root in the south; and to prevent serious economic collapse or political revolt.

Foreigners visiting the south in 1976-77 were surprised at how little it had changed. Churches were still open; the free market in consumer goods left over from the American occupation operated openly; food markets, retail shops, cafés and some transport remained in private hands. But banks, shipping, insurance and some import-export businesses were nationalized. Bank deposits were frozen. And two phrases were on everyone's lips: 'new economic zones' and 're-education'. Each was related to the problem of the workforce in peacetime Vietnam.

Despite the war, population had grown rapidly in both halves of the country. It almost trebled in the last half century to about 50 million, with north and south roughly equivalent.

Labour in post-war Vietnam was abundant. The workforce, which in 1976 totalled 22 million, was growing at a rate of a million a year. It was vital that people should be organized, trained and found jobs in agriculture, forestry, fisheries and light industries, where potential for expansion was greatest. Population increase and the redevelopment of the workforce and relocation of people between and within northern and southern Vietnam were inter-related issues raised during the fourth congress of the Vietnam communist party in Hanoi in December 1976.

The vice-chairman of the state planning commission, Che Viet Tan, said Vietnam's population growth – averaging 3 per cent – made improvements in living standards difficult. Vietnam's premier, Pham Van Dong announced that a redistribution of the workforce in Vietnam would start in 1977. The massive planned migration of some 10 million people, which would change the demographic shape of Vietnam, was to take place within ten to fifteen years. It was designed to reclaim more than 5 million hectares of arable land, re-afforest 7 million hectares of bare hills, supply manpower to new industrial centres to be established in the south, reduce the pressure of population on land and other resources in congested regions and create conditions for rapid electrification of the countryside. Most of the 10 million people to be moved would be from the densely packed Red River delta in the north around Hanoi and the central Vietnam plains. Some would go to the central highlands and the northern mountain areas, but most would go to southern Vietnam.

The 'new economic zone' (NEZ) was an integral part of the government's workforce redevelopment strategy. The heaviest concentration of these pioneer agricultural communities was to be in southern Vietnam, mainly in the Mekong delta and coastal plains along the east coast.

A great deal of controversy surrounds the NEZs. The US state department has described them as 'primitive communes generally located on remote agricultural land. People assigned to [them] received little if any real assistance from the state; they are expected to be self-reliant. Many Vietnamese, particularly urbanites, regard transfer to a new economic zone as a death sentence'. One western journalist who visited several of the NEZs called them 'the equivalent of being sent to Siberia'.

The Vietnamese authorities did not attempt to disguise some of the problems initially encountered in NEZs. One report by a Vietnamese journalist published for external consumption looked at the experience of Tan Hung village, about forty kilometres north of Ho Chi Minh City in Song Be province, in 1976. This NEZ was sited on 'what had been a big military base and was still cluttered with bombs, mines, blockhouses, carcasses of vehicles and barbed-wire entanglements'. It contained 5000 people 'of various trades and with a most heterogeneous set of personal records'. Most – nearly 1000 families – were from Ho Chi Minh City and two-fifths of them were said to have had at least one member who had collaborated with the Americans and the former administration.

The Tan Hung zone was supervised by a team of six local militiamen. Much of the land was levelled by bulldozers but quickly became overgrown with tiger grass and sprouting tree stumps. However, the settlers reportedly got considerable outside help. From Ho Chi Minh City and Song Be province they received bulldozers, road-making machines, trucks, building materials and teams of vanguard youth and carpenters; from the north they got seeds, breeding stock, young trees, fertilizers and food.

After 'six hard months' a new village of about a thousand wooden houses with fibro-cement roofs was built, with an administrative committee office, a primary school for over 400 children, a twelve-bed hospital run by an assistant doctor with four nurses and a midwife, a foodstore, a general goods store, a market, water wells and a playing field. Each family had a garden plot of about 2000 square metres with the produce for sale or for personal consumption. A thousand hectares was to be planted with rice, groundnuts and soya beans in the first season. This area was farmed on a collective basis 'day and night' with settlers working in rows, digging, raking, weeding, felling trees.

The report readily acknowledged that life in the early days of Tan Hung NEZ was 'not plain sailing'. Some of the people had never done manual work before, or they had given it up long ago. Some, it appeared, were not yet accustomed to the climatic conditions. Added to these difficulties, saboteurs were out to distort the truth, exaggerate the hardships and even occasionally lay mines and throw grenades into crowded places to demoralize the settlers. Many 'began to waver'; some moved back to the city. Some left their families behind so as to continue receiving settler allowances granted by the state. Others, 'leaving the children to look after their belongings . . . went back to the city to have a try at small trading'. However, things gradually settled down. 'Although they had experienced a hard life on the land, those who left for the city found their days even harder there, asked to return to the NEZ, and were welcomed back; those who had wavered now definitely plumped for Tan Hung'.

Life on these 'socialist co-operatives' being established in southern Vietnam was not always the hardwon success depicted on Tan Hung. In the same province, Song Be, a visitor reported that an estimated 10 per cent of the people sent to NEZ gave up the struggle and left. Living and working conditions were harsh and very different from those familiar to the majority of settlers, who were from urban backgrounds. The southern middle-class had no desire to carve out a new life with a pick and shovel in the central highlands and even those who had previously been slum-dwellers sometimes returned to the cities.

The effort to persuade and induce hundreds of thousands of southerners to head for the countryside began shortly after the communists won control in 1975. In Ho Chi Minh City special offices in all districts and wards were created to register those leaving. Free transport was arranged for them and some of their possessions. Food and a small amount of money was provided for the trip. On arrival, local authorities were supposed to provide each family with certain essentials: land, farm tools, seeds, fertilizers, building materials and six months' rice. Once in the zones, families were to buy basic supplies on credit at state-run stores, paying for them after the first harvest.

The NEZs were not simply a way of cutting an intolerably high level of urban unemployment, boosting agricultural output and making Vietnam more self-sufficient. They were part of a process of restructuring society along socialist lines. They served to disperse people from potential centres of dissent and resistance formerly under the control of the old régime. Once in an NEZ, southerners could expect to be mixed with settlers from the north. Northern cadres could shepherd the ideologically uncertain southern flock.

'Re-education', which was intended to reform through 'study, practice and labour', is as controversial a subject as NEZs. It began on a large scale in June 1975, when members of the defeated armed forces were ordered to register. Numbers involved were huge. The regular forces – army, navy, air force and marines – as well as the regional and popular forces, totalled about 1.2 million men. They were commanded by 40 000 to 50 000 officers. Paramilitary forces added another 1.2 million men to the tally; the national police another 125 000. Many of these military personnel had shed their uniforms and weapons, donned mufti and merged into civilian life rather than surrender to the communists. However, a left-wing French journalist who was in Saigon after the takeover and had close links with the new rulers reported that they had captured one of five American computers. In its memory bank was a 'Who's Who' that included information on the political affiliations of members of the disbanded army. Computer cards for the police and civil service were also reported to have been recovered. In addition to the military and police, there were about 300 000 civil servants, politicians, and others closely associated with the previous régime who were eligible for re-education.

The authorities outlined their approach to the subject in these terms: Political courses have been organized to help the persons concerned to see more clearly the crimes and schemes of the Americans and the traitors, as well as the duties of Vietnamese citizens in the new stage of national reconstruction and socialist construction, and to mend their ways in order to find a place for themselves in the new society. Three broad categories of 'the persons concerned' were established. In the first were ordinary soldiers, NCOs, and low-ranking members of the administration and political organizations of the previous government. They completed on-the-spot courses in less than a week. Secondly, there were the more senior functionaries and officers, up to the rank of captain. They remained in re-education centres for anything from ten days to a year and were then liable to administrative surveillance for six to twelve months. Then there were the 'difficult' cases from the second category. These were held longer and merged with inmates of camps set up for those who had held important political, military and police posts.

Evasion was considerable. In Saigon for example, official figures suggest that in one district 5000 out of 25 000 military did not register. Also, although the authorities promised to err on the side of leniency, so that those who were found to have made real progress would be authorized to return to their homes and to recover their civil rights earlier than the regulation time, many detainees have still not been released. Most are believed to be military and police officers. With them are an unknown number of ex-civil servants, politicians and local officials. In 1976 Vietnam's ambassador in Paris claimed 'only 50 000' people were still being held. In April 1977 a senior communist official reported that 96 per cent of those formerly associated with the defunct Saigon government had been 'enfranchised'.

For many, re-education was a simple stepping stone to reintegration in society and recovery of civil rights, but for others it was a tougher transition to probationary or second-class citizenship and for some (the 'stubborn' cases) it was bleak detention. The US state department in December 1978 estimated that Vietnam held from 150 000 to 200 000 political prisoners. Whatever the actual number, they are apparently kept in two types of camp – those for long-term incarceration and those from which releases are progressively made. Most are believed to be in the latter. They live under conditions that can be survived by people in robust physical health but would certainly be damaging if not fatal to the ill and weak. They have to undergo long hours of manual labour, trade training, political indoctrination and 'self-criticism'.

Hanoi's policy statement on re-education also mentioned refugees for the first time: 'Those who have committed numerous crimes against the revolution or against the population and have zealously served the US imperialists, and now, following the day of liberation, seek to leave the country in the wake of their masters, will be punished by law. Not included in this category are those who have been duped by enemy propaganda, taken fright, and have fled abroad'.

These were the circumstances in which the second wave of boat people took their leave of Vietnam.

*   *   *

The motives of the first wave of refugees from the south – those who left with the departing Americans – were clear. They had become so closely associated with the American presence or had become so dependent on it as a way of life that they feared for their lives or their livelihood under a communist régime. Some of those who formed the second wave decided within weeks or months of the fall of the Saigon government to make their escape. Others awaited developments. Despite Hanoi's decision to move cautiously in the south, pressures on the lives of middle-class people, especially those who, as Catholics, opposed communism, or who were in private business or the professions, were sufficient to keep warm the hope of getting out. While some were well off, others escaped with little more than their lives. Unlike the first wave and the later mass exodus of refugees in 1978 and 1979, they were better organized, planning their escape in secrecy in small groups, often families, and were therefore less vulnerable to commercial and official exploitation. Vietnam's coast is long, indented with many bays and hard to police.

Typical of the second wave of boat people was Nguyen Hoang Cuong. He was a business man with interests in manufacturing and export, but his character was that of an intellectual rather than a tycoon. Aged forty-nine, he taught business administration at Dalat university and he took at least as much pride in his academic post as in his business interests. When the communists arrived, he had to surrender his share in a joint venture with Japanese partners in a radio and television assembly plant in return for a job on the factory floor.

He had never been so closely associated with the previous régime that he felt in danger of death or conventional imprisonment. He was too old to be drafted for national service and was not required to register for re-education or a new life in an NEZ. He left Vietnam because he could see no future for himself or his family. He had been a busy and, in a modest way, influential member of society before 1975: now he could not endure what he regarded as a deliberate policy of discrimination against anyone who was not in the favoured circle of revolutionary families, industrial workers and peasant cadres. Bribery and corruption were 'about as rampant as they were under the former régime', also, food prices were high and jobs hard to find, but the impression he created, as he told his story in a refugee holding camp at Tengah in south Malaysia late in 1977, was that of a man whose pride had been trampled on.

It took nine months and three failures before he succeeded in escaping. One of his friends was arrested when the first attempt was discovered. The final plan required his brother-in-law to work as a fisherman for six months, selling the catch to a state co-operative, in order to stockpile 250 litres of scarce diesel fuel. With his wife, three sons, some relatives and fishermen (eleven in all in an eleven-metre boat with a 10-horsepower engine) they slipped out of Tra Vinh village on the coast of the Mekong delta. They left without compass or charts. In the South China Sea they signalled passing ships for assistance but none stopped, so they headed for Malaysia, arriving on the north-east coast of the peninsula where villagers gave them food and clothes and police gave them fuel. They intended to go to Singapore and apply for resettlement in the US or Australia. But their entry to Singapore was blocked: they were towed out to sea first by a marine police launch and then by a naval vessel. They were given fuel, water and food, but their appeals to have the disabled engine repaired were rejected (after reference to authorities ashore) and they were left drifting in international waters late at night. After several hours they succeeded in starting the engine and by a stroke of luck beached the boat not far from the Tengah camp.

Mr Cuong was interviewed in December 1977, standing on the beach at Tengah with the makeshift thatch of huts of the refugee camp as a backdrop. A thin man, he seemed to personify the combination of frailty and resilience that marks many Vietnamese. He is now settled in America with his family.

* * *

The world was slow to react to the boat people. They seemed a strange, romantic, almost unnatural phenomenon that would surely pass. Why had they taken to the seas in such flimsy craft? Did they not understand the risks they were taking, what their chances of finding refuge were? On ships on the high seas binoculars were averted from the unfamiliar faces and frantically waving hands. If ships did pick up boat people they would probably never be able to put them down. In June 1977 an Israeli freighter *Yuvali* picked up sixty-six boat people a hundred kilometres off the Vietnamese coast. Their boat was sinking and most of them, including a pregnant woman, were sick. Among them was a professor of geography, a surgeon, two dentists and a bank director. Four ships had passed by before the *Yuvali* rescued them. In Taiwan, permission to land the refugees was denied. They were not even allowed to stand on the pier. Japan refused them as did Hong Kong and Thailand. So they were taken back to Israel, where they were accepted. Before they were taken on board the *Yuvali*, some of them (despite, evidently, the presence of the professor) had not heard of Israel.

Early in 1977 an old American minesweeper was used in a controversial operation to rescue refugees. The *Roland*, a forty-metre vessel able to carry several hundred people, was chartered by an organization called the World Conference on Religion and Peace (WCRP), which included representatives from all major religions. With no assurance of acceptance, the minesweeper hoped to land the refugees in the United States and Australia. The scheme was described by the United Nations high commissioner for refugees as 'misguided philanthropy' but 300 refugees were attracted on board.

The minesweeper left Singapore well stocked with food, clothing and medical supplies, purchased with money supplied from foreign countries. The Japanese chapter of the WCRP donated about $50 000. But, after a change of plans by the WCRP in response to criticism, the vessel remained stranded in Malaysia while it awaited permission to unload. Malaysia would not allow the refugees to disembark until western states had made commitments to resettle them. It was not until June that the refugees were resettled. During that time they were captive on board the *Roland*. Also an investigation revealed that some of the refugees had each paid $800 for their passage to a member of the crew.

The numbers of boat people in 1975-76 rose steadily, but they constituted a trickle compared with the flood yet to come. In 1975 they were 377; in 1976: 5619; in 1977: 21 276. These were the numbers of safe arrivals (either in camps or resettled), not of departures; nor, of course, did the figures include those who had been caught while escaping.

Gradually the dilemma posed by the Indo-Chinese refugees sharpened. The refugee camps in Malaysia and Thailand became crowded. The ruthless Pol Pot régime in Kampuchea, which had killed half a million or more of its people (estimates of up to two million have been made) after taking power in 1975, forced refugees into Thailand and also (about 200 000) into Vietnam. But it was the boat people, with their peculiar mobility, who caused the first stirrings of international tension. Ships' captains were criticized for turning a blind eye to boats in distress. Countries in the region were criticized for turning the boat people away. In turn, rich countries were criticized for refusing to resettle refugees. The prime minister of Singapore trenchantly defended his policy of refusing permission to land without guarantees of resettlement. His island-state was 'a small, weak, over-populated country not in need of labour of the kind that comes in these perilous journeys in unseaworthy boats', he said, in an ambiguous reference to the quality of the boat people.

The boat people themselves did not escape criticism, usually directed at their apparent wealth. Organizing an escape required money and the currency of the boat people was gold, because it was easily convertible. When Saigon fell, a great deal of gold was in private hands and was the basis of a parallel banking system. Also, some escapees were able to get money from relatives overseas, which was then turned into gold. Stories of boat people staggering ashore with gold bars or gold leaf in their pockets fed rumours of the wealth of the refugees. One family, after spending a week in a hostel in Australia, bought a house valued at $50 000. Also, some of the boats made more than one journey, suggesting that a profitable traffic could have been organized during the early period of emigration.

However, the numbers of the boat people were still small and the criticism was often niggardly. There was a sense of something impending, but not yet a crisis. It was not until 1978-79, when powerful factors of politics and history began to bear down upon the boat people, that the region and the world realized it had a crisis on its hands.

Chapter 2

Legacy

The history of Vietnam is a pattern of recurrent themes, each of which bears on the refugee crisis: resistance to China politically while absorbing its culture, an internal struggle for unity, a claim on its smaller neighbours, rejection of western imperial power.

The French scholar Paul Mus says that Vietnam 'entered history' in 208 BC, somewhere around the southern edge of China. His phrasing raises an old question about the meaning of history, especially the history of people who live under the shadow of others and who had gathered in communities, tilled the soil, made artefacts and worshipped, long before their existence was confirmed by a superior political calendar. South-East Asia appears to have been the home of one of the earliest branches of *homo sapiens* and some of the earliest artefacts have been found in what is now northern Vietnam. The Annamites, who form the main ethnic group in Vietnam, are thought to have come from Tibet, the source of many migrations before the Christian era (and also of the great rivers Yangtse, Mekong and Salween which flow into the rice plains). The Khmer people who became dominant in what was Cambodia are believed to have arrived from the north-west around 2000 BC. What did they do before they entered history through the annals of the civilization of India and China? Recent research in anthropology and archaeology is responding to the insistence of local nationalism: they were advanced in horticulture, bronze-casting and navigation. South-East Asians can now point to a culture that pre-dates not only the impact of European colonialism but even the more ancient and pervasive influence of China and India. Today, as the great powers once again vie for influence in South-East Asia, this nationalism is being tested.

However, for the Vietnamese, China has always cast a long shadow. It is impossible to understand modern Vietnam, especially Vietnamese nationalism, without an appreciation of the contradictory impulses of attraction and repulsion that bind it to China. For a thousand years (111 BC to AD 939) northern Vietnam was governed as part of a Chinese colony. During that time the Vietnamese thoroughly absorbed Chinese cultural tradition while rebelling whenever they judged the power of a dynasty in China to be weak. Perhaps the most famous of the rebels were the Trung sisters, who led Vietnamese armies in a desperate stand against the Chinese in AD 40-43 and who had become goddesses in Vietnamese mythology by the twelfth century. (They were still being honoured in ceremonies in both the communist north and the anti-communist south during the Vietnam war.)

After the Vietnamese broke China's hold, armies from the north invaded many times (in 981, 1075-77, 1250 and 1280, 1406-27 and 1788) always ultimately unsuccessfully. This history of rejection of China, while at the same time drawing from the deepest resources of Chinese culture and paying appropriate homage to Peking, fostered the historical ideal that has sustained Vietnamese nationalism until today: that a united Vietnam has always existed, that its antecedents are as venerable as China's and that its internal harmony can only be managed by a single ruler. The ideal ruler was one who could resist China while absorbing its tradition.

As they established themselves in the narrow, mountainous country shaped like the letter S, which stretches for 2000 kilometres north to south and is only 50 kilometres wide at its narrowest point, the Vietnamese came into conflict with their southern neighbours. The Hindu-Buddhist kingdom of Champa, which had established itself on the central Vietnamese coast in AD 192 and had at times held sway in southern Cambodia (sailing up the Mekong in 1177 to sack Angkor), was eliminated after bitter wars. The Vietnamese pressed upon the Khmers, who were also harassed in the west by the Thais. By 1672 the Vietnamese had pushed south to Saigon and from there they spread to occupy the Mekong delta. Cambodia paid tribute to the Vietnamese court and for a while was incorporated into Vietnam.

The Vietnamese also fought among themselves. A struggle for supremacy between the Trinh family in the north and the Nguyen family in the south lasted from 1620 until 1777, during which the Nguyen built walls across the waist of Vietnam near the seventeenth parallel which became the dividing line between north and south in 1954 (after the Geneva agreements which brought French rule to an end). Vietnam was finally united in 1802 with three main regions, Tonkin (capital: Hanoi) in the north, Annam (capital: Hue) in the centre and Cochin China (capital: Saigon) in the south.

The Vietnamese absorbed little of the Hindu culture of their neighbours. Some influence of Cham music has been detected and Vietnamese generals used elephants, which are potent in Hindu lore, while the Chinese favoured horses, but this was probably simply because the elephants were more mobile and some accounts suggest the horses were afraid of them. But the Vietnamese never adopted the symbols of Hinduism that had become established in South-East Asia – the lingam, the guru, the mountain-temple, Sanskrit, nor, indeed, religious tolerance. Their strength was a village-based society linked in the mind, especially of the peasant, with a higher order of values expressed in the Confucian idea of a governing élite. Their methods were social integration, physical occupation and political unity. They moved relentlessly across the flooded rice fields of the southern delta and peninsula, hard-working and self-sufficient, and it is probable, had the French not arrived, that they would have occupied a substantial part if not the whole of what became known as Indo-China. On the other hand, of course, if the Vietnamese had not stood against China, the Chinese might well have occupied all of Indo-China themselves. This argument continues today in the contrary claims made by Peking and Hanoi about each other's intentions in South-East Asia.

The first Europeans in Vietnam (1535) were traders and missionaries and although the Dutch and the Portuguese meddled occasionally in the epic Trinh-Nguyen feud, European governments did not become interested in Vietnam until the end of the eighteenth century. A missionary, Pierre Pigneau (de Behaine), was responsible for the first gestures of official French interest. He became a supporter of Nguyen Anh and journeyed to France in 1787 to plead his case at the court of Versailles. With him, given as a pledge, was Nguyen's four-year-old son and heir, Canh. The court, which was on the verge of the French revolution, gave little thought to the political worth of the priest's mission, although the boy created excitement in the salons. However, a treaty was signed between France and Nguyen's fiefdom, Cochin China, with promises of help, but no hardware. Pigneau raised private money in France and on his way back to Vietnam stopped at the French settlement of Pondicherry in India where he recruited volunteers and bought provisions. Eventually four shiploads of stores and a couple of hundred volunteers arrived in Vietnam in 1788 and helped Nguyen Anh to power.

When Nguyen Anh became the famous Emperor Gia-Long (1802- 20), the first to rule over a united Vietnam, he granted privileges to those Frenchmen who remained in his service. However, unfortunately for the French, Prince Canh, who no doubt retained vivid memories of his visit to Paris, died in 1801. His brother, Minh-Mang (1820-41), who was a strict Confucian, revived the persecution of Christianity. His successors were even more severe. Vietnamese Christian communities were dispersed and their lands redistributed. Christians were branded on the cheek (with characters meaning 'infidel') and missionaries were imprisoned and even executed.

At this stage of the nineteenth century, western intervention in China was intensifying. The British fought a war with China (1839-42, the first opium war), acquired Hong Kong, and five Chinese ports were opened up to European trade. The era of concessions, 'unequal treaties' and 'extraterritoriality', in which the Europeans established sovereign enclaves throughout China, had begun. French interest in Vietnam was an aspect of its wider interest in the wealth of China. So although French warships forced the release of missionaries from time to time in Vietnam simply by threatening to bombard coastal towns (especially the port Tourane, now Da Nang, south of Hue), it was not until French forces were released from China that the subjugation of Vietnam began in earnest. In 1858 an Anglo-French task force seized Canton. In the same year a Franco-Spanish force (Spain then occupied the Philippines) took Tourane in reprisal for the execution the year before of the Bishop of Tonkin, who was a Spaniard.

By 1861 the war in China had ended and French naval and army units were released. Even so, it was one thing to capture a city with superior weapons and quite another to hold it. Supplies were short, sickness endemic, the population sullen and occasionally rebellious. Rebels who had escaped from southern China during the anti-

Manchu T'ai P'ing uprising roamed northern Vietnam, merging with robber bands and insurgents. Also, France was affected by her defeat in Europe in the war with Prussia (1870-71). She was successful in gaining control of Cochin China and by skilful diplomacy added Cambodia which was at that time threatened by the Thais, but it was not until the 1880s that Tonkin was secured.

In 1887 the three regions, Tonkin, Annam and Cochin China, as well as Cambodia, were formally brought together in what was then called by France the Indo-Chinese Union. Laos was added in 1893, not by diplomacy, as in the case of Cambodia, but by marching French troops along the Mekong and despatching two warships up the river to Bangkok, where the Thai government saw reason and agreed that the land east of the Mekong was Lao and therefore France's.

In the case of both Cambodia and Laos, the rivalry between Thailand and Vietnam was an important factor in the passive attitude they adopted towards France. When the Thais felt themselves to be outmanoeuvred by the French they turned to the British (on their western flank in Burma) for help, but the British offered only impeccable diplomatic advice, which was that the Thais would be wise not to irritate the French. So the Thais settled for less than they wanted, but remained free of overt imperialist entanglements, becoming a buffer state between the French and British eastern empires and, indeed, the only state in South-East Asia not to be occupied during the period of European expansion and colonialism.

French imperialism in Indo-China was not markedly different from French imperialism in Africa, the West Indies, Latin America and the Pacific, nor in essentials from other forms of European imperialism. Gradually, the economy of Indo-China came to depend on the economy of France. Slowly the local economy was changed in order to serve metropolitan interests more efficiently, so that the old system of village-centred production, with the landless cultivating communal land, was replaced by large estates and plantations. Tenant farmers paid a high proportion of their produce to landlords and borrowed money at risky rates.

The ethnic Chinese, who settled in Vietnam in the seventeenth and nineteenth centuries during periods of unrest in China, became middlemen, monopolizing the trade in rice, which was the major export. Money for French expansion in Indo-China came partly from local taxes but also from loans raised exclusively in France. France deliberately kept out other European capital. The second-biggest investor was China: even during French rule, the influence of China continued to be felt.

A distinctive aspect of French rule, as in other parts of the French empire, was the almost total lack of political development within Vietnam. The French passion was for civilization. In this they were generous, passing on freely their language and culture and their instinct for romance and sharing with the Vietnamese one of the world's most fascinating ways of life. Of all the colonial powers they were the most intense about language, education and culture, even if these were intended only to civilize inferiors. There was also an element of rivalry with Britain and of national pride in the French experience in Indo-China.

A people as nationalistic as the Vietnamese naturally opposed their French overlords. At first the main opposition came from the aristocracy, which prided itself on its Chinese traditions and whose superior role in society was undermined by the French. Several emperors had to be deposed after they led guerilla movements against the French. Journalists and scholars formed nationalist movements, modelled on the Kuomintang in China. Fleeing nationalists sought refuge in Japan (which after its successful war against Russia in 1905 had begun to consider itself the leader of Asian nationalism) and then later, when the Japanese succumbed to economic pressure from Europe, in southern China.

It was during the resistance to the French that the career began of the most remarkable Vietnamese of modern times. Ho Chi Minh was born of middle-class parents in 1890 in central Vietnam, was expelled from a French school at the age of thirteen, went to sea as a mess boy on a French liner in 1911, and worked in London as a kitchen helper during the first world war before moving to Paris, where he earned his living as a retoucher of photographs. He was thus in Europe when the Russian revolution broke out and he began his long association with international communist politics from that time. He was for twenty years a functionary of the Communist International (Comintern) and during this period became the founder-in-exile of the communist party of Indo-China in 1930. Perpetually on the run, his aliases became known to immigration officials all over the world. (He was born Nguyen That Thanh, although he chose as his 'real' name Nguyen Ai Quoc, which means 'one who loves his country' or, as he preferred, 'the patriot').

Ho Chi Minh spent 1933-35 in Moscow and was in China from 1936-41. His broad base in the international communist movement became important later, when Peking and Moscow factions developed in the Lao-Dong (or workers') party. Vo Nguyen Giap, who became famous as the military strategist who defeated the French at Dien Bien Phu, was closer to Moscow, while Dan Xuan Khu, better known as Truong Chinh ('Long March'), had joined the party, as his name suggests, after training in China.

During the late 1930s Japan pushed south in China, seizing Hainan Island off the coast of Vietnam in 1939 and thrusting into Kwangsi province, cutting China's railways and strategic roads with Indo-China. In 1940 the Japanese signed a treaty with Thailand and when the Nazis overran France, the Vichy government and Tokyo reached an agreement that allowed Japanese troops to enter Vietnam. Vietnam was thus still controlled by the French during the second world war, while occupied by the Japanese. This defined Ho Chi Minh's strategy. He returned to Vietnam and organized the partisan forces (Vietminh) against both the French and the Japanese, making the rice fields and the villages, not the towns, the shifting centre of his power base. This brought him for the first time into contact with the Americans, through the Office of Strategic Services, the precursor of the CIA, which was operating within Vietnam from positions in southern China.

It has been suggested since by some French writers that the Americans catapulted Ho from obscurity into national leadership by allowing him to present himself to the Vietnamese people as the man chosen by the United States to lead Vietnam when the second world war ended. Certainly American policy was opposed to a return of the French to Vietnam. In 1944 President Roosevelt had written his famous minute to Secretary of State Cordell Hull that France had 'milked' Indo-China for a hundred years and the Vietnamese people were now entitled to something better. Washington at that time believed that the colonial territories of Asia would have to become independent. The British, who had their own colonial interests to consider and with empire-minded Churchill in command, differed from the Americans. The decision taken by Roosevelt, Churchill and Stalin at Potsdam in 1945 was that, on the defeat of Japan, Vietnam would be occupied below the sixteenth parallel by British troops and above the line by the Chinese. The British ushered back the French in the south. In the north the Chinese eventually allowed them back also (in exchange for some privileges) but not before 150 000 Chinese soldiers had ransacked the route into Hanoi in a manner that is still referred to with awe. They moved through the countryside like locusts, stripping houses of even their roof-tiles and doors, and sending a shiver through the Vietnamese population which some historians believe strengthened Ho's hand.

Choosing brilliantly a moment of chaos (the Japanese had added to the confusion earlier by staging a coup against the Vichy French) Ho proclaimed in Hanoi in September 1945, on behalf of the Vietminh, the declaration of the democratic republic of Vietnam. The opening words of the declaration were: 'All men are created equal. They are endowed by their Creator with certain unalienable rights, among these are Life, Liberty and the Pursuit of Happiness . . .' Ho's luck, or his charm, was remarkable. As the ceremony proceeded, a flight of American aircraft passed overhead. Seeing the crowd, they dipped wings to take a better look, so it is said – but the Vietnamese (and many French) believed that the dip was a salute.

Ho's peaceful seizure of power, under the benevolent gaze of the victorious Americans, revived folk memories for the Vietnamese people. This was the leader who, having the 'mandate of heaven', could unite the country. It was the only place in the whole of colonial South-East Asia where leadership passed directly to the communists. Elsewhere leadership passed to the nationalists, like Sukarno, Tunku Abdul Rahman and Lee Kuan Yew and the communists tried in subsequent years to wrench power from them, unsuccessfully. Ho's national leadership was now established; party membership rose from 20 000 in 1946 to 168 000 in 1948. In view of what was to come, which would demonstrate to the world the qualities of both Ho Chi Minh and the Vietnamese communists, it is a little too easy to attribute his quick success in 1946 to a quirk of fate.

Nor is it possible to suggest that, in becoming communist, Vietnam simply followed China, as it had done in all other important matters. In 1945 China was four years away from communist rule and, while Ho followed Mao Tse-tung in the strategy of peasant-supported partisan warfare, the rice culture of Vietnam is different from that of China north of the Yangtse, where grain is the staple, and even in southern China the rice culture is different from Vietnam's because of the absence of the South-East-Asian monsoon. Vietnam is not China. Ho Chi Minh, in spite of his many years abroad, remained intensely Vietnamese, with a hard-headed political approach that has reminded writers as much of Gandhi as of Mao.

So began the last stage of the struggle for Vietnamese unity and independence for which millions had been sacrificed in the past and for which millions would be sacrificed during the next thirty years.

For, although a compromise agreement was signed between the French and Vietnam, and Ho Chi Minh adopted a strategy of conciliation (even dissolving the communist party), clashes between the Vietminh and French troops continued. In November 1946 the French navy bombarded Haiphong, killing 6000. Ho Chi Minh returned with his government to the jungles and the paddy fields and war with the French began. The emperor of Annam, Bao Dai, was persuaded to head a pro-French government.

With the death of Roosevelt and Washington's preoccupation with restoring western Europe, American anti-colonial sentiment became subdued. The cold war brought a US commitment to NATO (1949) and America's first military aid to the French in Vietnam arrived the next year. Although outgunned, the Vietminh took the offensive in the classical manner of guerilla warfare, controlling the rural areas of Tonkin and Annam and penetrating into Cochin China. The battle of Dien Bien Phu in north-west Tonkin was decisive. After a siege of fifty-five days, on 7 May 1954, 10 000 French troops surrendered to General Giap and the French nation was ready to negotiate.

The Geneva agreements of 1954 confirmed at an international level that Vietnam was an independent, sovereign state, but at the same time destroyed the unity that had been maintained since 1802. The country was split along the seventeenth parallel, with the intention that general elections in two years time for the entire country would restore unity. If the elections had been held, there seems little doubt that the Vietminh would have won handsomely. The mandate of heaven was again theirs. But the elections were never held. Instead, the policy of John Foster Dulles, who had become US secretary of state under President Eisenhower, required a stand to be made at the seventeenth parallel as part of the grand strategy of containing China and communism, and thus preventing the dominoes falling throughout South-East Asia and the south-west Pacific. It also required someone who could compete with Ho Chi Minh for the mantle of national leadership.

The man chosen was Ngo Dinh Diem. Like Ho, Diem also came from central Vietnam and was somewhat the same generation, being born in 1901. There the similarities ended. Ho Chi Minh was an austere bachelor who had lived most of his life abroad in obscurity and secrecy. Diem came from a large Catholic family active in Vietnamese public life. He had held office under Bao Dai in the 1930s but had resigned as a protest against French influence. He had been sought out early by the Vietminh but had become strongly anti-communist. It was thought that a man with a record of opposition to both the French and the communists would have the kind of nationalist integrity needed to make a stand against Ho Chi Minh and the Vietminh.

The formation of the South-East Asia Treaty Organization (SEATO) in 1954 brought South Vietnam, Laos and Cambodia under the American security umbrella. With the division of the country into two internationally recognized states, without a prospect of unity in the foreseeable future, some major movements of refugees began. Thousands from the north went to Thailand, where many of them remain. Some 800 000 crossed from the north to the south. Most were Catholic and opposed to reunification if this meant conceding victory to the Vietminh. These refugees provided the Diem regime with its central staff and its cadres. The Vietminh had felt that they could negotiate successfully on the basis of the Geneva agreements with Bao Dai and the French, both of whom had signed, but they were confronted now by the Americans and Diem, neither of whom had signed. The Vietminh complained to no avail about the failure to implement the agreements. They received little support from the Soviet Union and China, nor, indeed, from non-aligned states like India and Indonesia. In the late 1950s they decided to fight back. By 1960, the National Liberation Front (NLF) had been formed in South Vietnam. Working as always in the rural areas, it intimidated villages and assassinated petty officials. Its propaganda always stressed the unity of Vietnam.

With the backing of the Americans, Diem set about reforming South Vietnam. He deposed Bao Dai (by referendum) and established himself as president of the republic of Vietnam. He hunted down the communists, brought in land reform and gained control over several religious-military sects who had supported Bao Dai and sometimes the Vietminh, and who monopolized piracy and banditry as well as running brothels, gaming houses and opium dens in Saigon. His rule was authoritarian, as if he wished to return to a former age when Vietnamese society was hierarchical and stable.

Given by Saigon the derogatory description 'Vietcong' (Vietnamese communists), the guerillas gradually moved from sporadic raids to partisan warfare. In addition to Chinese weapons, they were armed with captured French and American equipment. In 1961 President Kennedy sent military advisers to Vietnam. At that stage, Vietnam was still on the fringe of American strategic thinking (the Cuban missile crisis of 1962 being central). But after the Sino-Indian conflict in 1962 and Peking's flirtation with Sukarno, who was 'confronting' the British in Malaysia, Washington began to take the view that a firmer stand needed to be taken in Vietnam.

Political unrest intensified in South Vietnam as pressure on the insurgents increased. Buddhist and student groups became openly hostile to Diem, who responded with mass arrests and the declaration of a state of siege. Late in 1963 a decision was made in Washington – although the details are still argued – that Diem's unpopularity, his patrician aloofness and unwillingness to work closely with the Americans had made him a liability and that he should be replaced. His brother Ngo Dinh Nhu was also suspected of secretly negotiating with Hanoi. A nod in the direction of a group of generals was enough. In November 1963 the President's palace was stormed. Diem escaped with his brother but they were found hiding in a Catholic church in the Chinese suburb of Cholon. They were shot dead in a car taking them to army headquarters.

The Americans were shocked at Diem's brutal murder; their understanding was that he would be given safe conduct. But they had encouraged the removal of the man they had built up as a patriot against Ho Chi Minh. No figure of national reputation was now offering. And in three weeks President Kennedy was assassinated at Dallas, Texas.

The war now became America's war. President Johnson committed ground troops and Hanoi moved larger tactical units into the south. American bombers pounded the north. American allies (Australia, New Zealand, South Korea, Philippines and Thailand) gave military support. Eventually 500 000 American troops would be in Vietnam and the bombing would exceed three times all the tonnage dropped on Germany, Italy and Japan during the second world war. This huge effort had a single aim: to secure the independence of the republic of Vietnam in the south (or, put in historical terms, to keep Vietnam divided). Ho Chi Minh also had a single aim: to unite Vietnam under his leadership.

There was no prospect that Vietnam would be united under the leadership of the south. While controversy over the war raged in America and the world, President Johnson claimed that the policy of attrition was working and that 70 per cent of the south was free of communist control. But the fall of Diem had produced a succession of ineffective governments, until a former general, Nguyen Van Thieu, became president by election in 1967. The Vietcong struck a devastating blow during the Tet (lunar new year) holiday on 1 February 1968, launching a general offensive on cities and towns, including Saigon and Hue, and on military installations throughout the south. They were repulsed over a period of two or three weeks and suffered heavy casualties, but not before they had reduced many towns to ruins, killed thousands of civilians and demonstrated beyond doubt to the population that the south was not safe. President Johnson announced that he intended to stand down.

The year 1969 marked another stage in the war. Richard Nixon and Henry Kissinger came to power in Washington, Ho Chi Minh died and the struggle moved into the sphere of secret diplomacy, and indeed, secret war. Negotiations began openly in Paris but the real discussions were conducted secretly between Kissinger and Hanoi. An unannounced decision was taken in Washington to bomb Cambodia, and its head of state, Prince Sihanouk, was replaced in a pro-American coup.

There was great irony, and even greater tragedy, in Washington's destruction of Sihanouk, especially under a secretary of state who had become noted for his understanding of history (but evidently only of European history). For Sihanouk had written in 1963: 'Whether he is called Gia Long, Ho Chi Minh or Ngo Dinh Diem no Annamite (or Vietnamese) will sleep peacefully until he has succeeded in pushing Cambodia towards annihilation, having made it first go through the stages of slavery'. Sihanouk did not want a powerful reunified Vietnam. He wanted a neutral South Vietnam and a neutral Laos so that he would not have to share a border with communist North Vietnam which he saw as the strong one of the Indo-Chinese states. He also said in 1964: 'If our region must one day be submerged by communism, we would wish that it be China and not another socialist country which takes control of our country because we know that she understands us and that she will maintain ... our territorial integrity'. The complex balance which Sihanouk sought was rejected as too subtle or too devious by Washington, just as it had earlier rejected other Asian ideas such as Nehru's in its determination to establish American power and American ideas in Asia.

American and South Vietnamese troops carried out operations in Laos and Cambodia designed to cut 'the Ho Chi Minh trail' (actually a series of trails) by which supplies and troops had been moving from north to south through neutral territory. Kissinger also undertook secret diplomacy with China, which Nixon visited in 1972. With each side trying to negotiate from strength, the war went on. In 1972 Hanoi launched a military offensive over the border and the United States responded by resuming bombing for the first time since 1968. Yet despite publicly expressed resolve, the impression gained ground that the United States, or at least Nixon and Kissinger, wanted an agreement with Hanoi before the 1972 presidential elections. Agreement was reached in Paris a few days before polling day and President Nixon was returned with a massive majority.

The Paris accords brought clearly to the surface that, to use Kissinger's phrase, the Vietnam war had become a 'cruel sideshow' to the larger objectives of American foreign policy. The essence of the accords was a 'ceasefire in place' which effectively meant that the forces of the NLF could remain in the south while the Americans, who were withdrawing anyway for their own reasons, handed over the war to Saigon. As President Nixon became embroiled in the Watergate disclosures during 1974, and as congress hostility to the war increased, the NLF forces gained ground in the south and Chinese and Russian supplies to Hanoi increased. Thieu believed he had a written guarantee from Nixon that if the Paris accords were 'massively' broken by Hanoi, the United States would retaliate by bombing. But even when NLF units in the south were merged into Hanoi's military command and the drive south began, the American withdrawal continued. The South Vietnamese fought stubbornly but in the early months of 1975 the Vietnam people's army moved south province by province. Saigon fell on 30 April and within a few days the whole of the south was in their hands.

In July 1976 the country was formally reunited under the name of the Socialist Republic of Vietnam. Saigon was renamed Ho Chi Minh City. The flag and the anthem were those used since 1946 by Hanoi. The bloodbath predicted by some did not occur but the reunification nevertheless established the dominance of the north over the south. In the perspective of Vietnamese history, the adjustment of the south promised to be painful.

A prime purpose of the fourth congress of the Vietnam communist party in Hanoi in December 1976 was to endorse plans for dealing with southern Vietnam. What methods should be used to integrate it with the north, socially and economically? At what pace should this assimilation take place? How could such a large body of potential opposition in the south be neutralized, if not won over? As noted in the preceding chapter, prescriptions for asserting socialist authority over the capitalist, individualistic south were sometimes ambiguous and obviously difficult to apply. At the time, observers felt these prescriptions had been the subject of intense, possibly divided, debate within the communist hierarchy.

The congress changed the party's name from Vietnam workers' party to Vietnam communist party, thus underlining its commitment to social revolution. It increased the size of the central committee from 77 to 133 in an attempt to strengthen party leadership in economic work. It enlarged the committee's politburo, a key decision-making body, to 17 by formally adding 7 members, mainly to confirm or promote communist leaders prominent in the south, though not necessarily born or raised there.

In the central committee report to the congress and in speeches on the rostrum, the principal themes were economic development and socialist construction. But it also dealt with weaknesses and abuses in the party and government system. It was clear that many were caused or aggravated by the grafting of the laissez-faire south onto the socialist north. Corruption, maladministration and mismanagement were interrelated themes and are still the subject of remedial campaigns in Vietnam.

When the war ended, the condition of the party in the south, particularly in Ho Chi Minh City, was weak. Thousands of cadres in the Vietcong army and underground had been killed or arrested over the past decade. In the year preceding the congress, party leaders repeatedly expressed concern over the low quality of party membership, which was attributed chiefly to a relaxation of entry rules during the war years.

Le Duc Tho, a member of the politburo and negotiator with Henry Kissinger at the Paris peace talks, told the congress that membership of the communist party had doubled since 1966 to 1 553 500, or 3.13 per cent of the population. Too much attention to quantity had resulted in a lowering of standards and 'corruption, bureaucracy, arbitrariness, autocracy and lack of devotion' still existed.

Another leading figure in Vietnam's collective leadership, Le Duan, general secretary of the party, also spoke out about 'backsliding' now that the imperatives of wartime survival and solidarity had given way to the seemingly easier tempo of peaceful reconstruction. He called for the expulsion of 'degenerate and corrupt elements' from the party, as well as for effective measures to prevent state cadres and employees from becoming a privileged caste.

Much of the trouble was occurring in, and attributed to, the corrupting influence of the south, although many of the officials involved were from the north. Increasing numbers of civilian cadres and technicians were sent south to fill gaping holes in the administration. While 3.13 per cent of Vietnam's overall population belonged to the communist party, the proportion in southern Vietnam was substantially lower – not much more than 1.3 per cent or barely 250 000. Only about half these southern members had a primary school or higher education. Many, perhaps 20 per cent, had been recruited since 1975. Some later became known as '30th of

April cadres' because of the suspicion that they only sided with the revolution after it became an accomplished fact with the fall of Saigon on that date. In the south, the party's youth group included only 10 per cent of those in the fifteen to thirty age-group; the figure in the north was about 30 per cent.

The October 1976 edition of the Vietnam communist party's theoretical journal, *Hoc Tap*, noted the cadres had been 'tempted and bewitched by a materialistic side of life', suggesting that the takeover of the south had spread unwholesome influence throughout the country. The blandishments of the higher material standards of living in the south, and the ready availability on the black market in 1975 and 1976 of all kinds of consumer goods that were rare or unobtainable in the north, affected the army as well as the civil administration. In the early days after the occupation of Ho Chi Minh City, regular soldiers (Bo Doi) were often seen buying matches, sewing machines and other consumer goods available in the black, but still officially tolerated, market.

For years the Vietnamese communists had drawn attention to the vice and graft that flourished under successive anti-communist governments based in Saigon, and used the undertones of foreign exploitation implicit in 'western-style' culture for propaganda purposes. After April 1975 they were in a position to purify the city of sin, but they found the task of turning Ho Chi Minh City into a 'revolutionary, civilized, healthy, joyful and fresh' place a protracted and difficult one. But the effort was in contrast with what happened in Cambodia (renamed Kampuchea) in April 1975, when the young cadres of the Khmer Rouge forced a brutal evacuation of cities and appear to have murdered almost an entire middle class.

The differences between the south, which had always been more available to western commercial culture, and the frugal bureaucratic north do not promise to become another Nguyen-Trinh epic. But they placed a strain upon a leadership that had grown old under the forced circumstances of a long war. Much of the argument about cadres and correct behaviour may have masked emerging differences among leaders who had before functioned almost as a family.

Two other themes of Vietnamese history – resistance to China and dominance of its neighbours, Cambodia and Laos – developed quickly in 1978 and 1979 and also had a bearing on the refugee crisis.

Vietnam's treaty with Laos in July 1977 and its military subjugation of Kampuchea in 1978 and early 1979 were classic demonstrations of its ancient determination to keep China out of its western approaches, while China's invasion of Vietnam in February 1979 was equally classic. Its troops crossed into Vietnam's northern provinces and, after some heavy fighting, withdrew in stages following an announcement by Peking that it had 'taught a lesson' to its truculent neighbour.

Anyone aware of the major themes of Vietnam history could not have failed to be impressed by the repetition of a familiar pattern. The Chinese troops entered Vietnam by the route they had used for centuries. To revert to the language of earlier times, they administered 'a dose of frightfulness' to the Vietnamese, as a punishment for their defiant behaviour, and then withdrew. Vietnam, united and independent again at last, was once again facing a test of its will to survive.

The new element was the Soviet Union, with whom Vietnam signed a 25-year treaty in November 1978. The split between Moscow and Peking had been submerged (although never mended) during Hanoi's war with America. The Vietnamese communist leadership remained cohesive even after the death of Ho Chi Minh, but the pressures of 1978 and 1979 produced a first major defection. Hoang Van Hoan, deputy chairman of the national assembly, and a party veteran who had helped Ho Chi Minh found the Indo-Chinese communist party in 1930, in August 1979 slipped his aircraft at Karachi and flew to Peking, where he accused the Hanoi leadership of subservience to the Soviet Union. He was expelled from the Vietnam communist party for treason. Observers in Hanoi noted that Hoan's star had been waning for some time (he had been dropped from the politburo in 1976). Nevertheless his defection to Peking at a time of virtual war with China provided a glimpse of the strain under which the leadership of Vietnam is now working.

A PRAYER FOR LAND

Lost in the tempests
Out on the open seas
Our small boats drift.
We seek for land
During endless days and endless nights.
We are the foam
Floating on the vast ocean.
We are the dust
Wandering in endless space.
Our cries are lost
In the howling wind.
Without food, without water
Our children lie exhausted
Until they cry no more.
We thirst for land
But are turned back from every shore.
Our distress signals rise and rise again
But the passing ships do not stop.
How many boats have perished?
How many families lie beneath the waves?
Lord Jesus, do you hear the prayer of our flesh?
Lord Buddha, do you hear our voice
From the abyss of death?
O solid shore,
We long for you!
We pray for mankind to be present today!
We pray for land to stretch its arms to us!
We pray that hope be given us
Today, from any land.

A poem written by an
unknown Vietnamese at a
refugee camp in 1978

Chapter 3

Armada

Ten days after they were shipwrecked on a barren atoll in the South China Sea, Tran Hue Hue's aunt, Cam Binh, died. Because the old lady was the first to go, her niece did not know what to do with the corpse.

Finally a group was assigned to tie her body on a large board and dispose of it in the sea. On a strip of cloth they wrote in English and Vietnamese: 'We are fifty people stuck on a coral isle. Please help us. sos'. The piece of cloth was bound around Aunt Binh's arm; then she was dropped into the sea. The corpse floated away for some minutes before the board broke and Aunt Binh disappeared.

It was a macabre, futile gesture; only people in desperation would have considered it. But for Tran Hue Hue, a striking young woman of sixteen, the ordeal was only beginning. She should have died. She should have gone mad. Somehow, she kept her sanity and survived.

When she was recovering later at a navy centre in Puerto Princesa, the capital of Palawan Island, south-west of Manila, she wrote an account of her experience. It was translated into English by two fellow refugees. Western refugee officials who spoke at length to Miss Hue are convinced it is true.

Her family lived in the bustling Mekong delta town of Can Tho, where her father owned a business selling and repairing watches. Food was short; her father did not like life under the communists: the family decided as a group to get out. The night escape on 12 September 1978 began badly. She, her uncle and aunt, and her brother Trung were among those safely on board when someone raised the alarm. They sailed in panic, leaving her parents and two younger brothers behind. For six days they travelled slowly across the South China Sea towards the Philippines. The wooden hull leaked; the engine was unreliable; food and drinking water had to be rationed. Two ocean-going ships passed them by. A third ship was avoided because it was thought to be Russian. Then their boat struck a coral reef and was too badly damaged to continue the voyage. Tran Hue Hue, with the forty-nine other occupants, began life on a tiny atoll in the South China Sea.

The atoll on which they were stranded was a graveyard of wrecked vessels. They sought shelter in one of them, a bleached hulk which became for Miss Hue 'the white ship', and the centre of her world. This is what she wrote after her brother died:

After Trung went away, I didn't eat. I just lay in the cabin weeping. There were times when I found myself home, living happily with my family. My other younger brothers and grandma too. When I awoke with nobody around, I would start crying again. After some time, I got used to my loneliness. I went around asking my companions for some dried food. We were still a crowd. We tried to live on oysters and snails even though the number of people dying by diarrhoea increased.

A month after they sought refuge in the white ship the number of survivors had dwindled from fifty to seven. One of them suggested they should all go to live on the wreck of a black ship because it was much larger and would be more visible, offering a better prospect of rescue. So they tried to wade across.

Miss Hue wrote:

Halfway to the black ship, the tide got higher and higher. We were scared, and had to get back. The wind started to blow harder, and through the green water I could see sharp spikes of coral and rocks. The last two to reach the ladder on the white ship – a girl of eighteen and a boy of nineteen – were swept away by a wave.

There were five left now: three women – Huong, 35, Lan, 18, and herself; and two boys – Cuong, 18, and Quan, 14.

We loved one another very much. We shared our food. We slept in the same corner and treated one another as blood relatives. And we were no longer a crowd, so the seagulls came back. In the day, when the seagulls flew away, we slept. When they came back in the evening to sleep, we tried to catch them. There were nights when we got as many as twenty birds, and we dried some to save for days when we caught none. We still had some water, because when it rained we used every kind of container to catch it.

But the blistering heat during the day, dehydration and malnourishment gradually took its toll. As their strength ebbed, the five refugees found it more difficult to catch food, fetch water and withstand illness. Miss Hue recalled: 'Whenever I wanted to sit down or stand up, somebody would have to help me. We walked with our hands supported by the wall. Later, we crawled on our hands and knees.'

Finally, the last of her companions, the 14-year-old boy, Quan, died in his sleep.

I was in a panic, thinking I would have to live alone on this phantom ship. I cried aloud, for a long time, but nobody answered. Around me there was nothing but dreadful silence. I was not scared of ghosts or demons, not even of Quan's body lying beside me. I was scared of loneliness. Who was going to talk to me? Who was going to catch seagulls with me? These thoughts made me cry more. The sun began to shine down and Quan's face got paler and paler. His hollow cheeks made his teeth show. With all my strength I sat up, pulled the corpse by its two cold feet to the deck and let him drop into the sea.

Miss Hue's story continued:

Living all by myself, I usually sat up late at night to catch seagulls. There were strong birds that fought back, tearing pieces of skin from my hands, but I never let loose. When I called Buddha, gods, I promised to offer them a chicken if a ship would come to save my life. There were days when I didn't catch a single bird, and lying there with my empty stomach, I dreamed of a meal with fish. I was scared of death no longer. I wished to die, but couldn't. I believed strongly that a ship would come to save me, and I prayed: 'If I was sinful, let me die at once. If I wasn't, bring a ship here and don't let me live in prolonged torture'.

It was raining when the Philippine fishing boat passed near the island, but fortunately she could still hear the engine. She stood up and ran out of the cabin. She wonders now how it was that she could even stand up, let alone run. With a white shirt belonging to somebody already dead, she waved to the ship which came closer. 'I was paralysed with joy. It stopped raining, but drops of water were running down my face. I touched the water lightly, thinking it was still another dream'. By the time Miss Hue was rescued, she had been on the atoll for five months.

* * *

The most dangerous of the routes taken by the boat people was the one Tran Hue Hue and her ill-fated companions had attempted – the 1500-kilometre, east-west crossing of the South China Sea. Boats going this way soon cross the main international sealanes and pass into the deserted waters beyond. If they have engine trouble, run short of supplies or spring a leak, they are unlikely to find help. On the latter half of the crossing, refugee boats faced another hazard in the hundreds of small reefs, atolls and islets that form a scattered chain lying west and south-west of Palawan Island. It was in this area that Miss Hue's boat ran aground. In July 1979, not long after she was rescued, Philippine officials reported that six Vietnamese refugees had committed suicide and seven others had died of thirst and hunger while crossing the South China Sea. The deaths of these unlucky thirteen brought to more than sixty the number of Indo-Chinese who died in one week in July trying to get to the Philippines. They included a boatload of fifty, mainly children, who drowned in one of the storms that strike with ferocious suddenness in the South China Sea. It is hardly surprising that less than 10 000 boat people have arrived in the Philippines since 1975.

Since the American evacuation of Saigon in 1975, when the first wave of Vietnamese left, the exodus of boat people from Vietnam had been only a trickle; by 1977 it became a flow – 21 276; by the end of 1978, a flood – 106 489; and in the first six months of 1979 a torrent – 166 604. In May alone, the outflow totalled 51 139; in June it peaked at 56 941. By the end of July 1979 the number of people who had left Vietnam on boats or ships since 1975 amounted to a staggering total of 292 315. A study made in June 1979 by the Hong Kong government, of the ages of nearly 20 000 boat people (just under a quarter of them from the southern and central parts of the country, the rest from the north), showed that 3.1 per cent were under the age of one, 29.4 per cent between one and twelve, 8.8 per cent between thirteen and sixteen, 10.7 per cent between seventeen and twenty, 23.2 per cent between twenty-one and thirty, 15.5 per cent between thirty and fifty, 8 per cent between fifty-one and seventy, and 1.3 per cent over seventy. On an average boat, about half the passengers were children, women and old folk.

Of the 292 315 people who left by boat from Vietnam, about 77 000 got to Hong Kong. Most of the rest – just over 200 000 – chose the sea route leading south-west from Vietnam to Thailand, Malaysia, Singapore and Indonesia. Virtually all of them were residents of southern Vietnam. They travelled by motorized boats, with an average speed of about 7 knots. For them, the shortest sea crossing was from ports in Vietnam's Mekong River delta to the north-east coast of peninsular Malaysia or southern Thailand's Kra Isthmus. From the fishing port of Rach Gia, on southern Vietnam's coastline facing the Gulf of Thailand, to the Malaysian state of Trengganu is 555 kilometres by sea; from My Tho in the Mekong delta to Trengganu is 759 kilometres; from Vung Tau, a port east of Ho Chi Minh City, to Trengganu is 722 kilometres.

*   *   *

Trieu Phieu remembers vividly the day before Christmas 1978. His wife and their four daughters, aged between two and seven, were like most of the other 249 Indo-Chinese on the overloaded boat: frightened and so weak from seasickness they could hardly move. They were in any case packed in so tightly that moving at the best of times was difficult; in rough weather it was impossible.

It was their second day out. The first few hours of the voyage from Ca Mau, the southernmost point of the Mekong delta, on the nineteen-metre fishing boat were uneventful. But they were tempting fate by travelling at the height of the north-east monsoon season. Their destination was Malaysia; however, the fury of the storm that struck them made them change course for Thailand. There was no way out of its path. As huge waves crashed about them, the boat started taking water. 'Very few of us had ever been to sea before. We could not swim. We had no life jackets. We thought we were going to drown,' Mr Phieu recalled later. About forty people on the boat were Vietnamese. The rest, including Phieu and his family, were members of Vietnam's Chinese minority. The panic and helplessness felt by this forty-year-old, one-time manager of a Japanese import company in Saigon, was especially real. Two months earlier, in October 1978, his mother and one of his younger brothers had drowned about ten kilometres from the port of Vung Tau after their boat sank in an abortive escape attempt.

Mr Phieu was lucky. His boat survived the storm and shortly afterwards they were rescued and brought to Singapore by a 10 566-tonne container ship, *World Lion*, owned by a US shipping company.

Thousands of boat people were saved by the lights of offshore petroleum rigs, either those drilling for oil and natural gas off the coast of southern Thailand or those operated by the US oil company Exxon off the north-east coast of peninsular Malaysia.

The presence of the rigs, and the relatively short distance between Vietnam and Malaysia, helps explain why nearly all the 200 000 people who left southern Vietnam in the eighteen months to mid-1979 first headed for Malaysia. The rigs also help explain how several thousand small boats, many of them built for use only in coastal or inland waters, were able to complete the sea crossing even when those on board were inexperienced mariners, armed with little more than a compass and a school map. The rigs literally served as signposts in the sky at night.

By August 1979 there were five Exxon production platforms tapping oil from seabed reservoirs about 190 kilometres off the coast of the Malaysian state of Trengganu. They lay to the east of the state capital, Kuala Trengganu. But for most of the duration of the large-scale exodus of boat people that started in 1978, only two production platforms were in place. They were about fifty kilometres apart. Each of the eighteen-metre-high, steel towers was illuminated night and day not only by powerful floodlights but also by jets of waste gas burning brightly about thirty metres above the sea.

In good weather the glow from the gas flares could be seen more than a hundred kilometres away. This meant that if a refugee boat leaving a Mekong delta port set a reasonably accurate course for the first twenty-four hours, it could expect to see, on the second night out if not the first, the beacons of light on the oil rigs. Western refugee officials say that even if the course steered by a refugee boat leaving southern Vietnam was 30 degrees out, it would still have a good chance of spotting the glow from the flares.

Fast crossings to Malaysia were accomplished in less than two days. Those dogged by misfortune could take a week, a fortnight or even longer. Some never made it and disappeared without trace. But for those that got through, the oil rig 'lighthouses' were an invaluable source of encouragement and help. Many refugees speak with gratitude of the assistance they were given by the international crews on the production rigs, standby barges and supply boats. Those in unseaworthy craft, or boats that were deliberately scuttled as they drew alongside an oil facility, were eventually ferried by supply ships or Malaysian navy vessels to resettlement camps run by the UNHCR. Other refugee boats were given the water, food and fuel they needed to continue their journey.

*   *   *

Before 1975 Mrs Le Thanh Van was a lawyer with a successful practice in Binh Duong province, just north of Saigon. After the communists took over she was not allowed to continue her professional career. So she remained at her family home in Ho Chi Minh City and plotted her escape. She made several attempts. In July 1975 she sailed from Nha Trang, but the captain of the boat became afraid they would not reach their destination in the Philippines and turned back. In 1976 she was about to leave on someone else's boat, but she felt the escape would not work and pulled out. Her hunch was right: the plan failed. On her third try in 1977, Mrs Van was arrested in Rach Gia on her way to meet a departing vessel on Phu Quoc Island. She was gaoled in Rach Gia for eight months. Late in 1977 she paid her share to be included in another escape plan out of Vietnam, but it turned out to be a swindle.

With her savings running low, she was determined not to fail again. She and a small group of would-be escapees clubbed together and bought a boat nine metres long by two metres wide. In the months before they left, they sent a small boat down the Saigon River, checking the frequency and location of police patrols and checkpoints. Their escape boat left Ho Chi Minh City on 31 May 1978. They boarded it downriver on 1 June. To avoid detection they changed the appearance of the boat between each of seven known checkpoints so that it would not match reports of boats heading towards the sea. The craft was fitted with two engines, one of 5 horsepower and one of 20 horsepower. When near security patrols, they would shut down the large engine and use only the small one, which was plainly too weak to power a boat on the high seas. They reached international waters without difficulty. But the one thing they forgot was a map. They got lost at sea but eventually found themselves near the south-east top of peninsular Malaysia where they landed at Mersing and later entered the Tengah Island refugee camp.

In the controversy about the officially approved exodus from southern Vietnam that developed after 1977, it is often forgotten that clandestine escapes continued at the same time as officially sanctioned departures. The latter were started mainly to get rid of members of Vietnam's Chinese minority, although ethnic Vietnamese were able to buy their way into this channel. On the other hand, some Chinese continued to leave secretly, although Vietnamese made up the majority of the boat escapees. Overall, a reliable estimate is that about one-third of all the people who have left Vietnam since 1975 did so covertly.

Towards the end of June 1979, communist authorities in southern Vietnam, apparently in response to international criticism, began to impose measures of unprecedented severity to prevent people leaving the country by boat. These reportedly included public warnings that anyone caught at sea trying to escape would be shot on sight. Coastal patrols were intensified and big rewards promised to those who informed officials about secret departures.

Even before this move, however, attempts to leave by stealth involved a high element of risk. Some escapes were made successfully on the spur of the moment, but most required careful planning. They were often ingenious, resourceful and daring. Boats had to be acquired surreptitiously. Fuel, food and other essential supplies were obtained on false pretences from the government or bought on the black market. There was an ever-present risk of discovery and arrest. On the way to departure points where the boat was waiting, security officials had to be avoided or bribed.

*   *   *

The big wave of boat refugees from Vietnam swept into Hong Kong in 1979. From New Year's day to mid-August, 531 small boats carried 45 928 men, women and children from northern Vietnam to the British territory on China's south-eastern flank. Another 14 323 came to Hong Kong in 169 small craft from what used to be South Vietnam. Most of these came from the ports along the central coast of Vietnam that were in territory overrun by the communists in 1975. They included Hue, Da Nang, Qui Nhon, Vinh An, Nha Trang, Cam Ranh and Phan Rang.

Why, having decided, or having been forced, to leave their homeland, did people strike out for Hong Kong in the north-east instead of south towards Thailand or Malaysia? It was largely a question of distance, the type of boats available and conditions at sea. Also, foreign radio reports had suggested that they would be accepted in Hong Kong. From Da Nang, in central Vietnam, direct to Hong Kong is 879 kilometres; from Da Nang to peninsular Malaysia is about double that distance. All the boats leaving southern Vietnam for Hong Kong had engines, like those going from Mekong delta ports to Thailand, Malaysia and countries further afield. This was in marked contrast to the craft that flooded into Hong Kong from northern Vietnam, the overwhelming majority of which were sailing junks.

These boats arrived in Hong Kong harbour crammed with men in khaki-coloured pith helmets, women in mollusc-shaped straw hats and children of all ages. Most of these twin- and single-masted vessels were between eight and thirty metres long, with a raised stern and sails in a style as ancient as the hand-hewn plank hulls. Some of the sails were made of patched and mildewed canvas; others of woven reed matting. There was little room below to shelter and most passengers squatted on the decks under makeshift cover. It seemed a miracle they could sail so far. But they did – by island-hopping across the Gulf of Tonkin after leaving northern Vietnam, nipping between China's Hainan Island and the mainland, and then hugging the indented coastline of southern China until they reached the Portuguese colony of Macao and nearby Hong Kong. This voyage by sailing junk usually took between six weeks and two months. The boats seldom lost sight of land. That way they could shelter from the rough weather, especially in the typhoon season from May to November. They could also call at Chinese ports for repairs and supplies, or barter with Chinese fishermen and villagers along the coast for food and water.

Mrs Tran Thi Chi, thirty-four, is half Chinese and half Vietnamese. She left Haiphong in northern Vietnam towards the end of March 1979 with her husband, their small baby, three other young children, her mother, an older brother, a younger sister and about a hundred other passengers in a twenty-metre sailing junk. In communist Vietnam she used to work for herself selling traditional Chinese medicine and made 'quite a lot' of money. Her husband was a factory worker.

Interviewed in a Hong Kong camp, Mrs Chi was dressed in typical northern attire. She wore a pale blue working shirt of thick cotton and a pair of baggy black trousers. She was lively and humorous, recalling the voyage as though it were an adventure.

We had just been at sea for a day or so when we met a big storm. That scared us. We dropped anchor and waited for it to go. We all sat below deck until it finished. Some of the old ladies were crying with fear. When the storm ended a day later, we carried on. But we were very slow. The people in charge of the boat knew how to crew it. But nobody knew exactly where Hong Kong was. We were always getting lost!

We were at sea for over a month, but spent two weeks in different places in China, repairing the boat. It was always leaking. Once the mast broke. I don't know where we were in China. I didn't really pay any attention – I don't speak much Chinese. We cooked our food together. When the supplies ran out, though, each family bought more at the places we stopped. If we were near a coastal town on the Chinese mainland, people would come out and offer us food. When we went into harbour, people would bring things right up to the boat to sell to us.

Payment was made in gold leaf, jewellery, wrist watches or anything else of value the Chinese villagers were prepared to accept. Mrs Chi said no one was seriously ill on the voyage, 'but we were seasick all the time for the first couple of weeks'. Her experiences were fairly typical of the refugees sailing to Hong Kong from northern Vietnam. Chinese authorities generally allowed boats from Vietnam heading for Hong Kong to stop for as long as necessary to make repairs or to take on urgent supplies. In some cases the Chinese helped with the repairs and gave food and water free of charge.

Of the 68 678 refugees from Vietnam who arrived in Hong Kong between 1 January and 15 August 1979, 56 per cent were ethnic Chinese from northern Vietnam and 26 per cent Chinese from southern Vietnam. Those from the north, like Mrs Chi, say they were expelled. Few Chinese from either the north or the south had to escape secretly. They say they were driven out by the Vietnamese authorities.

Miss Ly Thi Oanh is a fourteen-year-old Chinese girl who left Vung Tau, in southern Vietnam, in mid-April 1979, with her mother, father, brother aged four, and a lot of other ethnic Chinese. Several boats were moored side by side as they boarded in the rain. Headlights shone from a car and men walked about with lamps.

We had to form a long line. My father and mother were each carrying two suitcases and I had to hold onto my brother. Mother kept on saying 'Keep hold of him! Hold on to him!' and I kept hold of his hand. When we got near the plank that went up onto the boat there were two men in uniform who started asking my father questions and we stopped moving forward. They made my mother and father open the suitcases in the rain, and they started going through everything inside.

Somebody picked up my brother and carried him up the plank. I still kept hold of him and went up onto the boat. Looking back, I could see my parents pleading with the two men. My mother was kneeling on the stones in front of them. I kept on calling to her because I knew she thought we were still with her and didn't know we were on the boat.

The boat left without the parents. The two children arrived in Hong Kong believing they would never see the parents again. But six days later another small boat brought their mother and father to the British territory and they were eventually reunited.

Tran Van Tuyen is a cocky fisherman's son who thinks he is eighteen but doesn't know his birthday. His family is still in Hoi An, an attractive old town on the coast of central Vietnam not far from Da Nang. He arrived in Hong Kong in August 1979, with his ten-year-old nephew and five other Vietnamese friends and acquaintances. The family fishing boat was taken over by the state eight months earlier, though he and his mother continued to fish in it, selling the catch to the government for what Tuyen considered a scandalously low price. So one night, while the three soldiers supposed to be guarding the harbour were having dinner, Tuyen and his group sneaked aboard and took off. They reached Hong Kong about a week later.

Stepping off his sturdy, twenty-metre, motorized fishing boat at the Canton Road government dockyard in Kowloon, which serves as a reception centre for all small boat arrivals in Hong Kong, Tuyen wore a jockey's cap tipped jauntily on the back of his head. His clothes were filthy, his face grimy and his hands greasy. He grinned with delight as he told his story. He and his six companions left Hoi An with barely enough diesel fuel to reach China's Hainan Island, roughly half way to Hong Kong. They were towed into what was apparently a Chinese navy base by a patrol boat and allowed to land. A meal was provided. Describing it, Tuyen made a face: 'It was lousy – salted vegetables'. The Chinese then gave them 400 litres of fuel for the boat. 'I cried,' said Tuyen grinning. 'I said we would die at sea unless they gave us more. So they handed over another 300 litres and some food.'

But the Chinese also handed over sixty-eight extra passengers, all Vietnamese from Phan Thiet on the south central coast of Vietnam. All were Catholic. They had escaped on the spur of the moment by stealing a thirteen-metre fishing boat on the night of 31 July 1979, in the hope of being picked up at sea by ships of the US Seventh Fleet and the Italian navy. They knew these western warships were looking for refugees in the South China Sea because they had heard the news on BBC and Voice of America broadcasts. If they missed the warships, their plan was to head south for Malaysia. But on 2 August, heavy seas and high winds generated by the tail end of a typhoon drove them northwards. On 9 August the engine broke down and they had to rig a temporary sail. Most of their food and water was exhausted, and they started drinking seawater even though it made them ill. What rice they had left they cooked on deck using pieces of wood ripped from the boat. The vessel was water-logged and close to sinking when they finally drifted into Hainan on 12 August. Within a few days Tuyen came along and the Chinese handed them over. They were carried on to Hong Kong in Tuyen's boat.

*   *   *

For large numbers of boat refugees – possibly as many as one-third of all who left before mid-1979 – the voyage from southern Vietnam to a country of first asylum in non-communist South-East Asia was relatively uneventful. But, particularly from 1978 onwards, several factors narrowed the chances of a safe crossing and quick entry into a UNHCR-protected camp. One was the failure of the advanced industrial democracies, where the boat people wanted to settle, to take them at anywhere near the rate at which they were pouring into Vietnam's hard-pressed neighbours, especially Malaysia, Thailand and, later, Indonesia. Another was that Thailand, followed by Malaysia, pushed boat people back to sea, partly out of frustration at the failure of the west to do more to alleviate the refugee burden. The third factor that diminished chances of a safe passage from Vietnam was piracy.

One of the enduring myths of the refugee exodus was that many of the boat people carried fortunes in gold, jewellery, precious stones and convertible foreign exchange, especially US dollars. A small minority did bring out wealth of more than $10 000 each. A few had fortunes. In late 1978 a former Chinese jeweller from Cholon came to Malaysia with uncut diamonds worth $1.25 million. They were hidden in a can of lubricating oil which he had placed in the boat's bilge. No one was any the wiser until he declared the diamonds on departure for the United States. Also in late 1978, another Chinese businessman from Cholon stunned Malaysian authorities, shortly after he stepped ashore, by requesting them to take into safe custody $200 000 in gold and $350 000 in currency. In Darwin, northern Australia, an Indo-Chinese woman, when asked to declare her assets, unbuttoned her blouse and proudly displayed a special corset containing $250 000 in cash, jewellery and gold.

But these Midas figures were exceptional. Large numbers of Indo-Chinese smuggled out gold, jewellery and cash worth anywhere from a few hundred dollars to a few thousand. Many more were destitute. The gold – a traditional hedge against inflation for both Vietnamese and Chinese in southern Vietnam before 1975 – was usually in thin, beaten strips called taels. One of these weighed 1.2 ounces, and was worth about $300 (a rough average of the rapidly rising price of gold between early 1978 and mid-1979).

The valuables carried by individual refugees were hardly enough to attract the attention of sea robbers, but collectively the wealth could be substantial, particularly when, in 1978, the boats became larger and started carrying not a few score but as many as 600 or

700 people. Most of the passengers on these slow-moving, overladen and usually defenceless craft were Chinese. But all boats – Vietnamese, Chinese and mixed alike – were liable to pirate attacks.

Who were these sea robbers who operated in waters between Vietnam's Mekong delta and the coasts of southern Thailand and northeast Malaysia? Initially, it appeared they were Thai fishermen with a sharp eye for easy pickings. Piracy is still common in South-East-Asian waters and the line between smuggling, fishing, normal trading and preying on other boats has long been a fine one. Nearly a century ago, a British traveller aptly described the extended archipelago curling around mainland South-East Asia as a breeding ground for corsairs. He wrote: 'As surely as spiders abound where there are nooks and corners, so have pirates sprung up wherever there is a nest of islands . . .'

Fear of the Thai pirates was a factor that induced many refugee boats to head for the friendlier coast of Malaysia. The upsurge in piracy coincided with some harsh measures taken by Thai security forces to repel boat people, prompting speculation that the pirates may have been given a semi-official licence to keep Indo-Chinese refugees away from southern Thailand. On the other hand, it was difficult to detect and suppress this kind of piracy. Its practitioners purported to be, and probably often were, fishermen. They had their nets and their gear on board to prove it. Although they operated from ports in southern Thailand, they struck in international waters. Some of the pirates had guns, but their usual weapons were daggers, long-bladed knives, marlin spikes, cudgels, iron bars and hammers. That was usually all they needed to intimidate and overpower a defenceless refugee boat.

In only a few cases were refugees able to repel attacks at sea. One was in April 1978. Thirty-six Indo-Chinese, most of them Vietnamese, had taken over a government-owned fishing boat in south Vietnam by drugging the food of the guard stationed on the vessel and bringing him along, together with his Soviet-made AK-47 automatic rifle and his pistol. About half way across the Gulf of Thailand, heading for Malaysia, they met a Thai boat about twenty metres long and dark grey in colour. They tried to evade it but the Thai vessel eventually drew alongside. Two Vietnamese who crossed over to the other boat to find out what it wanted were threatened with knives.

As they leapt back to their own vessel, one of the Thais produced a gun and started shooting, wounding one of the Vietnamese. The refugees then opened up with their weapons and the other boat quickly broke away and left them alone. Another successful defence occurred in May 1979. In this case the sea robbers were scared away by brandishing long-bladed knives and light bulbs painted to look like hand grenades.

Lam Van Dai, a 28-year-old former electronics technician, said his fourteen-metre boat with 183 passengers was raided ten times by pirates. Women were forced to strip naked. Their clothes and bodies were thoroughly searched for gold, necklaces and other jewellery. In the second attack, the pirates used a derrick to remove the pump engine from the refugee boat. By the tenth attack, nothing of value remained, so all those wearing jeans were ordered to hand them over. Lam Van Dai said he arrived in Malaysia early this year 'with just my underpants and a shirt'.

A number of the pirates appeared to be well organized. They worked in packs of two or three marauding boats, each maintaining radio contact with the other. Not all were brutal; some robbed, but provided food, water or fuel in return. However, in 1978 and 1979 the incidence of violent attacks increased. US refugee officials interviewing victims often wrote the initials 'RPM' in their case histories: it meant 'rape, pillage and murder'. An American official estimated in June 1979 that 30 per cent of all refugee boats leaving southern Vietnam had been 'hit' by pirates; of those about a third suffered 'RPM'.

In Malaysia's Bidong Island camp, files in the section of the refugee self-government committee that deals with welfare contain an account written by two Vietnamese women, Quach Si Khuynh, thirty-five, and Ta Thich, forty-three. After several days at sea in October 1978 the water pump of their boat broke down. A Thai boat approached and about thirty people, mostly men, were taken aboard from the refugee craft. The women wrote:

The pirates tied them up and threw them into the water. The remaining people were tied up too, and locked in the hold after being stripped of their belongings. After this, the pirates came again to our boat to pillage and rape people. One person was killed after being dealt a blow with an iron bar.

Another had his finger cut off because he was unable to pull off his wedding ring. When everything was looted, the pirates hurried to go. They released the men they kept in the hold, and kicked them back to our boat. Some fell into the water and drowned with their hands bound behind their backs.

Among those murdered were the husbands of the two women.

In mid-1978 pirates raped an unmarried woman in her late twenties who was in a boat with about a dozen other refugees, including her brother and several sisters. When her brother, one of his legs atrophied by polio, tried to intervene, the assailants beat him up, threw him overboard and let him drown. In August 1978 there were three separate cases in which distraught parents reaching Malaysia reported that their teenage daughters had been raped by Thai pirates and abducted, presumably to be sold into prostitution. In May 1978 a boatload of about forty men, women and children from southern Vietnam was rammed and halted at sea by pirates. All the refugees were forced to strip naked on deck while a thorough search for valuables was made below. The men were then driven into the hold and the women systematically raped while terrified children watched. When the orgy was over, the women and children were thrown into the hold and the hatch cover nailed down. The pirates then tried to hole the refugee boat. But the Indo-Chinese men, mad with rage, managed to break out of the hold. The pirates opened up with automatic rifle fire, killing twelve and wounding several others. Two other pirate boats raided the refugee boat before it finally limped into Malaysia.

*   *   *

Afterwards, Phan Van Thieu seemed more astonished than embittered.

Mr Thieu, a former US aid employee in Vietnam in his early fifties, is very small and slight, his thin limbs and body giving him the appearance of a bamboo man. He left Ca Mau on the southern extremity of Vietnam's Mekong delta on 17 April 1979, in a twelve-metre wooden boat that he and thirty-three relatives and friends on board had acquired and fitted out in secret. He said security guards opened fire on them three times as they nosed along a river towards the sea under cover of darkness. However, no one was hit and the boat was not damaged. They were heading across the Gulf of Thailand for the nearest landfall on the north-east coast of Malaysia, a trip that should have taken no more than two or three days. But on their first day out about forty Thai pirates armed with knives swarmed aboard and robbed them of most of their valuables – five wristwatches, some gold, jewellery and about $100 in cash. Then their main engine broke down and neither of the two mechanics on board could fix it. A small spare engine was substituted. On 19 April they hailed a passing Thai freighter and asked to be towed to Malaysia. But they could not pay the charge of $1000 proposed by the ship's captain, 'so he sailed off leaving us with a bucketful of lubrication oil'. While alongside the ship, the propellor of the refugee boat had hit the steel hull, disabling the substitute engine, so they had to rig a makeshift sail from blankets.

Later in the day a Thai fishing boat with a crew of about thirty young men took them in tow, allowed them on board, provided some food and promised to take them to Malaysia. But fifteen kilometres from the Malaysian coast, opposite Kota Bahru, the good samaritans turned pirates. Each of the outnumbered and unarmed Vietnamese, including the five women and fourteen children, was stripped and searched for valuables. Mr Thieu's brother-in law was hit over the head and pushed into the sea. Fortunately he could swim. Mr Thieu's seventeen-year-old niece was not so lucky. She fell overboard – it is not clear how – and drowned. The robbers took the tool box as well as the spare engine from the refugee boat, so there was no hope of repairing the main motor. On 22 April, after being towed by two different Malaysian fishing boats, the Vietnamese landed near Kota Bahru and were allowed to join about 400 other Indo-Chinese in a temporary camp.

On 11 May local authorities put the thirty-three onto another refugee boat with a disabled engine. With another boatload from the same camp, they were taken in tow by a Malaysian navy vessel and told they were going to Bidong Island (where 42 000 of the 76 000 displaced Indo-Chinese then in Malaysia were held). However, late in the afternoon of 12 May, both boats were cast adrift by the Malaysian navy ship and told to cover the remaining fifteen kilometres to Bidong Island on their own. Mr Thieu said the refugee boat travelling with his disabled craft agreed to pull them. 'But after only ten minutes the tow rope was cut and they went on their way, leaving us alone at sea again.' Deserted by their fellow castaways, Mr Thieu and his companions had food for seven days but drinking water for only two. From 14 May they drifted without water for four days. 'We pooled our urine and drank it. On 16 May a two-year-old baby boy died of dehydration. The next day a four-year-old boy died. We had to throw the bodies into the sea. The other twelve children were close to death. Without water we could hardly eat. Everyone was exhausted'.

Mr Thieu claims at least sixty ships passed them, including some with Japanese and French names, before a Norwegian freighter rescued them and took them to Singapore. He added sadly, 'We waved white cloths and called for help, but none of them stopped. They all saw us. Some of them passed within a hundred metres'.

One ship that didn't bypass boat people in trouble at sea was an 11 462-tonne British container vessel, *Sibonga*, going from Bangkok towards Hong Kong to load cargo. Early in the morning of 21 May 1979, crew sighted distress flares about 150 kilometres south of Vietnam. The ship's master, Captain Healey Martin, forty-one, from Lisburn in Northern Ireland changed course to investigate. He later wrote an account in his log of what he saw, what action he took and why he did it. His first move, after reaching the boat, was to allow one of the refugees to board. The man said they had left southern Vietnam on 18 May with about 600 people. They were now short of fuel, water and food. Five babies had been buried at sea the night before. The boat was leaking badly and the pump was broken.

Looking over the side, Captain Martin described this scene:

Women and children on the twenty metres long by three metres wide boat were screaming for help; the smell on the boat, which was tier-decked for maximum capacity, was terrible. The weather had been fresh south-westerly for the previous forty-eight hours. Prolonged seasickness, lack of food and water and the horrible way the people were crowded together in their own dirt and urine had reduced them to a very weak physical condition. Merely to give them stores would have been to condemn a large number of people to death.

He decided to take them on board.

Having been in such tightly packed conditions for almost four days, some could hardly stand, their badly cramped limbs refusing to take the weight of their bodies. Cargo gear was rigged and a large box inside a cargo net was used to hoist those aboard who could not climb the shipside ladders. A couple of the ship's crew went onto the refugee boat to lift people into the box and prevent it being overloaded, as refugees, afraid I would leave without them, kept throwing exhausted children into the box in an attempt to ensure their safety. It was a heart-breaking scene and one I shall never forget.

Captain Martin's wife, Mildred, who was travelling with him, was also appalled by what she saw. As the *Sibonga*'s crew – thirty-eight Indians, seventeen Britons and two Australians – made rush preparations to receive and look after the Indo-Chinese, Mrs Martin and Rosemary Blyth, a trained nurse from Harrogate in Yorkshire, whose husband was a second officer on the ship, worked frantically in a two-bed clinic to treat sick refugees. Many of the survivors were close to exhaustion, dehydrated and covered in filth; a few were unconscious.

Shortly after completing the rescue, crew members on the *Sibonga* spotted another boat about eight kilometres away sending distress signals. The second boat was about fifteen metres long and three metres wide, with over 300 people aboard. The majority were women and children. Martin took them all onto the *Sibonga*.

The hospital and customs cabin was turned into a sick bay area and in the first few days was at full stretch dealing with cases of exhaustion, dehydration, dysentery, nursing mothers with no milk, hungry babies with colic ... a woman recovering from a recent operation, three pregnant women, another threatening to miscarry, one old man and a young girl who had severely injured her toe between the pilot ladder and the boat.

Captain Martin sent a message to the *Sibonga*'s owners, Bank Line in London, telling them he had picked up about 900 refugees from Vietnam. When an accurate head count was finally made the actual tally was 1003 – 328 men, 272 women and 403 children under the age of sixteen. Most were Chinese. Although eight of the refugees were ferried to hospital in Hong Kong after the freighter anchored off the British territory on 24 May, the rest were confined to the ship until the newly elected government of Prime Minister Margaret Thatcher in London finally agreed on 28 May to accept responsibility for the derelicts on the *Sibonga* and on a second British-registered freighter, the *Roach Bank*, also owned by Bank Line in London. The *Roach Bank*, which had rescued 393 boat people from Vietnam in the South China Sea, had been refused entry to Kaohsiung harbour in southern Taiwan.

But the Conservatives in Britain disowned an undertaking given by the former Labour government in December 1978, that all Indo-Chinese saved at sea by masters of British-registered ships would be given homes in Britain if no other country would accept them. In Hong Kong the press, reflecting official feeling, reacted angrily. Some cynical Hong Kong officials believed the new Conservative administration was obliged to offer quick asylum to the refugees stranded on the *Sibonga* and the *Roach Bank* because the chairman of the company was a member of the House of Lords and the situation was costing his firm well over $5000 a day.

The case of the *Sibonga*, which finally steamed out of Hong Kong for Vancouver on 4 June 1979, well behind schedule, epitomized the conflicting pressures that masters and owners of commercial vessels faced as a result of the swelling exodus of boat people from Vietnam. The time-honoured code of chivalry at sea – to help those in distress – came under challenge. Governments that had signed international conventions on safety of life at sea flouted the spirit if not the letter of this law. Only about a dozen western states, led by the United States, were prepared to guarantee that all people rescued at sea would be taken by the rescuing ship's home country if they had nowhere else to go. Other nations, like Britain and Japan, shuffled their responsibilities onto masters and owners of ships by saying that they, rather than the government, had a legal and moral obligation to render assistance to people in trouble at sea.

In 1978 and 1979 dozens of ships that had saved boat people in the South China Sea converged on ports in the region, particularly those of Singapore and Hong Kong which are among the busiest commercial shipping centres in the world. Singapore would not allow refugees rescued by ships to land unless it had guarantees that they would be accepted for resettlement in other countries. By September 1979, only the United States, West Germany, France, Denmark, Norway, Holland, Belgium, Italy and Australia were ready to offer such standing guarantees. Britain merely promised to deal with requests on a case-by-case basis. Israel and Brazil took a similar approach. Japan guaranteed to offer temporary asylum to stateless Indo-Chinese brought to Singapore by any of its flagships, but on condition that the UNHCR undertook to resettle these refugees in other countries once they reached Japan. If a vessel that had not managed to get a resettlement guarantee from a third country wanted to dock in Singapore to unload cargo, its principals had to furnish a bond of Singapore $10 000 (about $4665) for each refugee. The bond was forfeited if anyone jumped ship. Other governments in the association of South-East Asian nations (ASEAN) – Indonesia, Malaysia, the Philippines and Thailand – applied similar policies.

The difficulty in finding places to disembark refugees led to some marathon voyages around the world. One group of thirty-one Vietnamese – ten women, fourteen children and seven men – who were plucked from their drifting fishing boat in the South China Sea by the Panamanian-registerd freighter, *Cape Erimo*, were taken on an odyssey of rejection that lasted well over two months. They were refused permission to land in Singapore and at their next stop on the other side of the Indian Ocean, Yemen. They were finally allowed to land when the ship reached Japan.

In mid-1978, well-placed shipping industry sources in Singapore confirmed that certain owners, especially those with vessels registered in Asia or sailing under flags of convenience, had instructed their masters not to stop for refugees because of the costs and trouble involved. A big part of the problem was that 'flag-of-convenience' countries, like Panama, Honduras, Liberia and Greece, would not offer resettlement guarantees on behalf of the thousands of ships on their registries. Nor would Asian countries, such as Singapore, which offered relatively easy registration conditions. More cautious masters were also reluctant to approach refugee boats on the high seas because of reports of boat people feigning distress and then scrambling aboard the rescue ship and scuttling their own craft.

Despite the costs involved, hundreds of ships from many countries inside and outside the region helped refugee boats in trouble. Seaworthy craft were given fuel, food, drinking water, medicines, maps and other help. Sometimes people were saved from boats in danger. Between 1975 and early September 1979, ninety-five commercial vessels landed about 4800 rescued refugees in Singapore alone. Nonetheless, if refugee accounts are even partially believable, hundreds of ships bypassed boat people in distress at sea.

* * *

Singapore was the first of Vietnam's non-communist neighbours to start fending off boat people. It regularly turned away small craft from southern Vietnam after resupplying and refuelling them. By late 1977 Thai security authorities were regularly rejecting boat people, in some cases putting them on different craft when their own had sunk, been scuttled or had engines damaged beyond repair. A lot of these 'push-off' cases ended up in Malaysia. As the sea exodus from southern Vietnam intensified and boats converged on the north-east coast of peninsular Malaysia, central and local authorities started blocking seaworthy craft and giving them supplies to continue their onward journey.

In late 1978 the policy of turning 'seaworthy' boats away was intensified. In early 1979, after a special task force under the command of an army general was created to control the refugee influx, the coastal cordon was tightened. Western refugee officials estimate that in February about 25 per cent of those who tried to land in Malaysia were 'shooed off'; in April, 50 per cent; and by mid-1979, 80 per cent. Even so, more than 17 500 slipped ashore in May. In June the government in Kuala Lumpur announced a hardening of its policy towards what it called 'illegal immigrants' from Vietnam. No more would be permitted to land. Naval surveillance of the coast was intensified. Warships kept refugee boats away from the offshore oil rigs.

Since the communist takeover of South Vietnam in April 1975, 117 778 Indo-Chinese had arrived in Malaysia by sea. By June 1979 a total of only 42 248 had been resettled. The home affairs minister, Tan Sri Ghazali Shafie, said that, in the first six months of 1979, Malaysia had successfully towed out to sea 267 boats carrying more than 40 000 Indo-Chinese.

The 'castaway' policy created a special class of Indo-Chinese refugees, the so-called 'beach people'. While many boats were blocked from landing in the first half of 1979, a large number managed to dodge Malaysian patrols and beach, scuttle or dock their boats, or sabotage engines. These blockade runners were allowed ashore. Some were transferred to camps under UNHCR protection, but more and more were put into makeshift centres under armed guard, often on or close to the beaches where they landed, and kept under Malaysian control. UN and western refugee officials were denied access to them, as were journalists. They were literally living in limbo, not knowing whether they would be transferred to UNHCR camps for resettlement, or sent back to sea.

From mid-February to June, more than 5000 of the beach people were put onto boats and towed back to international waters. By mid-1979, refugee officials estimated that, of the 75 000 Indo-Chinese in Malaysia, only about 65 000 were in UNHCR camps and transit centres. The rest – about 10 000 men, women and children – were in the limbo camps under imminent threat of expulsion. They were being loaded onto repaired refugee boats, and in some cases even onto requisitioned Malaysian fishing craft.

At a squalid beach camp at Jambu Bangkok, on a desolate stretch of coast south of Kuala Trengganu, visited by journalists without permission on 25 June 1979, refugees complained they were short of food and that Malaysian guards charged them the equivalent of $30 for five-kilogram bags of rice (nine times the price on the local market) and $1.00 per item for posting urgent letters abroad.

On 3 July 1979 they were put onto four Malaysian fishing boats and towed out to sea for twenty-four hours by a navy patrol boat. The refugees said later they were cut adrift and left with little fuel or drinking water. The night after the four wooden craft were abandoned, they drifted apart. Miss Lieu Minh Tran, a Vietnamese high-school teacher who was in one of the boats, said she believed the other boats had sunk. 'As far as we know they had no more fuel than us. They couldn't have got far with their engines. Then they would have been blown about by the strong winds and knocked by the waves as we were. We were lucky. A passing ship saw us and stopped'.

The ship was a 1524-tonne freighter, the *Seasweep*, owned and operated for refugee relief by a Christian aid organization, World Vision International, with headquarters in California. The captain of the refugee boat found by the *Seasweep* was Hua Hien Minh, a 31-year-old mechanical engineer, who said they had been given about twenty litres of fuel – enough for about eleven hours – by

Malaysian authorities. When the engine broke down there were two litres of fuel left. For six days the wind blew them north. They became frightened that they would be blown back to Vietnam. The *Seasweep* found the disabled refugee craft with its ninety-three passengers, including about twenty children and many women, about 190 kilometres off southern Vietnam. The survivors were guaranteed resettlement by the US government and the *Seasweep* was allowed to land them in Singapore.

*   *   *

From Hong Kong through Thailand, Malaysia, Indonesia and the Philippines, there were depressing common factors about the camps for refugees, these half-way houses on the road to a new life in a foreign country. They were congested. Facilities were rudimentary. Above all, they were haunted by uncertainty. How long would a refugee have to wait before a country would offer a place? Where would he or she go?

Some camps like those in Malaysia and Thailand were tightly guarded. Others, like those in Indonesia's remote Anambas Islands, were far removed from centres of population and inmates could move at will. Not that there was anywhere to go. The most civilized conditions for Indo-Chinese boat people were in Singapore – but the camp at Hawkins Road was an exclusive club: to qualify for membership you had to be rescued in the South China Sea by a passing ship.

The most humane administration of camp life was in Hong Kong where the government progressively let the UNHCR take over the running of most of the centres. They had a total refugee population of some 67 000 in September 1979, the largest concentration of boat people in Asia. Most residents were allowed to come and go freely except when they were about to fly abroad for resettlement. The UNHCR and the Hong Kong authorities also pioneered a successful experiment in refugee self-support in 1979. There was a shortage of labour in the territory and the cost of paying for free food to the camps was running into millions of dollars a year. So maintenance subsidies were ended except in special cases and the refugees were helped to find employment.

Each camp for boat people in Asia had its own characteristics, but one in particular encapsulated the difficulties and frustrations of being a stateless Indo-Chinese in an alien land. In mid-1978 Bidong Island was uninhabited, its steep flanks smothered in jungle and fringed with coconut palms and coral sand beaches. A year later it bore the scars of a sudden, massive human invasion. Almost the whole of one side of a hill 300 metres high had been denuded of vegetation and stripped of all but the sturdiest trees, the result of a desperate scavenging for firewood and building materials.

But Bidong reserved its most intense shock for close range. One stepped ashore into a violent, tragic, sordid, but also indestructibly resilient world. Bidong was a dangerously congested slum; a tropical island ghetto; a chunk of south Vietnamese society pre-1975, unrepentantly capitalist, anti-communist and predatory, grafted onto a bit of offshore Malaysia; a shanty town with a population of 42 000 confined to a living area of less than one square kilometre.

Like nearly all others in Asia, the camp on Bidong was sponsored by the UNHCR, using cash contributions from the international community. It was run largely by the refugees themselves through elected representatives. They divided the camp into seven zones, each with its local council. Committees were set up for administration, architecture and engineering, health and social welfare, information and culture, security and supply. The refugees provided the labour but relied heavily on the UNHCR and the Malaysian Red Crescent for supplies of food, medicines, building materials and equipment. To keep the peace, there were some Malaysian police, soldiers and militiamen – about three dozen in all, most of them armed.

Near the administrative centre of the camp, at an intersection of some alleyways leading into the packed suburban heart of Bidong, was the most important noticeboard on the island. It listed arriving mail and departing refugees – two events that formed vital strands of hope in the fabric of a stateless person's life. Since the island started taking refugees in July 1978, 52 516 (453 boatloads) had arrived. A year later barely 10 500 had left for new homes in North America, Australia and Europe.

Mr Choy Wong Hong, a Chinese from southern Vietnam who spoke English, Mandarin and Cantonese as well as Vietnamese, had been on Bidong for seven months. He served as a translator for the camp committee. But he was lucky and he knew it. He had a definite future. He was twenty-three and a trained computer programmer. Soon he would leave to join an uncle in the United States. Some Bidong residents had been there for ten months and had still not qualified for resettlement.

Mr Choy told his story overlooking the 'front beach', one of Bidong's most coveted – and expensive – residential areas because it was close to the market, administrative centre, water and rations distribution points and such other modest facilities as the island had. Behind him lay a warren of shanties, some three storeys high. The main beams of these houses were of hand-hewn timber from the hill. Upper rooms had slat floors. The walls were made of cardboard, tin, bark and timber; the roofs of blue plastic sheeting or bone-coloured, waterproof sacks that once contained a popular brand of Malaysian sugar. An average room was about three by two metres, in which several families might crowd to sleep at night. The well-to-do on Bidong – those who managed to bring some valuables onto the island or who had made money since arriving – lived less congested home lives. Some even had lights drawing electricity from car batteries.

The beach was fouled with heaps of rubbish rotting in the heat and humidity. At one end near the jetty an incinerator was nearing completion. Flies swarmed everywhere and the stench of human excrement was oppressive. At the end of the beach furthest from the camp centre, figures squatted on rocks defecating into the water. Nearby, other refugees were fashioning a crude screen around the hulk of a twenty-metre boat lying in the shallows: it was destined to serve as a temporary latrine. 'We face many difficulties,' said Father Le Ngoc Trieu, former president of the Catholic education board in south Vietnam. 'We have run out of space to bury rubbish. We had to fill in some of the old latrine pits to build more houses over them.'

Shortage of water for drinking and cooking was acute. A crowd of children gathered around a well 'fishing' for water from a meagre pool at the bottom. Of 120 wells, only about 20 were still in use. The rest were polluted or dry. Weather permitting, a barge ferried water to the island from Kuala Trengganu every couple of days. Since the start of the dry season, quotas had been cut from five litres to two litres per person per day. A pair of water storage tanks were being built on the front beach and about a hundred fibreglass containers lay there awaiting installation. In the meantime the queues for water were long. Tempers flared and fights sometimes broke out as patience dried up under the burning sun.

Dr Nguyen Van Quoc, aged thirty, was one of eighty doctors, twenty pharmacists and twelve nurses in Bidong's refugee population. They staffed a tin-roofed clinic in the centre of the camp. There had been 371 births on the island and 78 deaths. The babies were born on a slightly inclined tabletop with a pale-blue plastic rubbish tin at its foot to catch the natal fluids and the afterbirth waste. Some of the deaths could easily have been prevented. 'I am afraid we do not have enough medicines. We use what we can get. We need more antibiotics, vitamin pills and drugs for treating asthma and tuberculosis,' said Dr Quoc. Early in 1979 a bout of infectious hepatitis struck about 500 refugees. Isolated cases of meningitis and typhoid, but fortunately no cholera, had also occurred. There were twenty-eight cases of mental illness, most of them 'RPM' piracy victims. One was a young boy who had watched his father die at sea.

Deaths generally fell into two categories: the old and the young. Dr Quoc said malnutrition among children in the camp was common. 'The diet is not adequate for children. There are not enough vitamins and proteins in the food they get. Their resistance to illness drops. That can be fatal.' For babies, the diet was potentially lethal. For more than a month, refugee architects and carpenters had been working sixteen hours a day in two shifts to finish a new wooden hospital before the departure of the French ship *Isle de Lumière* which had been serving as a floating hospital for serious cases.

The UNHCR's standard ration pack contained 900 grams of rice, a tin of condensed milk, three tins of canned meat, fish and vegetables, two packets of noodles, sugar, salt and two small teabags. One pack was distributed to each person over the age of three and had to last for three days. Children under three got milk powder and dry biscuits. Fresh vegetables were officially available only every six weeks or two months.

The monotony of this diet – and of life itself – on Bidong was relieved by a booming black market. The island was a monument to entrepreneurial talent. Tailors, barbers, mechanics, pawnbrokers, bakers, cakemakers, and hawkers of all kinds sold their skills, brawn and goods. There were woodcutters, watch repairers, acupuncturists and artists. A thriving, though illegal, real estate market existed. No one was officially permitted to sell a house, but many did when they left the island. Prices could range from about $350 for property in a central location to $20 for a rudimentary shelter on the sides of the hill where the climb was hard work and the distance for hauling water was long.

Bidong boasted several 'restaurants' and 'coffee houses'. One of the most successful, the Vien Du (The Venture) was started by four ex-army friends on borrowed money. At night, patrons were entertained with taped and live music, and a constellation of vocalists including two female movie stars popular in south Vietnam before the communist takeover.

The black market was the single biggest source of business activity. The police winked at it (and refugees claimed they were paid to do so). The camp committee said the black market sapped community spirit, but was essential nonetheless. 'It provides food and other items that are needed and would not otherwise be available,' one committee member said. Most of the trade was financed by a group of the wealthiest Indo-Chinese on the island. One man was reputed to have made the equivalent of $100 000 in black market real estate and loan and currency dealings. Australia, the United States and other resettlement countries refused to accept him: he retorted that he was happy to stay on Bidong.

The black market worked like this: Malaysian fishermen smuggled goods from the mainland at night to pre-arranged rendezvous points at sea, up to several kilometres from the island. Vietnamese, pushing body-length homemade boats in front of them, swam out, bargained and lugged their haul home for distribution to retailers. It was a cut-throat business. Thirty-five people were listed as missing from the camp and a substantial number were presumed to be victims of this torrid trade.

Hawkers offered an array of consumer goods: nails, wire, fishing tackle, soap, hair shampoo, talcum powder, torches, kerosene, lamps, joss sticks, pencils, ballpoints, aerograms, writing paper, stamps, scissors, face washers, Nescafé, rice flour, curry powder, cigarettes, canned soft drinks and many other items, even sewing machines.

The black market managed to produce most of the things a refugee might need – if he could afford to pay.

The Reverend Nguyen Xuan Bao spent most of his day on top of a rocky promontory known as 'religion hill'. When the former moderator of the Presbyterian Church in Vietnam arrived in Bidong in November 1978, there was no church on the island. Seven months later, in addition to his own Christian reformed church, there was a Catholic church next door and a Buddhist pagoda nearby run by Vietnamese monks. The Rev. Mr Bao had lots of ideas for improving life on Bidong and had applied some of them. His 'library' was the cabin of a refugee boat positioned so that its balcony looked out over the sea. From it, the chants of an English class conducted by one of his volunteer teachers could be heard: 'Take me to Kennedy Square', 'Where is the Haymarket?', 'Where is the taxi?'

There were some 1800 orphans and unaccompanied minors in the camp. The Rev. Mr Bao wanted to see a home established for them. There were also many widows with children and war veterans who lived in hardship and required help. He was thinking of starting vocational classes and a youth organization. Perhaps a school eventually.

*   *   *

Whatever the conditions in the camps, the boat people were very happy to get there. The catalogue of horrors afflicting boat refugees from Vietnam was seemingly endless. One of the most shocking incidents occurred in June 1979, when a boatload of ninety-three men, women and children from Nha Trang, who were heading for the Philippines, were driven by bad weather in the South China Sea onto one of the Spratly Islands controlled by Vietnamese forces. Philippine marines stationed on a nearby island heard artillery, mortar and machine-gun fire. Only eight refugees emerged alive. They claimed Vietnamese guns had accounted for twenty-three of their companions; the other sixty-two drowned trying to swim to safety. Of the eighty-five victims, forty-five were said to be children. In the same month as the Spratly massacre, on a boat jammed with 358 passengers, about twenty Chinese from southern Vietnam died when the sheer weight of bodies on the roof of the deckhouse caused it to collapse.

How many boat people perished in the four years or so to the middle of 1979? One of the most often quoted figures is up to 50 per cent. In June 1978, the US assistant secretary of state for East-Asian and Pacific affairs, Richard Holbroke, said in a speech that many refugees 'set out in rickety boats with few supplies, and estimates are that only half make it to another port'. Australia's minister for immigration, Michael MacKellar, said several times between April and July 1979, that about half the boat people perished at sea. He said this conclusion was drawn from talks with refugees and intelligence sources. 'We are looking at a death rate of between 100 000 and 200 000 in the last four years'.

Some estimates ranged even higher. They concentrated on what was undoubtedly the special horror, and susceptibility to mishap, of the boats that brought tens of thousands of Chinese from southern Vietnam after March 1978. These wooden vessels were seldom suited for a sea passage and often grossly overloaded, often having as many as 600 or 700 men, women and children crammed into two or three layers below deck. The passengers were virtually entombed amid the noise and fumes of the engine, and the dreadful press of human bodies, for as long as the voyage lasted. Air was forced into the holds through funnels from the deck.

In July 1979, the US state department handed a 'dossier' to journalists alleging Vietnamese government complicity in the export of refugees. One of the documents appended to this report quoted comments of 'a western observer in Hanoi' to the effect that Chinese in Vietnam estimated that about 70 per cent of refugees were now being lost at sea. This high rate of loss was attributed to the use of smaller and less seaworthy vessels, compounded by the use of small diesel engines, originally imported for light work in the delta waters, which were breaking down or exploding during the long sea journeys.

We know that 292 315 people who left by boat from Vietnam between May 1975 and mid-1979 reached other countries. But no one knows, although Vietnamese authorities may have a rough idea, how many people actually set out in boats. Nonetheless, estimates of an overall death rate of 50 per cent, or even higher, appear to be exaggerated. On the basis of the numbers that arrived, this would have meant a figure of nearly 150 000 lost.

Refugee officials and those knowledgeable about conditions at sea, agree that the casualty rate among boat people heading for Hong Kong was low. Unlike the southern route from Vietnam, the way to Hong Kong was not beset with pirates. Moreover, even though many of the boats that crept towards Hong Kong were powered only by sail, they stuck close to the coast of China and so could escape bad weather and stock up on essential supplies. The refugees in Hong Kong constituted a sizeable proportion of the total exodus – 77 000 out of 292 315.

Also, many of those boat people forced out to sea, especially by Malaysia, managed to sneak back. There are documented cases of at least 500 drownings as a result of Malaysian policy, but it is clear that the overwhelming proportion of more than 40 000 Indo-Chinese towed out to sea by the Malaysian navy in the first six months of 1979 returned to Malaysia or landed in Indonesia. Many of the boats were towed to within a few hours sailing of Indonesia's Anambas Islands. By the end of July, there were 33 000 Indo-Chinese in camps in these islands, virtually all of them rejected by Malaysia. Only for a period of a few weeks around mid-1979 was the Malaysian navy known to be towing refugee boats straight out into the South China Sea, rather than towards Anambas or other islands of the Indonesian archipelago.

Spokesmen for western governments, such as those of the United States and Australia, may have felt it politic to heighten the tragedy of the boat people in order to generate international sympathy for the refugees and win domestic support for resettlement programs. They may also have wanted to blacken Vietnam's already tarnished image on the human rights issue and, perhaps, justify their own policies of hostility to communist Vietnam.

However, the differences between several and many thousands, while reducing the scale of the tragedy, does not diminish its force. While dismissing as excessively inflated claims of a 50 per cent death rate among boat people, one experienced western official said he believed that between ten and fifteen per cent of refugees leaving Vietnam on small boats were lost at sea. This means that some 30 000 to 40 000 people died.

Chapter 4

Exodus

Why in 1978 and 1979 did the boat people become an exodus that set off shock waves through the region and across the world? This question has been at the core of international polemics about the boat people: an attempt to answer it is made in this chapter. Of the main exodus of 163 000 people who left Vietnam between March 1978 and mid-1979 for nearby non-communist countries, 65 per cent were from Vietnam's Chinese minority. In the same period about 250 000 Chinese left Vietnam for China. Clearly, an explanation for the exodus must be sought, at least partly, in the position of the Chinese in Vietnam.

Numbering in all about 1.7 million, they came originally mostly from southern China and the island of Hainan in the nineteenth and twentieth centuries, although some had come earlier, escaping famine and civil war. They spoke Hakka, Cantonese, Hokkien and Teochew, Cantonese speakers being the most numerous and Hokkien speakers generally the most prosperous. In the south, where they numbered some 1.4 million, the vast majority were in trade, although some were engaged in specialist agriculture such as the cultivation of pepper or ginger, and fishing. Cholon ('great market' in Vietnamese) soon took over from Hoi An, on the central coast, as Vietnam's Chinatown. In the north, where they numbered about 300 000, they lived mainly in the six provinces bordering on China and, while also engaged in trade, were usually farmers, fishermen, dockers, coalmine workers and manual labourers. The Chinese in Vietnam rose to prominence during the French period, when they enjoyed economic privileges as middlemen, leading to their control of banks, transport companies, insurance agencies and the marketing of many basic foodstuffs, such as pork, flour and monosodium glutamate, an ingredient in Chinese cooking. Most importantly, the Chinese middlemen established a monopoly of the rice trade, buying paddy from the peasants (who were frequently in their debt), milling it, transporting it and selling it overseas.

After partition in 1954, governments in both Hanoi and Saigon took steps to integrate the Chinese, without much success. In 1956 President Diem introduced legislation to force the Chinese to adopt Vietnamese citizenship or go out of business, in several Chinese-dominated areas. Many Chinese adopted Vietnamese citizenship, if unwillingly, but a substantial minority resisted. Some went into businesses not prohibited by law; some hired a Vietnamese partner or married Vietnamese citizens and carried on as before. Others took advantage of a loophole that allowed second-generation Vietnam-born children to own 51 per cent of an enterprise. In 1955 China urged Chinese in north Vietnam to take Vietnamese citizenship. In the countryside, compliance was widespread; in the cities there was greater reluctance. Hanoi gradually transferred ethnic Chinese into the bureaucracy, factories and co-operatives, but pockets of private enterprise remained, even in the socialist north, and Chinese traders and shopkeepers came to dominate the north's small private sector.

Because of history, the proximity of China, their clannishness, entrepreneurial talents and opportunism, the 'Hoa' (as Chinese living outside China were known) in Vietnam were to be inextricably caught up in the events of 1978–79 that caused the exodus.

* * *

This is what interested governments said about the refugees from *northern* Vietnam.

Vietnam's secretary of state for foreign affairs, Nguyen Co Thach, in an interview in the *New York Times* on 7 August 1979:

[Ethnic Chinese in northern Vietnam are] caught in a crossfire. If they support the Vietnamese against [China] the Chinese are suspicious. If they support the Chinese against the Vietnamese, the same. If they are neutral, they are doubted by both sides. So it's very difficult for them to stay.

China's vice foreign minister, Han Nianlong, in a speech on 5 July 1979:

The Indo-Chinese refugee problem is a product of the reactionary domestic and foreign policies of the Vietnamese authorities. To suppress popular resentment and shift the burden of their economic difficulties onto others, the Vietnamese authorities have been inciting ethnic animosity. They not only persecute Chinese nationals who have lived in Vietnam for many generations, but also persecute Vietnamese citizens of Chinese descent, other ethnic minorities and those Vietnamese who disapprove of their reactionary policies. They deprive those people of their means of livelihood by various despicable methods and forcibly expel them from the country.

The Soviet Union's deputy foreign minister, Nikolai Firyubin, in a speech to the UNHCR Geneva conference on 21 July 1979:

The main reason for the departure of ethnic Chinese from Vietnam is actually instigation from the outside, as a result of which hundreds of thousands of the deceived ethnic Chinese started leaving . . .

The governor of Hong Kong, Sir Murray Maclehose, in an interview with the *Asian Wall Street Journal* on 9 August 1979:

This is something that has been in most Vietnamese minds a long time. They just don't like Chinese, and are suspicious of them, and have always had the feeling that they tend to get the cream out of the country.

US state department spokesman, Tom Reston, on 16 June 1979:

It is clear that Vietnam has adopted a centrally directed deportation policy aimed at the wholesale expulsion of . . . ethnic Chinese . . . We and other governments know why refugees are fleeing Indo-China and we do not accept the concept that a government can simply shift the obligations it has to its people to the international community.

Britain's secretary of state for foreign and commonwealth affairs, Lord Carrington, in a speech to the UNHCR Geneva conference on 20 July 1979:

One can only conclude that they have left because the policies of the Vietnamese government made it impossible for them to remain.

*   *   *

The exodus from northern Vietnam into China probably started in 1977, but it was not until April 1978 that Peking chose to make an issue of it, accusing Vietnamese authorities of persecuting and expelling tens of thousands of people of Chinese origin who had long been resident in Vietnam. Hanoi hit back with accusations that Peking was threatening Vietnam in order to panic the Hoa, using 'bad elements' among the local Chinese to spread concern. Fear that they would be caught in the crossfire of a war between Vietnam and China caused a rumour-prone community to stampede. The exodus was further stimulated by China's ready acceptance of refugees until it closed the border in July.

From refugee interviews, it is clear that, for the most part and certainly in the initial stages of this sudden mass movement, Vietnam tried to discourage people from leaving, while not actively preventing them. In Hong Kong in August-September 1979, a number of Hoa refugees from Hanoi, Haiphong and Mong Cai said reassuring measures had been taken by the authorities. A noodle-maker from Haiphong said officials in his home precinct toured the streets telling people that there was nothing to fear, there would be no massacres. A peasant from Quang Ninh (where some 55 per cent of all Chinese in north Vietnam lived) watched several neighbours leave, but was told by government officials: 'If you want to go you can, but we would encourage you to stay'. Several Hanoi residents said they went to meetings of the government-sponsored 'fatherland front' and the official Lien Hoa (union of Chinese residents). One of them, an accountant, recalled the speaker at one meeting urging 'Hoa relatives' to remain calm and denouncing 'reactionaries' for trying to sabotage the friendship between the Vietnamese and Chinese peoples.

In the summary of a US state department publication entitled 'Vietnam's refugee machine', which was handed in draft form to journalists at the UNHCR Geneva meeting in July 1979, American officials claimed that the Vietnamese leadership decided in March-April 1978 that

worsening relations with China made Vietnam's Chinese minority . . . a fifth column that had to be eliminated. Chinese were encouraged to leave through a systematic campaign of persecution. Ethnic Chinese, including those who had lived peacefully in the north since 1954, were dismissed from their jobs and threatened with conscription or transfer to a new economic zone.

Parts of the summary appear to be tendentious, designed to make a case against Hanoi while glossing over China's role in encouraging the refugee exodus. The main evidence given for the assertion that from early 1978 it was official Vietnamese policy to drive out ethnic Chinese from the north was an interview in the dossier with a refugee described as a former member of the Haiphong public security bureau's office of alien affairs. He was quoted as saying that in March 1978 the ministry of the interior issued a directive stating that it was government policy to expel ethnic Chinese from the cities in northern Vietnam, and that the Haiphong office expanded its activities accordingly. Independent interviews with refugees did not support this: if such a directive were issued, it was more likely to have been in March 1979, after the border war with China than in March 1978.

Two interviews in the same dossier tell more convincing stories. A refugee who left Haiphong in early June 1978 said that, by the time he departed, 60 per cent of Haiphong's 35 000 Chinese residents had already left, because of rumours that Haiphong would be a first point of attack if China invaded and that if this happened 'overseas' Chinese in Haiphong would be rounded up by Vietnamese police and imprisoned or executed. The city's administrators tried to counter these rumours by mounting loudspeakers on trucks that toured the Chinese sectors of Haiphong, broadcasting that war was unlikely between the two communist neighbours and that, even if it should break out, Chinese in Vietnam would not be punished so long as they remained loyal to Vietnam. Special editions of Chinese-language newspapers and meetings with Chinese leaders in Haiphong were also held.

The same refugee said that in another place (believed to be Hanoi) in late May 1978, only 20 per cent of the Chinese residents had left. He believed this was due to better control over news media available to the Chinese, as well as the greater difficulty of leaving Hanoi which is inland. In his view, the Vietnamese government tried to persuade Chinese not to leave, because many of them held important positions in industry and mining; the trouble was caused by deliberate spreading of rumours intended to panic the Chinese. It was easy for him to understand why Chinese in southern Vietnam wished to leave, as they were traditionally merchants who saw no future for themselves in a socialist economy, but Chinese in northern Vietnam were different. They were veterans of the socialist system and respected citizens.

Another interview in the dossier, with an ethnic Chinese refugee who had formerly been a government employee in northern Vietnam, indicates that, while official policy was to encourage Chinese to remain in Vietnam, in strategically sensitive regions near the border with China measures were applied to test their loyalty. He said that in early February 1978 in the area of Lao Cai, a provincial capital on the Red River close to the frontier with China, Vietnamese public security forces had escorted to the border those Chinese who had come to Vietnam since 1950 and had refused Vietnamese citizenship. They were allowed to take with them only their clothing. Subsequently, stories circulating in Hanoi and Haiphong that they would be well treated in China and helped to find good jobs prompted tens of thousands of Hoa throughout Vietnam to journey by train to Lao Cai and cross into China's Yunnan province. Initially, Vietnamese authorities allowed those departing to enter China without a border check. As the numbers increased, the authorities began confiscating valuables, perhaps in an attempt to deter so many from leaving. He said that, on average, one or two members of every Chinese family in northern Vietnam had left for China. Most Chinese in Vietnam did not want to be sent to the countryside under the government's new economic program, so nearly all were seeking a way out.

While allegations that Hanoi was responsible for the Chinese exodus are not always borne out by independent interviews with refugees, neither are Hanoi's allegations that China was responsible for instigating these mass departures. The movement out of Vietnam and into China could not be stopped because it was fuelled by a potent mixture of rumour, panic and the increasingly virulent propaganda war between Peking and Hanoi. Once started, it became self-generating. The shock waves from the northern exodus to China almost certainly spread to the Chinese community in southern Vietnam, just as nationalization measures and currency reform in mid-1978, which hit the Chinese-dominated business community in southern Vietnam hardest, also had an unsettling effect on Chinese in the north.

After China announced in July 1978 that it was sealing its 1287-kilometre land border with Vietnam, thousands of Hoa, including some from southern Vietnam, continued to slip into southern China. Others started sailing to Hong Kong by boat from northern Vietnam. Interviews by Hong Kong authorities contained a number of refugee accounts claiming that measures designed to force Chinese to leave were imposed by the Hanoi government in the first half of 1978. Several of these accounts made dubious source material, either because of imprecision (it is not clear whether the refugee is referring to measures affecting Chinese in northern Vietnam, southern Vietnam, or both) or because some of the claims made are contradictory. However, several said they had lost their jobs late in 1978. A factory worker who left in April 1979 said that since the beginning of that year the government had put pressure on ethnic Chinese to leave Vietnam. They were not allowed to conduct any type of business or work in a factory, and Chinese working for the government, including those with many years service, were dismissed. Almost daily, public security officials came to Hoa houses and warned them to leave as soon as possible. An unskilled factory worker who said he was a seventh-generation Vietnam-born Chinese, complained that in March 1979 government-run Chinese schools were closed down, leaving Hoa children no opportunities for education. A Chinese truckdriver from the north said that until mid-1978 ethnic Chinese in the north had been treated quite well but, once started, the persecution gradually became unbearable. The reason, he thought, was the growing tension between China and Vietnam; although war broke out in February 1979, he believed the Vietnamese had been preparing for such a conflict since mid-1978.

Interviews by the *Age* in Hong Kong with Hoa refugees who left northern Vietnam in 1979 did not yield much in the way of firm recollections about anti-Chinese measures in 1978, even from Hoa who were highly indignant at the treatment meted out by Hanoi in 1979. Perhaps the period between the closure of China's border with Vietnam in July 1978 and the month-long Chinese invasion of northern Vietnam in February-March 1979 can best be described as a twilight phase in which the Hoa were viewed with increasing suspicion by Vietnamese authorities on national security grounds. However, refugee after refugee interviewed in Hong Kong said measures against them tantamount to expulsion started in the latter part of March 1979, in the wake of the Chinese attack on Vietnam.

Tran Van Bao, a Hoa in his early fifties, a graduate of Hanoi university and a teacher of Vietnamese language and literature in a secondary school, left northern Vietnam by boat on 31 March, ten days after he was dismissed from his job. He summed up the situation in this way: 'Last year was different. The Chinese government mobilized a number of patriotic Hoa to return to the motherland. Last year the Chinese government mobilized them. This year the Vietnamese pushed them out.' The rate of small boat arrivals in Hong Kong supports him and the supposition that the situation became drastic after the Chinese invasion (the average sailing time from northern Vietnam to Hong Kong was six weeks). In January just over 2000 refugees arrived, in February and March about 3000 each month, in April 6143; but in May there were 17 683, June 19 651, July 8797 and August about 3000. Over 62 per cent of the 68 678 boat refugees who flooded into Hong Kong in the seven and a half months to mid-August were from northern Vietnam – and the overwhelming proportion of northerners were Chinese.

Most Hoa were given a 'choice' at very short notice, either after being summoned to public meetings or confronted by security officials at their homes and workplaces. They were told to leave by boat or to be prepared to go 'to the interior'. This is what happened to Hanoi bus driver, Huynh Ngoc Ba, a father of five.

Some people went to China last year. A lot of people from my street. And some of the bus drivers. I'm not sure why they left. They must have been scared of a war. This year, though, things got bad after the war broke out. The local security police went from house to house. What did they say? Well, they just told us to go! The second time one came around to our house, he just said: 'Why haven't you gone yet?'

Ngoc Lien, a 23-year-old ethnic Chinese, worked in an artificial flower factory in Hanoi. Her husband, an ethnic Vietnamese, worked for the state railway. He left with his wife rather than face separation. She said:

In March when the meetings were organized to tell us to leave, cadres said that the government couldn't guarantee our safety if the Chinese invaded.

We would have to go to the mountains if we didn't have the money to go abroad. Everybody in my neighbourhood was afraid of working in the mountains – we're used to working with machines. We don't know about farming. So most of the people wanted to leave. We sold all our belongings to buy a boat from the government, but couldn't get good prices for anything . . . When we'd sold everything, the government locked up our houses and wouldn't let us go back in. So we had to go to Haiphong and sleep on the boat.

Duong Van Minh, a 38-year-old graphic designer whose father was Chinese and mother Vietnamese, worked in the ministry of culture as head of a workshop. His wife had a job at the ministry of education. They lived in Hanoi's Hai Ba Trung district, not a predominantly Hoa area. He said:

Until 1978, relations between Hoa and Vietnamese were normal. Occasionally, though, there would be some discrimination. After 1978 the atmosphere changed in my workplace. Hoa people with responsible jobs began to be demoted. It was all very subtle. Take my case, for instance. At first people higher up began to suggest I might be tired of my present job; perhaps I'd like to do something else. Finally at the end of 1978 I received an official typewritten notice removing me from my post. I continued to work as an artist though – designing posters and things like that.

On 25 March 1979 he was called to a meeting, where an official, reading from a document, announced the new policy towards the Hoa. 'I'd wanted to go abroad for a long time. The economic situation [in Vietnam] was so bad. Then when the political situation got worse, I knew we'd have to go.'

Khai and Lien were both part of Hanoi's artistic élite. He was artistic director of one of the country's main cultural groups and earned 70 dong (about $20) a month. Lien, his wife, was a soloist in the group and earned 80 dong. Their combined income was well above average. They enjoyed a number of other privileges reserved for only a few people in Vietnam: during the group's performances they would receive extra food rations – three kilos of meat a month (as opposed to the usual rate of less than one kilo a month); they had also travelled widely – several times to China, the Soviet Union, Bulgaria and other countries of the communist world. They speak Vietnamese perfectly while their Chinese is, they say, 'limited'.

Despite their privileged situation they share a number of traits in common with other ethnic Chinese who left this year. This is Khai's story, as told in Hong Kong:

My parents were traders – most of them went south in 1954. I would have gone too, but I couldn't get there in time. My uncle became the director of the big French brewery in Saigon: he left in 1975 with the Americans. He's now living in California, working as an accountant. That's where we want to go too. He's making good money there. Compared with most people in the north, we were very comfortable. But still, it was nothing like what even the most ordinary worker has here [in Hong Kong]. I used to deal in foreign currency – on the black market of course. Gold, diamonds, antiques, and occasionally watches. If they'd caught me it would have been life imprisonment. The official bank rate for a dollar now is 3.70 dong: on the black market it's 10 dong. Our main customers used to be the Soviets and other socialist countries, with occasionally a few Swedes. Our main customers, at the end, were Hoa, though. Most of them have brought dollars out with them. I brought a few thousand out, as well as some antiques. I'm going to sell those in Europe. I used to collect the antiques as we went around the countryside with the cultural group.

On 8 April the people in their neighbourhood – Hoan Kiem, one of the largest Chinese areas of Hanoi – were called to a meeting in their local government office. Khai went on:

The cadres went round personally, to announce the meeting. No radio or press announcement – very clever. The cadre who addressed the meeting said that the policy of the government in the present war was to protect all the Hoa by moving them as far away from the front lines as possible – to safe areas in the countryside, where we could support ourselves by agriculture. But if we wanted, the cadre said, we could go abroad and the government would help us. Two days later we decided to leave. A group of us got together and I was asked to make the arrangements. First I wrote a request [to leave] and took it to the district public security office. They gave me a letter of introduction to the alien's office – that's part of the Hanoi city public security office. They authorized me to contact a co-operative in Haiphong. The ship we were offered had been badly holed by US bombing. It took two weeks to repair and ended up costing us 370 000 dong ($100 000). There were 295 of us. We raised the money by selling our belongings – furniture, bicycles, motor-bikes. But we couldn't get a decent price for anything – the people who were buying agreed beforehand to keep prices low . . . we left Vietnam from a point eight kilometres outside of Haiphong at 4 am on 25 April.

Like many Hoa, Khai expressed a certain disdain for the government:

I've been involved in propaganda work for twenty years – that's what cultural work is: mobilizing the troops, workers or whoever. I got fed up with changing the line every time the government made a new decision. But you have to understand the mentality of people in the Vietnamese government – they've been promoted not because of their educational level, but because they are from worker or poor peasant background.

Neither Khai nor Lien had ever thought of leaving before. Said Lien:

I never believed this would happen to us. When people began to leave last year I didn't even consider going. All my nine brothers and sisters went to China. Three of them have already made it here, to Hong Kong. I expect the others will come too. When I left this year, the people in the cultural group were very sad. They said they did not agree with the new policy, but had to carry it out. They said they hoped I'd understand . . .

Le Van Dung, a Chinese who belonged to the Vietnamese communist movement, was born in 1930 – 'the same year as the [Vietnamese communist] party'. He would not say exactly what his work was. 'I joined the party in 1950. At that time I was involved in political and military activities with workers in Haiphong . . .' Like some other expelled members, army officers (one an artillery expert trained in the Soviet Union), and senior government officials, he was extremely bitter. On one boat, a group of them ripped up their party membership cards and threw the bits into the sea as they left Vietnam's territorial waters. Dung said, 'We fought for the fatherland, we sacrificed, and now we're being thrown out . . . I have no skills – where do I go?'

For some of the Hoa from northern Vietnam, the forced departures were a chance they had been awaiting for years. For others – the fishermen, peasants and noodle-makers – it was a brutal turn of events which left them uprooted and bewildered. Why did it happen so suddenly and in such a drastic way immediately after the Chinese invasion? In Vietnamese pamphlets published soon after the China war, mention was made of Hoa who left Vietnam in 1978 but returned in 1979 – as guides or in guerilla units with invading Chinese forces. At a big meeting in Hanoi in mid-March that was organized by the public security department and addressed by a senior security official, Hoa cadres, party members and officials were given details of what the Vietnamese government claimed were acts of treason by a considerable number of Hoa (including military officers and party officials) in the areas taken over by the Chinese. Several of the refugees in Hong Kong apparently attended this meeting, but were studiously vague about it. This may be because attendance at the meeting would mark them as having been fairly senior bureaucrats, intellectuals or army officers and such status, implying communist party membership, would prejudice their resettlement chances in the west. What follows is an account primarily provided by one refugee, with supporting evidence from others.

The meeting, which was in the Kim Mon theatre in the centre of Hanoi and lasted two or three hours, began with a lengthy review of Sino-Vietnamese relations and an expression of the Hanoi government's gratitude towards the people of China and the Hoa of Vietnam for the aid they had given Vietnam in the past. Recently, however, said a senior security official, the 'gang of reactionaries' in Peking had joined hands with US imperialists and were opposing the socialist camp. They had provoked a war along Vietnam's borders and were trying to force the Vietnamese into submission. Vietnam had to resist and a dangerous situation had arisen. A number of Hoa serving in the security forces and the army had turned their guns on their fellow-countrymen. Some of the traitors were party officials. The head of the public security for Lang Son, for example, had deserted to the enemy at a critical time. Other Hoa, the speaker continued, led Chinese troops to bunkers where Vietnamese cadres were hiding and were thus responsible for their massacre. Still others showed the Chinese the location of Vietnamese supply dumps and other important installations. Some Hoa were forced to co-operate at gun point; many others, however, had betrayed Vietnam willingly.

The government had therefore decided that Vietnamese of Chinese origin in responsible positions in the party, the armed forces, the administration and co-operatives, must be ready to evacuate to other areas of the country. (Two main areas were mentioned – the town of Vinh, several hundred kilometres south of Hanoi, and the south central highlands.) One person asked how long would they be away. The answer was: until China abandoned its intentions of invading Vietnam. Another person asked how they would work in the new areas. The answer was: wherever possible, people would continue in their present employment, but 'While you are waiting to obtain appropriate work the local authorities will deploy you in productive labour'. At this meeting there was no mention of a 'second way' – going abroad.

Virtually all the northern Hoa interviewed in Hong Kong described relations between the two ethnic groups prior to 1978 as 'normal', 'good', or 'warm'. Nearly everyone, however, had some reservations. A number of manual workers complained of petty discrimination. They said their Vietnamese colleagues did not trust them, or said 'rude things' about them behind their backs. Hoa of various social backgrounds complained that the ethnic Chinese were always blamed for any rise in prices.

A Chinese couple – he a 30-year-old printer, she a 25-year-old confectionery worker – who left northern Vietnam on 15 April 1979, said that in Hanoi the average Vietnamese was still friendly towards Chinese. But because of the government's policy it was common for Vietnamese to tell their Hoa friends they could no longer associate. The wife had noticed that since the Sino-Vietnamese war, some Vietnamese kept watch on Chinese and reported their movements to public security officials who checked their homes regularly. The local radio station broadcast daily the names of ethnic Chinese who had been arrested for 'spying'.

How did the Chinese in Vietnam see themselves? How did they see Vietnam and China? Where did their loyalties lie? A sample of Hoa birth certificates, smuggled out by refugees from the Hanoi-Haiphong area and examined in Hong Kong, showed that while Hoa intermarried with ethnic Vietnamese, few had adopted Vietnamese citizenship. With striking consistency the entry 'Hoa' was followed by 'citizenship – Chinese'. This, given the efforts of the Vietnamese authorities to assimilate the Hoa, suggests a persistent identity with the 'motherland' China. One refugee commented tartly: 'They tried to assimilate us – but we opposed them'. The widespread citizenship bond with China also helps explain why so few Hoa went into the Vietnamese army (only volunteers joined, otherwise it would have meant conscripting foreign nationals of a powerful neighbour), and why Hoa could go to China every few years without much difficulty – a privilege not available to most Vietnamese.

Some Hoa lived in largely Vietnamese areas, had married Vietnamese, worked with Vietnamese and knew little or no Chinese language. However, when asked about their feelings when war between China and Vietnam erupted, many were sympathetic to China. Said one: 'Some of the [Vietnamese] leaders . . . are following the Soviet Union, even though China gave them so much aid during the war. When China struck Vietnam, I felt some sympathy for China.' Another said he thought the war was a result of Vietnam's 'mistaken policies'. A third said he was confused – his original sympathy for the Vietminh in the 1950s has been closely tied to pride at the success of the revolution in China and Peking's support for the struggle in Vietnam. Another man said that 'of course China had to invade – Vietnam was opposing it'. The bitterest words came from a young man from Quang Ninh province: 'I was born there, grew up there, but I'm not Vietnamese. When China attacked Vietnam, I was glad. If they hadn't chased me out I would have gone anyway.' For each person who was willing to discuss politics, however, there was one who was not, who felt Vietnam was his or her home and had wanted to stay there.

* * *

This is what interested governments said about the boat refugees from *southern* Vietnam.

Malaysia's home affairs minister, Tan Sri Ghazali Shafie, in an address published on 29 November 1978:

These people are not in fear of immediate reprisal for collaborating with the US or [former President] Thieu. They have tasted life in the new régime and . . . found it unpalatable for one reason or another.

Vietnam's secretary of state for foreign affairs, Nguyen Co Thach, in an interview published in the *New York Times* of 7 August 1979:

There was no bloodbath. We have shown our humanity to them, our clemency. But they could not stay. Why? Because they have guilty consciences and ... they were used to the easy life under American aid. They cannot work hard, so they would like to go ... The second group of refugees are the Chinese. They are mostly big businessmen and they don't like the socialist reformation of South Vietnam.

An official Vietnamese publication (1978) on the role of ethnic Chinese in the south:

In the work of socialist transformation in Vietnam, as in other socialist countries, including China, some years ago, the abolition of the bourgeoisie as a class is inevitable. This transformation was carried out in a fair and reasonable way. Most of the Vietnamese bourgeois of Chinese origin willingly accepted it, but naturally a small minority opposed it because of their class nature.

US vice president, Walter Mondale, in a speech to the UNHCR Geneva conference on 21 July 1979:

[Vietnam] is failing to ensure the human rights of its people. Its callous and irresponsible policies are compelling countless citizens to foresake everything they treasure, to risk their lives, and to flee into the unknown.

A spokesman for China's ministry of foreign affairs on 16 June 1979:

In the final analysis, the problem of Indo-Chinese refugees has arisen solely as a result of the fact that the Vietnamese government is pursuing a policy of aggression and war. After the end of their war of resistance against US aggression, the Vietnamese authorities showed no regard for the welfare of their people and failed to turn their attention to healing the wounds of war and embarking on economic reconstruction. To support their war of aggression in Kampuchea and maintain control in Laos, they press-ganged their young people into serving as cannon-fodder and bled the people white. This has ruined the economy and made the people destitute. Consequently, large numbers of Vietnamese inhabitants have had to flee the country.

Canada's immigration minister, Ron Atkey, in a television interview on 17 June 1979:

There is a case of genocide here against the ethnic Chinese and to a certain extent the entrepreneurial class in Vietnam.

Vietnam's secretary of state for foreign affairs, Nguyen Co Thach, in an interview with UPI published on 12 August 1979:

Many of the boat people in ASEAN countries were actually from China. More than 100 000. They [the Peking authorities] are very clever. We have arrested some ships from China going to South-East Asia ... many people do not realize this because the Chinese from China are the same as from Vietnam.

Australia's immigration minister, Michael MacKellar, in an address to the UNHCR Geneva conference on 21 July 1979:

We are again called to consider one of the most inhuman and unnecessary tragedies in the calendar of human suffering.

The leader of the French socialist party, François Mitterand, in a television interview on 21 June 1976:

We must not let a new holocaust happen under our eyes.

Sweden's foreign minister, Hans Blix, in a statement to the UNHCR Geneva conference on 20 July 1979:

The present dangerous and inhuman exodus should be substituted by orderly departures. We appeal to the government of Vietnam to pursue this line of action ... My government is aware of the immense difficulties which the government of Vietnam is facing in rebuilding the country after the ravages of war and in securing sufficient food for its people after several periods of natural catastrophes ... The chaotic outflow of people is not totally unrelated to that desperate situation.

*   *   *

The background to the exodus from the south was bad weather, a deteriorating economy, and pressures from outside, including conflict with Kampuchea. In particular, Hanoi authorities found they could not compete with the resilient private sector in Ho Chi Minh City, where in early 1978 they estimated that only 30 per cent of all goods in circulation were under state control and profiteering, hoarding, speculation and graft were rampant. On 23 March 1978, all 'trading and business operations' of 'bourgeois' elements were abolished. Small merchants would be permitted on a temporary basis to retail goods not controlled by the state, but the effect of the edict was nevertheless dramatic. In Ho Chi Minh City alone, perhaps 30 000 shops and businesses were closed and their contents confiscated. The Chinese in particular were hit hard.

On 3 May the government's grip on the economy tightened. A single currency for the whole of the country was introduced, dealing another blow to the rich and middle-class in southern Vietnam, many of whom were Chinese. (Hoarders in the north were also caught. In Hanoi, in the wake of the showdown, bundles of old money were found lying in the streets.) In 1978 the pace of socialization of agriculture was also stepped up to overcome resistance by rice farmers (mostly Vietnamese) and middlemen (mostly Chinese). Also, from July to October, typhoons and floods swept the lowlands of northern, central and southern Vietnam, causing losses in food, livestock and housing. In October Vietnam appealed for international emergency aid. In November rice rations dropped from eleven to four kilograms a month for city-dwellers and from eighteen to eight kilograms for the rural population.

External events also pressed hard on Vietnam. In an article in *Le Monde Diplomatique*, Paul-Quinn Judge reported being told, by the deputy foreign minister, Phan Hien, of captured Kampuchean 122-mm and 150-mm artillery, which had been supplied by China. This long-range artillery was used to bombard Vietnamese territory, China's support having emboldened the Pol Pot régime evidently to believe that Vietnam would not retaliate, just as later, Vietnam's treaty with the Soviet Union led it to believe that China would not attack it. Vietnam claimed that about 750 000 Vietnamese were driven away from the border provinces, because of Khmer Rouge shelling. It also requested the UNHCR for help to look after 321 400 refugees from Kampuchea (125 600 Khmers, 25 500 ethnic Chinese and 170 300 of the Vietnamese minority), who had fled into southern Vietnam since 1975, most of them in 1977-78. Even if Hanoi exaggerated these figures, they make the point that refugees moved into Vietnam as well as out of it. The conflict with Kampuchea meant that the army was removed from economic duties (such as preparing the new economic zones) and the draft was extended.

The big outflow of boat people from southern Vietnam started in April 1978. What sort of people were they? Why did they leave? Through access to the refugees themselves, either in their camps or through interviews with western officials and journalists, the following pattern emerged. There were two distinct groups. One was the Chinese, whose background was predominantly urban and 'capitalist'. The other was Vietnamese, most of its members were closely identified with the pre-1975 political, military and economic order in the south. Among the Vietnamese, a strong political motivation to leave their homeland was often clear. They included members of the former government's armed forces including police, civil administration and anti-communist political parties; employees of the US embassy and its aid agencies; teachers, academics and intellectuals, professionals, technicians, businessmen and businesswomen, rural landholders and fishermen. It is also interesting to note those not prominently represented. There were few labourers and not many farmers. A large number of the refugees were Catholics, many of whom had moved from the north to the south in 1954 when the country was partitioned. Also quite prominent were supporters of anti-communist religious sects, such as the Hoa Hao and the Cao Dai.

Ages of the boat refugees from the south ranged widely, but most were under thirty-five. There were many women and children. Some young men said they left to avoid conscription. Some people said they were the victims of politically inspired harassment and persecution; others said they feared such treatment. Fear of what might happen was a potent factor, sometimes taking grotesque forms. An old woman who left by boat with her son on 10 April 1978 said, 'I have heard that all old people who are taken to hospital . . . are given a needle so that they die, like dogs.' A feeling of alienation from the new communist administration and identity with the old régime was common, often mixed with an economic motivation: a conviction that their livelihood was better before and could only get worse. They felt the future was bleak for themselves and for their children. Fear of 're-education' and of being sent to a 'new economic zone' were also pervasive.

Mrs La Thi Thuy Quynh, a 24-year-old Vietnamese and her husband, Pham Bao Quang, were both studying chemistry at Saigon university in 1975. They graduated in April 1979, shortly before they left Vietnam by boat for Malaysia. Mrs Quynh did not like the regimentation and austerity in southern Vietnam, but what made her leave, she said, was discrimination. Her father was a lieutenant-colonel in intelligence before 1975. Her mother was in business selling clothes in Saigon.

My father was taken first to a re-education camp in Saigon, but in 1976 he was moved to Vinh Phu province in north Vietnam. The first and only time my mother could see him there was last December [1978]. A policeman was present when they met in the camp. He took notes of the conversation, so my father couldn't say very much. He wore the uniform of the defeated army and had no shoes. He said there were indoctrination and self-criticism sessions. But most of his time was spent labouring. He carried water from a stream to the camp farm, a distance of five or six kilometres, many times a day. When they first took him away, his weight was 62 kilograms: when my mother saw him he was 42 kilograms. His daily diet was sweet potatoes and virtually nothing else.

Mrs Quynh said the communists knew her family background. When she graduated in April 1979, she was told she would only be given her graduation certificate after serving as a teacher in an NEZ in Minh Hai, the southernmost province in the Mekong delta, several hundred kilometres away. Her husband was told he would have to go to a different NEZ, this one closer to Ho Chi Minh City because his father had had no connection with the old régime. Her 20-year-old sister was not allowed into university because of her father's background; she was now a seamstress.

Ma Xai, a 42-year-old doctor and a former deputy of the lower house of the national assembly in Saigon, had belonged to an anti-communist party and from 1966-75 was an adviser to the Hoa Hao sect. His home, An Giang province in the Mekong delta, was a centre of the sect's power and political influence. He said he could have left south Vietnam with the American evacuation a week before Saigon fell, but declined to do so because his wife and five young children were in An Giang and there was no way of getting them out. He registered for re-education on 16 May 1975, and was taken to a former orphanage at Long Thanh, some fifty kilometres east of Ho Chi Minh City. ('The director of the orphanage was pro-communist, so we had locked him up for a few years in President Thieu's time.')

The orphanage was part of a complex of camps that held about

3000 inmates including senior police, intelligence officers and political party officials. Two of the people in his section were former deputy prime minister, Duong Kich Nhuong, and a leader of the Saigon delegation to the Paris peace talks, Nguyen Xuan Phong. On some days, they spent from 8 am to noon studying and from 1 pm to 5 pm labouring, with further study in the evening. On other days they did manual labour the whole time, repairing roads or working in vegetable gardens adjacent to the camp. Studies took two forms: lectures in the theory and practice of Marxism-Leninism, given by senior cadres (about whom Xai was disparaging) and writing their life histories over and over again in great detail. There was no physical violence but camp authorities were 'very hard'. After checking personal histories against their own dossiers, they would call individuals back if anything was found to be 'hidden' or 'not correct'. Xai was specifically asked to give details about Hoa Hao organizations, and his connections with foreign intelligence agencies, which he denied.

He spent a total of sixteen months at the Long Thanh orphanage. There were a number of cases of beri beri and two deaths, one due to lack of insulin supplies. There were no escapes but more than a hundred people were released. At the request of public security officials in An Giang he was transferred to 'an old Thieu prison' in his home province in late 1976. In August 1977 he was placed under 'house arrest' for six months and then given probation, reporting every month. With his family, he started farming on land belonging to some relatives. In January 1979, at the request of the authorities, he became doctor to a village commune and remained there until April 1979, when he escaped by boat for Malaysia with his family. As the province of An Giang borders on Kampuchea and security was getting tighter because of fighting along the frontier, he was sure he would have been detained again if he had stayed. The government was concerned that Hoa Hao diehards would take advantage of the border troubles with Kampuchea to carry on their war of resistance. Questioned as to whether the Hoa Hao were doing this, Xai replied 'of course'.

Anti-communism emerged in many forms during interviews, especially from Catholics from the north who had a good educational background and who had moved to the non-communist south in the 1950s. One was Nguyen Truong Ba, fifty-one, a mathematician who had studied and taught at the university of Paris for sixteen years until 1966. He left for Malaysia by boat on 7 May 1979, after two unsuccessful attempts. Ba said he was automatically suspect in the eyes of the communists because he had studied and worked in the west for a long time and had come from a northern family that went south.

After they took over in 1975, I was removed from my position as director of basic sciences at the Phu Tho institute of technology and made an ordinary lecturer. They let me teach the unimportant subjects. Every morning I had to clock in to work by filling in a book. Teachers in southern Vietnam now have to undergo courses in Marxism-Leninism in the summer vacation: it is all brainwashing and lies ... Wherever I went to teach in Saigon, I was followed by two party agents ... I asked to resign in 1978. My superior, a party member, told me I shouldn't because I would then be considered a reactionary. If you do not collaborate with the communists they treat you as an opponent. Sooner or later if I hadn't gone, they would have sent me off to a re-education camp. At the institute I used to talk straight. The communists don't like people who talk straight.

Apart from embittering many people like Ba, the sackings and demotions that were widespread after the communists assumed power also had an effect on the living standards of families who until then had been comfortably off. Luong Xuan Minh, thirty-nine, and his wife left southern Vietnam for Australia by boat on 16 April 1978. In 1970-71 he was employed in America by the oil company, Esso, then returned to Saigon and joined the Shell oil company. In 1975 when the communists nationalized Shell he was an assistant manager in the transport section.

My family fled from the north in 1954 because they were Catholics. After 1975, freedom of religion was very restricted, although we could attend church. Certain church activities, such as the youth organization, were not allowed. The communists also started to use movies and other propaganda with an anti-religious theme. At work I was retained on a temporary basis and I was afraid that middle-level management, including me, would be dismissed soon. Employees were subjected to continuous indoctrination, and intellectuals like myself were singled out for criticism. We were accused of

Some of the 130 000 Vietnamese who fled with the Americans in the last hours before the fall of Saigon in April 1975 *(UPI)*

Overladen refugee boats are tossed by high seas off the Malaysian coast *(UNHCR)*

Vietnamese refugees wade ashore after their small boat sank off the coast of Malaysia *(UNHCR)*

Their boat sunk, their future uncertain, refugees huddle together on a Malaysian beach *(UNHCR)*

The *Huey Fong*, a ship carrying more than 2500 refugees, at anchor near Hong Kong *(Government Information Services, Hong Kong)*

Some of the 571 paying passengers who were crammed into a modified military landing craft that reached Hong Kong in 1979 from South Vietnam *(Government Information Services, Hong Kong)*

Cambodian refugees cling together in monsoon rains at Laem village near
the Cambodian border in Thailand where they had fled to escape Vietnamese-
Cambodian crossfire *(UPI)*

Mother Theresa, crusader for the world's destitute, called upon the US and the UN in June 1979 to persuade countries to admit more Indo-Chinese refugees *(UPI)*

Actress Jane Fonda, well-known for her views against US involvement in the Vietnam war, hosts a party to raise funds for the boat people in August 1979. Acto Mike Farrall from the television show *M.A.S.H.* was among the stars in attendanc *(UPI)*

A makeshift city provides scant shelter for refugees on the shores of Bidong Island, Malaysia, 1979 *(Age)*

Clothes dry out in the ramshackle beach camp of refugees on Tengah Island, Malaysia, 1979 *(Age)*

Vietnamese children, rescued from their sinking boat by a British ship in the South China Sea, arrive at Stansted Airport in England in October 1978 *(PAP)*

exploiting the workers under the old régime. I could have escaped with the Americans, but I wished to remain behind to help rebuild Vietnam. However, I found that the communists insisted that a person must be a true believer and, even if they were not technically qualified, gave promotion to party members or members of revolutionary families. I believe the communists were attempting to create a new political élite by controlling entrance to university and other educational institutions and only allowing sons and daughters of party members to enter.

Many of the young male boat people, ethnic Chinese as well as Vietnamese, said they left Vietnam to avoid compulsory military service. While they may have been instructed to register, few Chinese are believed to have been actually called up, and it was unusual for members of the former government and its armed forces to be conscripted as they were not trusted by the communists. La Quoc Quang, a 24-year-old Chinese who arrived in Malaysia with his wife and 3-year-old son in May 1979, had previously lived and worked in Cholon. The privately owned electrical company that had employed him was nationalized in 1976, but he kept his job. However, he found it difficult to earn enough to pay for food to support his family. Then, in January 1978, he said he was told to report for military service as part of the compulsory call-up for all men in Vietnam between the ages of eighteen and forty to bolster the armed forces in the fighting with Kampuchea and in case of war with China. So he went into hiding. If Vietnam's communist government mistrusted local Chinese, as he asserted, why was it instructing them to register for military service along with Vietnamese youths? Quang replied, 'Because they want to have us killed. Putting us in the army is one way. Vietnam is against China so the Vietnamese hate the Chinese in Vietnam.'

Ly Chanh Ba was a 19-year-old student in Cholon when her father's hardware shop was seized on 23 March 1978.

My parents noticed that the communists started visiting houses at the end of the street at night, and that the people were being taken away . . . Arrangements were made for my brother and me to be hidden in a friend's house. I went back to my parents' home three or four days later and found them gone. The house was occupied by a communist cadre so I did not go in. But neighbours in the next street told me that our mother and father had been trucked out at night to a new economic zone in Kien Giang province. I was unable to find out exactly where they were. When my father arranged for us to go into hiding he said we should make every endeavour to leave Vietnam and that is why we escaped by boat on 24 March 1979.

Ong Tin Loc was a 17-year-old Chinese high-school student in Cholon. His parents were general merchants. After the communist takeover in 1975, they stockpiled imported goods, prices of which were shooting up, so that they could sell gradually at a good profit. The shop was seized with its contents in March 1978. His father avoided an NEZ by becoming an approved state worker in a co-operative making wheat noodles. However, in September 1978, Loc was instructed to register for military service. Besides poor living conditions, surveillance ('whatever you did people watched you') and a desire to study medicine, which he did not think he could do as a Chinese in Vietnam, Loc said he left for Malaysia because he was determined to avoid the draft. 'We Chinese don't want to fight Chinese. We also hate the communists and don't want to fight for the communists.' But wasn't China communist? 'Well, they are closer to us. When war broke my family felt a little bit of sympathy for China. After all my grandmother is in China. Grandfather used to say to us: "China is our home. Vietnam is only our second home".'

Tran Xuong, fifty-six, was a wealthy Chinese rice trader with a mill near Soc Trang in the Mekong delta province of Hau Giang. He had several dozen hectares of good farming land that belonged to his wife, and houses in both Soc Trang and the Saigon area. His iron-grey hair is cropped short and he has a gold tooth that gleams when he smiles. Neither he nor his family of four boys and six girls were under pressure to go to an NEZ because they had established themselves as farmers on one of the family plots of land. Before he left Vietnam he took steps to safeguard his property by putting in relatives. He was furious about the loss of his rice mill shortly after the communist takeover in 1975.

We grew rice on a two-hectare plot, just enough for ourselves. What's the use of growing more if they take it from you? They say they are going to give you so much in cash but they never do. They speak very nicely but just give you bits of paper. For my mill they gave me an IOU saying the money could be collected from the local communist party office. If I'd tried, I'd have been arrested. The cadre several times described me as a 'capitalist' or an 'exploitive capitalist'. I couldn't live in Vietnam any longer. We had no future. I was fed up with working in the fields and then having to go in the evenings to listen to what the communists had to say in political meetings.'

Lac Chi Bang, a 28-year-old repairman from Cholon, set sail for Australia on 26 March 1979. He left with his two brothers and three sisters because the savings his parents had given him in March 1978 were running out. They had handed over fifty taels of gold (worth about $15 000) before leaving Vietnam with his younger sister. 'In a year we had spent ten taels on food and living. I also had to bribe cadres who came to our house every month so that my brother and I wouldn't have to do military service.'

Being officially regarded as unemployed increased the risk of being sent to an NEZ. Diminished opportunities for tertiary education, because those of less privileged backgrounds got precedence, meant many sons and daughters of the rich or middle class joined the unemployed. Those on declining incomes and without officially approved occupations, if they resisted pressure to transfer them from the overcrowded cities to the countryside, were liable to have their ration cards withdrawn. This increased their reliance on the black market, where costs of food and other basic necessities were many times higher than the government price, so that their savings dwindled even faster.

One of the early arrivals at the Le Minh Xuan NEZ outside Saigon, where 200 families lived, was a Vietnamese Catholic family of eleven who moved there from Ho Chi Minh City under pressure in August 1976. Nguyen Manh Hung, twenty-four, said a bus was supplied to take them there, together with some furniture and clothing. They were given a thousand square metres of land for their own use, some farm implements, and corrugated iron sheeting for a house. The land had not been cleared and the soil was poor. They tried to grow rice, then turned to pineapples. Supposed to be completely self-sufficient, they were given no food, even to start with. However, families poorer than his, who could not afford to buy rice on the black market, were given food by the government. Young people could do various jobs in the NEZ, being paid a maximum of nine kilograms of rice a month. After some time the family decided to quit. Leaving their parents, who had tuberculosis and could get treatment at the NEZ, the brothers and sisters split up. Hung went to an uncle who owned farming land around Long Thanh. In December 1978 he went to Rach Gia and escaped in March 1979 by boat for Malaysia.

Hung said that in his area of Ho Chi Minh City, ethnic Chinese were 'crafty': he did not know of any who were sent to NEZs. However, La Quoc Quang, a 24-year-old ethnic Chinese electrician, said that, when some of his relatives were forced to leave Cholon for NEZs after the clamp-down on private trading in March-April 1978, 'Some of them slipped back to Saigon [in 1979] and went into hiding because they said conditions were so bad.'

Many young boat refugees – teenagers and those in their twenties – objected strongly to the compulsory labour activities organized by the communists. Nguyen This Thanh Tam, nineteen, was educated at a French language high school in Dalat in the central highlands. Her mother was a shopkeeper and her father a lieutenant colonel in the defeated army. She gave two reasons for leaving Vietnam: firstly, the atmosphere was no longer 'relaxed' or 'easy-going' and, secondly, 'We had all sorts of duties, for example, labour duty. It was not just at school but outside as well. Once a year we did a month's service around the city digging irrigation canals or planting sweet potatoes.' Another young Vietnamese woman, Vu Thi Kim Chi, described life in the south under communism as being 'boring'. She also objected to labour duty. Once a year for a month she was sent from Ho Chi Minh City to the Le Minh Xuan NEZ, where her work was cooking.

Nguyen Van Le, seventeen, was a fisherman in Tha Vinh. Unusually big for a Vietnamese, most of whom are slightly built, Le has a barrel chest, strong arms, a thick neck, a gruff voice. With one year of formal education, he had been fishing since the age of ten. On 15 March 1979 he set out for Malaysia as the captain of an eighteen-metre fishing boat. 'Seven months earlier the communists nationalized our boat. We had to sell part of our catch to the government. If we caught two tonnes, we had to sell half a tonne to the government. But the government gave us a low price. We could get higher prices by selling privately.'

Among the boat people have been a sprinkling of Buddhist monks. Thich Thien Quang, thirty-eight, one of the Buddhist leaders at the An Quang pagoda in Ho Chi Minh City, which was a centre for

Buddhist opposition to anti-communist governments before 1975, escaped from southern Vietnam by boat in June 1979. Head shaven and dressed in black clerical robes, the monk agreed on 12 July to talk to a correspondent of the *New York Times* away from other Indo-Chinese refugees in Indonesia's Tanjung Pinang camp and in the presence of international refugee officials. Some observers of religious affairs in southern Vietnam who have made visits there since 1975 believe Thien Quang's account of religious repression and dissidence in the south is exaggerated. But even if it is, it provides an insight into the thinking of a leader of a significant Buddhist faction in the south. According to his account, his superior, Thich Tri Quang, who had become famous as a Buddhist protest leader before 1975, was turned into a skeleton-like cripple during eighteen months of solitary confinement in a Ho Chi Minh City prison. For most of that time he had been kept in a coffin-like hole in which he could not sit up, being let out for only fifteen minutes a day to relieve himself and bathe. Released in 1977 after his legs atrophied, he was now confined to a wheelchair at An Quang pagoda.

Thien Quang said his own mission now was to go to the United States and the United Nations to tell the world about religious persecution in Vietnam. He described the beginnings of a united religious struggle in the south, linking Buddhists, Catholics, Protestants, Hoa Hao and Cao Dai, as well as clandestine armed resistance groups who were organizing disgruntled Vietnamese along the lines of the Vietcong for an uprising in 1981. Asked where these groups got their arms, Thien Quang said many communist soldiers had become corrupt and often sold weapons. Protests against religious discrimination began in earnest in 1976 when twelve Buddhist priests and nuns burned themselves to death in a mass immolation ceremony in the Mekong delta city of Can Tho. In the last two years, he alleged, eighteen others had committed the same act in Ho Chi Minh City alone. Asked why the An Quang Buddhists, after causing Diem and Thieu so much trouble, were struggling against the communists, Thien Quang replied: 'Under Thieu, we were only protesting against corruption. Now, under communism, we cannot exist at all.'

Chapter 5
Trafficking

During 1975-77, both the numbers of boat people and the accounts they gave of their escapes suggest that the Vietnamese authorities were trying to stop them. From 1978, both the increase in numbers and the stories of the refugees suggest something different – a pattern of organization and semi-official or official sanction. Also, although in the later period refugees were still leaving in small boats, an increasing number were being carried in vessels that could hold up to 600 or 700 people, and an increasing number of these were ethnic Chinese. The first phase in the increased flow of refugees started in the first half of 1978 and reached a peak at the end of the year. This is consistent with the view that Hanoi, after the nationalization in March of small businesses in the south, allowed the exodus to continue until December 1978. Then, facing a UNHCR meeting on refugees, and needing the support or at least neutrality of non-communist neighbours for its decision to invade Kampuchea, it stemmed the flow. The second phase began in February-March 1979 and reached a peak in the middle of the year, when it stopped abruptly. This is consistent with the view that, after the clash with China, Hanoi decided that the ethnic Chinese were a potential fifth column and Vietnam would be better off without them. The flow then redoubled until another UNHCR meeting in July turned off the tap again.

Hanoi has vigorously denied that it was involved in the refugee traffic. In an interview in *Asiaweek* magazine, on 15 June 1979, secretary of state for foreign affairs, Nguyen Co Thach, said of refugees: 'Mostly they are from the south, from Ho Chi Minh City in particular. In 1975, we forbade them to go out. We were criticized by the west. We thought it over. We decided to give them the freedom to go. Now they [Vietnam's critics abroad] say we are exporting refugees. So now we say they [the emigrés] must ask to go. And we will allow them to go . . .' (under an expanded legal emigration system agreed in principle with the UNHCR in May 1979). On reports that the Vietnamese government was taking money from the refugees, Mr Thach said: 'That has not been our policy. Perhaps there have been low-level cadres who have done so, but that is not the same thing. You know in [America] you have had your Watergate and your Lockheed scandals. It is something similar.' In an interview in Hanoi with a group of visiting US newsmen in August 1979, Mr Thach said that stopping all refugee boats was difficult: 'You have difficulty in stopping crime in your cities . . .' (the reference to crime may serve Hanoi's case better than the allusion to Watergate, in which there was connivance at a very high level indeed).

According to refugee accounts, however, Vietnamese authorities were involved in the traffic, through the security police network known as the Public Security Bureau (PSB). Detailed accounts by the refugees suggest that this bureau was given the responsibility sometime early in 1978 for overseeing paid departures. Since the PSB is an important and sensitive government agency, the decision to develop the program would have been made at a high level. The PSB is under the interior ministry headed by a politburo member.

In southern Vietnam the PSB staffed or supervised several offices in Ho Chi Minh City, as well as in Cholon, the 'China town' where an estimated one million Sino-Vietnamese lived. Subordinate offices were set up in coastal provinces of the Mekong delta and central Vietnam. They were usually run by centrally appointed officials under a provincial chief of public security. The role of the PSB was usually limited to initial registration and approval of applicants wanting to go abroad, and to final checks before those leaving joined their boats. The actual organization of passengers was left to middlemen. Offices handling the organized exodus were seldom located in government buildings, the police and security officials were in plain clothes, and the program was not publicized in the media, merely by word of mouth.

By early 1978, refugees from those sectors of central Vietnam that had been part of South Vietnam before 1975 reported that provincial authorities were also concluding confidential agreements with Chinese community leaders in Da Nang city to organize sea passages for ethnic Chinese. A Chinese merchant and former member of the

Vietnam chamber of commerce from Cholon said that in southern Vietnam the authorities organized a network of go-betweens by quietly putting out the word to about fifty 'state-approved' Chinese business organizations. These organizations had commercial contacts stretching throughout South-East Asia and as far afield as the United States, and some of their members had relatives who had already left Vietnam.

Generally, one or more Chinese with access to gold or cash would finance the acquisition of a boat, which would often require repair or modification. Fuel and supplies essential for the voyage had to be purchased on the black market at inflated prices. Ship-building and repair, together with most forms of land and sea transportation, had been taken over by the state in southern Vietnam after 1975. One side-effect of the controlled exodus was the growth of a busy small-boat repair and reconstruction industry centred on state-owned or approved yards.

Organizers would negotiate with the PSB at the town nearest the intended departure point about access to the boat, the number of passengers to be carried, and the payments to be made, usually in gold. Fees were generally collected from the passengers by the boat owner or his agent. The price of a passage varied according to the age of the passenger, his capacity to pay, his relationship with the boat organizers, the honesty of officials, middlemen and boat owners, and the availability of boats and their place in the queue of departures.

Most of the boat people leaving through the 'assisted passage' channel were Chinese from around Ho Chi Minh City, including Cholon, but there were also smaller numbers of Chinese from other areas on these boats. Almost all had been businessmen or petty traders before the communists took power in 1975. The fare for each adult passenger during the 1978-79 period ranged between eight and ten taels of gold ($2400-$3000). For children aged from five to fifteen it was four to five taels ($1200-$1500), or half the amount for adults, and children under five were normally free. Refugees and organizers say that about half the money went to the government in the form of registration and departure taxes. The rest went on the boat, supplies and bribes; what was left over was profit for the organizers.

Both boatloads of refugees from southern Vietnam rescued by the British freighter *Sibonga* (described in Chapter Three), were government-approved 'escapes'. One of these boats was organized by six Chinese who themselves joined the group when it left My Tho, a bustling port on the Mekong River, on 18 May 1979. Seven months earlier, one of the six organizers, a 26-year-old Chinese dental technician, had with two of his colleagues been taken by a middleman to a private house in My Tho where they were introduced to a plain-clothes official whom they believed to be a provincial PSB representative. They were given permission to leave on payment to the local public security office of six taels of gold for every passenger over sixteen and three and a half taels for those aged ten to fifteen; no charge was levied for those under ten. They were also to present a 'tourist car' to the PSB office for every twenty adult passengers travelling. (Three new cars were eventually handed over.) Only ethnic Chinese would be allowed to leave Vietnam. Once these terms were agreed, the organizers were given permission to buy a boat.

About a week before the boat was due to leave My Tho, the PSB arranged to collect the gold from the organizers. Two plain-clothes security men came by car to collect the agreed 870 taels for the 200 passengers. Having paid the levy, the organizers claimed they needed more passengers to cover expenses since many of the original group of 200 were children, or adults who could not afford the full price. So another 200 people with a better capacity to pay were recruited to join the boat. The group of more than 400 men, women and children assembled and waited in an empty factory in My Tho for four days. Two ferries took them out to their boat. They boarded shortly before midnight and left with two other refugee boats (one of them was the other boat rescued by the *Sibonga*). They were escorted out to sea for six hours by a motorized vessel belonging to the PSB.

Similar arrangements were possible in central Vietnam. A refugee who left Da Nang during the early wave of officially approved departures in 1978, also reported that local Chinese community leaders had been requested by provincial authorities to provide lists of potential passengers for screening by the PSB. The Chinese leaders were responsible for acquiring boats, food, fuel and other supplies for the voyage. In this case, they got free passages for themselves and thirty relatives, plus two taels of gold per adult and one tael each for minors.

Thus, while the departure system and its cost varied from place to place, month to month and case to case, it had a basic uniformity. Security police screened applicants, registered the names of those qualified to leave and collected payments. Although adults generally paid eight to ten taels and minors went for half fare, families could arrange lower prices by bribing individual security officials with vehicles, furniture and other personal possessions before these were officially confiscated by provincial authorities. In a few cases, free passage was permitted for Chinese without money who were considered troublemakers, or those who had tried persistently to escape 'illegally', meaning without government approval.

After security screening, some passengers had to sign declarations of intent to leave the country and waivers of future claims against the Socialist Republic of Vietnam. They listed their property and signed statements donating it to the government. In other cases, Chinese refugees said they had to sign forms stating that the applicant who had applied for permission to leave wished to give all his property to the state so that he could go overseas and be reunited with his relatives. Heads of households and adult males handed in biographical details and had their photographs and fingerprints taken. They were instructed to declare all gold and jewellery in their possession. (Many refugees did not make full declarations.) Except for two taels of gold each, all declared valuables were confiscated.

* * *

An important difference between the exodus from south Vietnam and that from the north was that compulsion was more obvious in the north. The flight of refugees from northern Vietnam falls into two categories and, generally, into two different periods. The first wave of refugees fled to China, starting in March-April 1978, and accelerating between May and late July, when China announced the closure of its frontier with Vietnam. Almost all those leaving were people of Chinese descent. In mid-June 1978, Peking claimed that China's southern provinces had accepted 160 000 ethnic Chinese from Vietnam. Officials in Hanoi later offered a slightly lower figure

– 140 000; among them were 3500 from the 13 000-strong Chinese community in the Vietnamese capital.

The smaller but more visible exodus from the north was by boat to Hong Kong: 60 per cent of all the boat people who had reached the British territory by mid-August 1979 were from northern Vietnam and most of them were ethnic Chinese. They had begun to arrive in Hong Kong in relatively small numbers in the last months of 1978, after China closed its border, claiming that they had left Vietnam because of persecution. But the flood of northern Vietnamese into Hong Kong on small boats started after China's month-long invasion of its southern neighbour in February–March 1979. From then on, ethnic Chinese in northern Vietnam were, in effect, forced to flee.

As in the south, the government agency supervising departures of the boat people was the PSB's office of alien affairs. A refugee who had been a long-time employee of the alien affairs office in Haiphong, an industrial centre and port serving Hanoi, told western officials in late 1978 that the Haiphong office was organized on the same lines as that in Ho Chi Minh City. Both had subordinate units operating in cities and provinces with sizeable ethnic Chinese populations, such as Hanoi and Quang Ninh in northern Vietnam, Da Nang and Quy Nhon on the central coast, and Can Tho and Bien Hoa in southern Vietnam. The traditional work of the Haiphong PSB office, he said, included the monitoring and control of alien residents and visitors. While it was managed by Vietnamese army officers, most of the staff and informants were ethnic Chinese. He claimed that by insinuating its personnel into almost every illegal activity, such as private enterprises, smuggling and black-marketeering (all of which, he claimed, were rife in the north), the office kept effective watch on the Chinese population.

When the intense exodus from northern Vietnam started after the China-Vietnam war, ethnic Chinese in Hanoi, Haiphong and other centres were called to meetings or visited by Vietnamese cadres. The new policy was explained: Hoa (ethnic Chinese living in Vietnam) could choose between being sent to remote labour camps or leaving by small boat. The Chinese reacted by forming groups and appointing leaders. These organizers obtained 'letters of introduction', normally from the local PSB alien affairs office, that permitted them to purchase a vessel from a fishing or marine co-operative run by the state. Meanwhile, would-be emigrants tried to sell their personal possessions to pay for the boat, and for supplies bought mainly on the black market. Outside the big cities the system was much the same except that the Chinese farmers and villagers were often ordered to leave with little or no notice and so could not organize departures until they reached the coast. A 26-year-old bicycle-repairman from Vinh Phu, about thirty kilometres west of Hanoi, said that when he was forced out he had first to arrange to travel by truck to Mong Cai, on the north-east coast overlooking the Gulf of Tonkin. There he found many other Chinese sleeping out on the streets and on the beach while they waited to go to Hong Kong. He formed a boatload with about 150 others and, as he had worked on a boat as a teenager, he was named captain. The group approached the secretary of a Mong Cai co-operative to buy an old sailing junk that had been used to carry rice and lime. The secretary's opening price was 10 000 dong ($2858) but after several days' hard bargaining they succeeded in reducing it to 7800 dong ($2228), each contributing about 50 dong – a bit less than a month's wages for an average worker.

Because the government apparently wanted ethnic Chinese to go, it did not, in the north, insist upon heavy departure taxes. Moreover, in southern Vietnam there was a lot more hoarded gold and other assets that could be appropriated, because the Chinese in the south were more numerous and much wealthier than those in the long-socialized north. Most of the money demanded for exits from Chinese in the north was for boats and supplies. A noodle-maker from Quang Ninh province paid 700 dong for places on a boat for himself and his family of ten. A boat bought by 150 Chinese from the town of Bac Giang, north-east of Hanoi, cost 150 000 dong. In fixing the purchase price, government officials at co-operatives making the sale seem to have adopted the 'Robin Hood' principle: groups were charged according to their estimated capacity to pay.

The experience of a Chinese who had worked for the government before leaving Haiphong for Hong Kong in April 1979 was evidently typical. To find a boat for himself and sixty others he first contacted the state-run Quang Ninh transport company; then the group approached the Hon Gay City public security office for permission to buy it. This was given verbally. The transport company's opening price was 84 000 dong ($24 000), an unusually high figure because, unlike most boats going to Hong Kong from northern Vietnam, this one had an engine as well as sails. As the boat was in poor condition and the group could afford only 74 000 dong ($21 143), their offer was accepted and they were given a receipt signed by the head of the company. Each member of the group contributed as much as he or she could afford. The transport company sold them fuel, but for food they had to resort to the black market. After submitting a list of passengers intending to leave to the public security office, they were given a date and time for departure.

The experience of a Haiphong-born Chinese driver, who arrived in Hong Kong with his family in a sailing junk in April 1979, also indicates that the costs of leaving from the north were not so high. With more than a hundred others, he bought the boat privately in February for 20 000 dong ($571) plus a tax of 2000 dong. From his own life savings and the sale of possessions such as furniture, the driver contributed 4800 dong ($1371). After giving the passenger list to the public security office in Haiphong, a person called at his home to collect 12 000 dong ($3429) – 10 000 dong for the exit papers and the balance for himself as the middleman. Normally security officials would note the details of refugee boats and advise nearby ports to allow them to leave when the exit papers had been produced for inspection. However, the driver said, his boat had barely left the coast when it was approached by a vessel carrying Vietnamese militia who fired shots into the air and demanded another 4000 dong. The money was handed over and, the driver believed, was kept by the militiamen. The total cost of the exit of this group of more than a hundred from northern Vietnam was more than 40 000 dong ($11 429), or about 400 dong ($114) each (about eight month's wages for the average worker).

It seems, therefore, that corruption of officials and the use of go-betweens did occur in northern Vietnam, but not on anything like the scale that it did in the south. Allegations by boat people from the north of official corruption were directed mainly at the PSB aliens office in Haiphong. Certain categories of Chinese were expected to get special permission to leave the country: doctors, engineers, skilled craftsmen, and communist party members were among them.

Many circumvented the requirements by registering to leave under a false occupation. A Hanoi professor now in Hong Kong went out as a machine operator, a change of recorded occupation arranged for him by a corrupt official in the Haiphong PSB. One man in this office, who was known as Mr Cong, apparently branched out into private consultancy. He sold false Chinese identity cards to ethnic Vietnamese who wanted to leave by boat, at the price of about 5000 dong ($1429) apiece. Hundreds of Vietnamese probably managed to leave in this way, but they were still very much in the minority among the boat people. Statistics compiled by the Hong Kong authorities show that, of the 61 275 people who arrived there from Vietnam in small boats from 1 January to mid-August 1979, only 3972, or about 5.5 per cent, described themselves as ethnic Vietnamese from northern Vietnam.

*　　*　　*

The use of seagoing freighters to transport refugees added a new dimension to the exodus of the boat people. In late 1978 and early 1979, a succession of these aging tramp steamers slipped in and out of Vietnam and then dumped – or tried to dump – their unwanted human cargoes in neighbouring countries. These ships were conjured up by middlemen and syndicates in southern Vietnam, Singapore, Hong Kong, Macao and Taiwan, working with the connivance, collaboration and at times on the initiative of Vietnam's PSB officials. The system of soliciting passengers for these ships was basically the same as for the small boats, but the price and the proportion of gold going to Vietnamese authorities were generally higher.

The attraction of the freighters was that they were safer, minimizing the dangers of piracy and death at sea. The use of cargo ships gave the whole exodus a higher profile, and led to a more thorough investigation of the system that brought paying refugees out of southern Vietnam. In particular, three extraordinary voyages – those of the *Southern Cross*, the *Hai Hong* and the *Huey Fong* – exposed the system at its worst.

*　　*　　*

On 19 September 1978, word reached the UNHCR office in the Malaysian capital, Kuala Lumpur, that a 950-tonne freighter, the

Southern Cross, had rescued more than a thousand Indo-Chinese and wanted to put them ashore urgently. The Indonesian captain claimed that the refugees had abandoned their small boats and swarmed aboard the freighter while she was immobilized by engine trouble in the Gulf of Thailand. Anchored in international waters off Mersing, the *Southern Cross* was short of food and water so Malaysian helicopters and navy craft ferried supplies to her. By the following day it appeared that the 1220 Indo-Chinese cooped up in the tramp steamer had become victims of a 'catch 22' situation. The UNHCR tried to persuade Malaysia to let them land at the Tengah Island refugee camp near Mersing, so that they could be processed for resettlement abroad. The Malaysian government refused: it wanted guarantees of quick departure first, and argued that western countries able to provide permanent homes for displaced Indo-Chinese should come forward. Singapore also took a hard line: it placed its navy and marine police on alert to stop the freighter from landing there. The UNHCR continued to insist that it could not process the refugees for permanent resettlement until it could get them ashore.

The *Southern Cross* decided to break the deadlock. She steamed away from Mersing and marooned her passengers on the uninhabited Indonesian island of Pengibu, midway between Malaysia and Borneo. A radio message from the ship said she had been holed on a reef while landing the refugees and was now crippled. Shortly afterwards, the United States, Australia and Canada gave assurances to the UNHCR that they would each accept for resettlement a substantial number of the people on the *Southern Cross*. Indonesia then announced it would grant them temporary asylum and preparations were made to move the stranded group to the refugee camp on Bintan Island, south of Singapore.

At the same time, the French newspaper *Le Monde* published an article by its South-East Asia correspondent, who had just returned from Vietnam, reporting that officials there were letting wealthy Chinese buy their way out. He said that the human cargo of the *Southern Cross* – '1200 rich and unwanted Sino-Vietnamese' – had paid their way out with 'more than half a ton of gold'. Vietnam's embassy in Paris angrily denied the report and an official broadcast from Hanoi denounced the French journalist. In South-East Asia, few people took much notice and the world soon forgot the *Southern Cross*.

However, on 9 May 1979, a 35-year-old Singaporean, Allan Ross, was arrested with three others, under Singapore's Criminal Law (temporary provisions) Act, which permits detention without trial. The home affairs ministry announced that the four men were involved in traffic in refugees from Vietnam 'with the complicity of the Vietnamese authorities'. On 23 August 1979 the *Age*, with the permission of Singapore authorities, interviewed Ross at the Queenstown remand prison. What Ross said was checked against information available from other sources, including Indonesian and western refugee officials who had questioned passengers from the *Southern Cross*. This is Ross's account of what happened before the freighter arrived off Malaysia.

On 25 August 1978 the *Southern Cross*, her holds empty, steamed out of Singapore into the shipping lanes of the South China Sea. Thousands of vessels from all parts of the world use this route each week; the *Southern Cross* could have been going anywhere - Thailand, the Philippines, Hong Kong, Taiwan, Korea, Japan. The ship, once a Dutch coastal trader that used to ply between Singapore and Madras was old but in good condition. Her hull was black, her superstructure white, and she cruised at between 8 to 10 knots. The freighter's managing agents in Singapore were Seng Bee Shipping, headed by a young Singaporean Chinese, Chong Chai Kok. One of the directors was a swashbuckling Finnish captain, Sven Olof Ahlquist. The vessel, registered in Honduras, was owned by Iranian interests and Ahlquist was their local representative.

The *Southern Cross* had an Indonesian skipper and a crew of ten, mainly Indonesian. Also aboard was a rotund, 51-year-old, Singapore Chinese businessman, Tay Kheng Hong. Ross, who had been recruited by Ahlquist, had worked for Seng Bee Shipping before. On this voyage he was responsible for the cargo and was also to keep an eye on Tay. Before leaving he had supervised the clearing of the holds and the storage of supplies. Ross liked the Finn, describing him later as a 'tall, blond good-looking guy, easy-going'. Ahlquist, who had lived in Singapore for more than ten years, was married to a friend of Ross's wife. Ross himself was the son of a Scottish-Eurasian engineer and a Chinese mother. As his father had died in

1948, Ross had lived with foster parents until he was twelve, and although he had had only three years of interrupted primary schooling behind him and could not read or write, he spoke fluent English and Malay, as well as three Chinese dialects: Hokkien, Cantonese and Teochew. His heavily tattooed arms indicated his seafaring background.

The *Southern Cross* anchored at a rendezvous point about fifty kilometres from the Vietnamese coast, off the port of Vung Tau which lies on the northern lip of the Saigon River estuary. There they waited for several days. Then, at about 5 pm on 3 September, they saw a boat coming towards them from the mainland. Tay Kheng Hong told the crew to hang a sign over the ship's side. Painted in large letters on cloth, the sign was in code: the numbers 0044 and some Chinese characters. Tay told Ross: 'This is our friend coming to meet us and guide us in'.

The approaching boat was a steel-hulled fishing trawler flying the Vietnamese flag. A man came aboard the *Southern Cross* and talked to Tay. Shortly afterwards they weighed anchor and followed the trawler towards the coast for nearly three hours. The next day, 4 September, at about 10 am, a pilot launch, again flying the red flag with a yellow star, came alongside. The pilot, in uniform – blue trousers, white shirt and white cap – boarded and spoke to Tay in Vietnamese. The pilot then used the radio on the *Southern Cross* to contact Vung Tau for permission to enter the Saigon River estuary. Guided by the pilot, they travelled for about two hours until they reached a long, well-constructed wharf. There, two Vietnamese navy patrol boats were moored and a third prowled up and down nearby. The pilot left the ship. Later a jeep driven by a man in khaki army uniform came along the wharf and stopped. A Vietnamese in civilian clothes got out, climbed up the ship's gangway, and talked privately for an hour in the crew messroom with Tay. All the while several Vietnamese soldiers armed with rifles patrolled the wharf. After the Vietnamese visitor departed, the ship was provided with fresh water and vegetables.

The next day, 5 September, two more Vietnamese civilians arrived in the same jeep with the same driver. After speaking with them, Tay told Ross that they wanted the *Southern Cross* to load 800 passengers, although Ross protested that the ship's maximum capacity was 700. Later the four of them went to lunch at a dilapidated seafood restaurant about fifteen minutes' drive from the wharf. Tay introduced one of the Vietnamese to Ross as 'the man who is giving permission to people to leave Vietnam'.

The following day, 6 September, guided by the same pilot and now flying the Vietnamese flag, the *Southern Cross* steamed slowly for about two hours to a point Ross assumed must have been close to the entrance of the Saigon River, as they could see mangrove swamps from their anchorage. A fishing trawler, with uniformed and armed soldiers on board, remained close by overnight.

At about eight in the morning their cargo appeared. Ross said:

We saw three fishing trawlers [each about twelve metres long] approaching from a bend in the river. They were packed with men, women and children. The trawlers were followed by a steel barge, also packed with people. I saw two armed soldiers on each craft. On reaching the *Southern Cross* there was a mad scramble to get on board. No one was hurt, but the whole operation took about an hour. Then the trawlers and the barge left with the soldiers.

Ross saw two men he took to be Vietnamese civilians carry four sacks from one of the trawlers to the captain's wheelhouse on the *Southern Cross*. Later, when the ship was safely at sea, Tay told Ross the sacks contained gold. In his cabin he displayed some of the haul to Ross, who described it as 'bundled gold leaf – a helluva lot'. Tay said the agreed price for the passage was two taels of gold (about $600) for an adult and one tael ($300) for a child. Tay also said the passengers paid the Vietnamese government between six and eight taels each to leave the country. After loading, the *Southern Cross*, still flying the Vietnam flag, turned around and nosed back towards the open sea with the pilot guiding and his launch following. They saw several patrol boats but were not challenged. After two hours the pilot left them and the freighter sailed south towards Indonesia.

Several days later, at a point not far from Singapore just west of Bintan Island, the *Southern Cross* prepared for a secret, late-night rendezvous. A yacht was waiting for them: the signal was a flashing light. The gold was transferred to the yacht in two brief cases carried by Tay and Ross. Ahlquist was on the yacht to meet them. The three men were all on the trim white craft when it returned to its usual anchorage at the Ponggol Point boatel on the eastern arm of the

Johore Straits. 'No one tried to stop us. We were just another yacht coming back from a pleasure cruise,' Ross said with a smile.

Later, at the Seng Bee Shipping office, the crew of the *Southern Cross* was paid off. Ross said the ordinary seamen received $1370 –$1820. He, the Indonesian captain and the Singapore radio operator were each given $4650 by Ahlquist and a bonus of ten taels of gold ($3000) by Tay Kheng Hong. Seng Bee Shipping's share was 700 taels ($210 000).

*   *   *

On 15 October 1978, a down-at-heel tramp steamer called the *Hai Hong* ('sea breeze' in Chinese) left its home port, Singapore, with an Indonesian skipper, a crew of fifteen Indonesians, and two Singaporean passengers. The ship was an old tub of 1600 tonnes, built in 1948 to carry general cargo. She was 75 metres long and 12 metres wide and her single, eight-cylinder diesel engine pushed her along at a speed of about nine knots – when it was working properly.

The *Hai Hong* was supposed to be on her last voyage. She had been sold, it was thought, to a Hong Kong buyer for scrap. The broker in the purchase deal had approached the Panamanian consulate-general in Singapore to have the ship put on the Panamanian register for one month from 9 October so that she would be registered for the duration of the voyage to Hong Kong.

On 31 October, the *Hai Hong* appeared out of the blue in Tarempa harbour in Indonesia's Anambas Islands. On 1 November the captain radioed the UNHCR in Kuala Lumpur to say that he had more than 2500 refugees from southern Vietnam on board and wanted UNHCR assistance. But the ship was ordered to leave Indonesian waters, and she sailed from Tarempa on 6 November. The Singapore navy made sure she did not try to enter Singapore. Early on 9 November, claiming to be crippled with engine trouble, she slipped into the outer harbour of Port Klang, Malaysia's main commercial shipping centre. There she stayed, despite the best efforts of Malaysian authorities to get rid of her.

After talking to the captain and five of the passengers, the Malaysian police issued a statement. The captain had claimed, it said, that the freighter, having developed engine trouble on the way to Hong Kong, had been boarded by refugees while anchored in the

Paracel Islands; on attempting to return to Singapore, further engine trouble forced them to put into Tarempa. The police statement said it was difficult to believe the captain's story: it was inconceivable that 2500 people could have gathered in one place in the South China Sea and succeeded in boarding without prior arrangement with the ship. The statement accused the captain of trying to conceal a 'planned migration of a sizeable number of people from Vietnam'.

After a stand-off in Port Klang, with the refugees still crowded on deck and in the holds, arrangements were made for supplies of food, water and medicines to be sent to the ship. Refugees were confined there, in some cases for several months, before they could be airlifted abroad, mainly to France, Canada, West Germany and the United States. In December the Malaysian government announced it was detaining the Indonesian captain, fifteen crew members and three Singaporean passengers until police investigations into the illegal entry of the freighter into Malaysian waters were completed. Among the three Singaporeans arrested was Tay Kheng Hong.

According to the account Tay gave Malaysian officials, a rendez-vous had again been arranged about fifty kilometres off Vung Tau and the same Sino-Vietnamese contact man involved in the *Southern Cross* operation had again come out to meet them in a trawler. The arrangement was for the *Hai Hong* to carry about 1200 paying refugees, but the contact man claimed Vietnamese officials had forced him and his fellow organizers in Ho Chi Minh City to add another 1300 passengers to the list. He also told Tay that adults leaving on seagoing freighters had had to pay levies of ten taels ($3000) each to the Vietnamese authorities, with those under sixteen years paying half and those under five going free. If this were true, a conservative estimate of the total value of the 'exit levies' for the *Hai Hong* would be about $4 million.

The plan had been for the *Hai Hong* to sail on to Hong Kong and deposit the refugees there and, when the ship left Vietnam on 24 October 1978, it did head north towards the British territory. But rough weather and a malfunctioning engine made the captain decide to turn back. Tay had not gone with the freighter from Singapore to Vietnam, as he had done with the *Southern Cross*, but had joined the ship in Tarempa.

One of Tay's immediate problems had been to get to the owner of a Hong Kong company (a man Tay named as Andrew Siaw), the bulk of the 1200 taels due to him. Siaw had put up the money to buy the *Hai Hong* for the refugee trafficking operation. On instructions from him, Tay had registered the owner of the *Hai Hong* as the Rosewell Maritime Company of Hong Kong. The shipping merchant Tay called 'Andrew Siaw' has not been traced and there are reasons to believe the name was an alias. Tay said he first met Siaw in 1971 when both were in business in South Vietnam. Siaw had a shipping firm that operated two freighters between Saigon, Hong Kong, Taiwan and Singapore. Siaw used to export scrap iron - an abundant by-product of the Vietnam war - to Hong Kong. Tay also claimed Siaw was associated with a syndicate that smuggled Vietnamese draft-dodgers to Hong Kong. Faced with the problem of getting Siaw's share of the gold off the *Hai Hong*, Tay used the radio telephone, shortly after the ship was expelled from Tarempa on 6 November, to send a message to Chong Chai Kok, the managing director of Seng Bee Shipping in Singapore. Chong despatched a tug boat to meet the *Hai Hong* at sea and Tay handed over to it 1000 taels ($300 000) earmarked for Siaw, retaining for himself what he considered to be his rightful due - 200 taels ($60 000).

Tay Kheng Hong typified the Chinese middleman who formed the vital link between the internal and external arms organizing the refugee traffic on big ships from southern Vietnam that mushroomed after September 1978. Tay was born in Singapore but spent extensive periods living and working in Indonesia. In 1971 he left Singapore and established himself in Saigon, investing nearly $1.5 million in the timber industry. In the wake of the communist takeover, his business was confiscated by the state. He managed to fly out of Ho Chi Minh City on an Air France flight to Bangkok in April 1978, by bribing Vietnamese immigration officials with five taels of gold. From Bangkok he went back to Singapore. Tay had lost a fortune and he was anxious to recoup some of it.

*   *   *

The man who appeared to be the master-mind behind a third refugee ship, the *Huey Fong*, was a 48-year-old Hong Kong businessman by the name of Kwok Wah-Leung. Associates called him 'Kwok the Dwarf', or 'Shorty' Kwok, because of his diminutive stature. Like

Tay, he had close connections with the Chinese commercial community in southern Vietnam. Born in China, Kwok went to Hong Kong in 1954, living and working there until, in 1969, he moved to Saigon. In 1976, the year after the communists took power, he returned to Hong Kong, leaving in Saigon a wife, son, and two younger brothers. Kwok and his family were all on the *Huey Fong* when it sailed into Hong Kong shortly before Christmas 1978.

Like the *Hai Hong*, the *Huey Fong* was a dilapidated general cargo vessel flying the Panamanian flag. The *Huey Fong* was supposed to be on a voyage from Bangkok to Kaohsiung, a port in Taiwan. The Taiwanese captain of the ship first contacted the Hong Kong marine department on 19 December when he was off southern Vietnam: he claimed to have rescued boatloads of refugees at sea. When she anchored outside Hong Kong on 23 December the *Huey Fong* was crammed with 3318 men, women and children from southern Vietnam, mostly ethnic Chinese. Alerted by the case of the *Hai Hong*, authorities were immediately suspicious. The *Huey Fong* finally sailed into Hong Kong waters on 19 January 1979, despite the fact that she was advised to proceed to her original destination and the captain was warned that if he entered Hong Kong he would face the consequences of the law.

On 23 January, as the last batch of refugees went ashore into camps pending resettlement overseas, police started interviewing the captain and crew. Three days later the first cache of gold taels was found on board. On 7 February, 3500 taels (worth $1 050 000) were discovered hidden in the engine room. Twelve men were charged with conspiracy to defraud the Hong Kong government by bringing refugees in by 'illegal pretence'. They were the captain, six of his officers, a Sino-Vietnamese from southern Vietnam, and four Chinese businessmen with connections in both Hong Kong and Vietnam, one of whom was 'Shorty' Kwok.

The *Huey Fong* trial was the first court case to expose the organization behind the big-ship refugee racket. The hearing in Hong Kong from 7 June to 1 August revealed that the methods of the *Huey Fong* operation had been similar to those of the *Hai Hong*, the main difference being that Hong Kong rather than Singapore was home base. There had been the usual hard bargaining over splitting the profits. Coded communications between organizers in southern Vietnam and those outside had referred to potential refugee passengers as 'frozen ducks', the ship as 'the bride' and the proposed date of arrival in Vietnamese waters as 'the wedding date'. The captain had tampered with the log book in an attempt to cover up the unscheduled call in the Saigon River. In one statement, which he later admitted to be false, the captain had pretended he had no knowledge of 'Shorty' Kwok although the Hong Kong businessman was on board for the whole of the voyage.

Another of the three Hong Kong Chinese businessmen who were tried in the *Huey Fong* case was 58-year-old Lo Wing. He had arrived in Hong Kong from Vietnam in October 1978 with the intention of getting a ship to collect Vietnamese refugees. He was put in touch with Kwok who, in liaison with Vietnamese authorities or their ethnic Chinese agents, arranged for the *Huey Fong* to be chartered from a Taiwan company. In a statement to police read out in court, Lo Wing said respectable and influential Chinese group leaders in Vietnam had regularly been making arrangements for refugees to go to Hong Kong.

Another of the accused, Tiet Quoc Lien, a 44-year-old Chinese from southern Vietnam who had arrived in Hong Kong on the *Huey Fong*, said his father had asked Lo Wing, before the latter had left Ho Chi Minh City for Hong Kong in 1978, to help arrange the exodus of refugees. According to Kwok, Tiet's father, Kwong Shuk (known as 'Uncle' Kwong), who had supported the communists in the south before they came to power in 1975, was 'very influential' in southern Vietnam. Tiet Quoc Lien also said in his statement that the Vietnamese government had changed its policy towards refugees in October 1978. Since then, the government had ordered the security department to send plain-clothes officers to respectable Chinese in Vietnam who could arrange the exodus. Tiet said the Vietnamese government had invented a slogan: 'You Chinese should rescue your own Chinese people'.

Kwok said that the *Huey Fong* had been met off Vung Tau on 13 December 1978 by two Vietnamese gunboats carrying Tiet Quoc Lien and four plain-clothes police. The next day, after being guided to a position further upriver, a party of Vietnamese officials boarded; with them was 'Uncle' Kwong. Kwok, the officials and Kwong then went ashore in a small boat and drove to Ho Chi Minh City. They were taken to a heavily guarded building which he believed was a PSB office. (He could not remember the name of the street in which the building was located, but recalled that the number was 175. A Chinese refugee from Ho Chi Minh City who claimed to know the location of the office handling the exodus of people from southern Vietnam has said that the address was 175 Tran Hung Dao Street, opposite a cinema.)

On arriving in the building, Kwok said, he saw about ten people seated at a long table checking forms and counting and weighing gold, which was mostly in the form of tael leaves but included personal items such as rings and chains. He was told it was the gold given by Chinese so that they would be allowed to leave the country on the *Huey Fong*. Kwok said he asked Kwong why the office was not in a government building and was told that the matter could not be made public because, if world opinion were alerted, refugees using this channel would not be accepted.

On the evening of 15 December, Kwok and Kwong were taken by car to Cat Lai on the bank of one of the tributaries of the Saigon River, east of Ho Chi Minh City. About 1000 refugees, brought by truck, were processed that night in an area by the river that was enclosed by barbed wire. Guards patrolled the camp and street lights nearby were turned off. Several junks were moored at the end of a wooden bridge. Before people boarded they handed the guards tickets which, Kwok was told, were receipts for the gold they had paid. He joined the refugees on one of the junks around midnight. The slow and silent journey downriver to the *Huey Fong* took about four hours. The freighter was only supposed to carry 1500 refugees but, according to Kwok, Vietnamese authorities brought another two groups alongside for loading and by the time the *Huey Fong* left Vietnam on 18 December she was carrying more than double her limit.

'Shorty' Kwok featured as a star witness for the prosecution in the *Huey Fong* trial. He was granted immunity on condition that he gave evidence. Defence lawyers claimed that the Chinese businessman had invented a good deal of his testimony. They suggested that he had told the police and the court what he thought they wanted to hear. In his summing up, the judge described Kwok as 'a very clever rogue' who had told numerous lies to the parties concerned in the conspiracy and had 'led each by the nose' in order to arrange the voyage of the *Huey Fong*. 'Gold was the motive for this incredible story of deceit and intrigue,' the judge said. But he added that he did not think Kwok had told any 'real lies' in court: most of his evidence had 'the ring of truth and was rational, plausible and straight-forward'. All eleven defendants were found guilty of conspiracy to defraud the Hong Kong government by illegally importing refugees. Prison sentences ranged from fifteen months to a maximum of seven years.

*   *   *

Official investigations into the activities of the *Southern Cross*, *Hai Hong*, and *Huey Fong* provided insights into the extent to which the Vietnamese authorities 'encouraged' the exit of Sino-Vietnamese. Other incidents in the seagoing freighter traffic reveal other aspects of the refugee trade.

On 7 February 1979, Hong Kong received another unwelcome visitor. Without seeking permission or informing the marine police, a 3600-tonne freighter called the *Skyluck* dropped anchor in the western section of the harbour. The ship was carrying more than 2630 people claiming to be refugees from southern Vietnam. The Panamanian-registered and Hong-Kong-owned cargo vessel gave the British territory as her first port of call; however, no documents were produced to support this claim. When police boarded they found the Taiwanese skipper tied up and guarded by several refugees. The captain asserted that he and his twenty-five crew had rescued the refugees between 18 and 21 January in the South China Sea and that subsequently some of the refugees had turned on him, using weapons to force him to head for Hong Kong.

Preliminary investigations by Hong Kong authorities showed that the vessel had left Singapore on 12 January with a cargo of paper and wooden boxes. She took twenty-seven days to arrive in Hong Kong, a voyage that should normally take four to five days. The captain alleged the log book and the radio log were thrown overboard by the refugees. While held in Hong Kong harbour, a series of bizarre events occurred on the *Skyluck*, including one occasion on 11 March when about 150 refugees jumped overboard in an attempt to dramatize their plight, and another, on 29 June, when the ship's anchor chains were cut and she ran aground.

Inquiries in Hong Kong and the Philippines revealed the outline of an elaborately organized scheme. On 31 January 1979, around dusk, a ship remarkably like the *Skyluck*, but named the *Kylu*, was intercepted by a Philippine coastguard cutter near Palawan Island and told to move away. The *Kylu* headed out to sea, but, according to refugees on board who were later interviewed, the ship doubled back under cover of darkness to a rendezvous off Palawan. The plan was to leave all the passengers on the island but, about daybreak, two unidentified boats rounded the headland and the captain, thinking they were coastguard or navy, panicked. He hurriedly raised anchor and steamed at full speed towards international waters. (In fact, the two craft were only oceangoing fishing trawlers calling to take on fresh water.)

The *Skyluck* had left Singapore on 12 January, at about the same time as a ship called *United Faith* (Taiwan-owned and subsequently scrapped). The *Skyluck* had loaded passengers, and the gold in payment for carrying them, off the port of Vung Tau, leaving Vietnamese waters on 24 January. A few days later she met the *United Faith* near Indonesia's Naturas Islands in the southern part of the South China Sea. The gold was transferred to the *United Faith*, which was there ostensibly to supply the refugee carrier with food and water. The *Skyluck*, re-christened *Kylu* by the simple trick of painting out the first and last two letters of her name, then sailed north-east towards Palawan. The *United Faith* made a beeline for Hong Kong where she was met, in international waters, by a fishing boat which offloaded the gold and ferried it undetected into the British territory. 'A few days later, we saw Vietnamese gold popping up in the local market, but no refugees,' a Hong Kong official said. The refugees arrived with the *Skyluck* (her name freshly repainted) on 7 February after the plan to land them all on Palawan Island had been aborted.

In March 1979, a 900-tonne, Panamanian-registered trader, the *Seng Cheong*, 'disappeared' in mysterious circumstances while being towed from the Portuguese colony of Macao towards Hong Kong, where it was intended she would undergo repairs. The *Seng Cheong* had already undergone certain modifications in Macao, and this alerted the suspicions of the Hong Kong authorities. These were confirmed when it was discovered that a ship bearing a close resemblance to the *Seng Cheong* had been spotted off the Vietnamese coast. But she was difficult to track, and the Macao authorities, where the owner was based, could not provide adequate information on her movements. Somewhere in the vicinity of Vietnam, the ship's name was changed to *Sen On* by painting out the necessary letters. On her way north she 'disappeared' again when she put into China's Hainan Island for engine and hull repairs.

On 26 May the *Sen On* made a dramatic entry into Hong Kong. She was caked in rust, listing to starboard, her decks crowded with people. The launch signalled the freighter to stop but the message was ignored. As the police gave chase, the *Sen On* turned and headed straight for Lantau Island. She ran aground on the beach, to the astonishment of a few weekend holidaymakers who watched several hundred refugees leap into the shallows and wade ashore waving and shouting.

The escapees were rapidly rounded up by police reinforcements which had been rushed to the island, and the group of some 1400 Indo-Chinese was taken to the government dockyard for processing. Police discovered that the night before, when the *Sen On* had been in the Pearl River estuary, off the Chinese mainland, the refugees had taken command of the ship after the Hong Kong Chinese captain and ten crew had climbed overboard and sailed off on a junk. Before leaving, they had instructed the refugees on how to navigate into Hong Kong. They had also destroyed log books, documents and navigation equipment.

Until she joined the refugee trafficking business, the *Seng Cheong* had belonged to Japanese interests. The outline of her former name, *Kina Maru*, was still visible on the stern when she reached Hong Kong. In the last phase of her life, the *Seng Cheong* was owned by the son of a prominent Macao businessman. The passengers from southern Vietnam – almost all of them ethnic Chinese – told police that they had paid an average of twelve taels of gold per adult ($3600), and half that amount for minors, to travel to Hong Kong.

Another interesting case was that of a 2000-tonne general cargo ship with suspected refugee syndicate connections which left Hong Kong on 7 May 1979 for Bangkok. To reach Bangkok from Hong Kong, vessels had to pass through the South China Sea, around southern Vietnam and into the Gulf of Thailand. The freighter did not arrive at her destination and on 7 June was reported to be anchored beside the main channel of the Saigon River. These reports were based on US satellite reconnaissance photographs, sightings by other passing ships, information from refugees, and intelligence from within Vietnam itself. The position of the freighter could be precisely pinpointed in one of the serpentine coils of the river, about half way between Ho Chi Minh City and the sea. Hong Kong authorities also knew the ship's name had been painted over, and had information about passage money having been paid, and about ethnic Chinese in the Ho Chi Minh City area being readied for departure.

Armed with such information, and concerned about the influx of refugees in Hong Kong, the British foreign office summoned the Vietnamese ambassador in London and delivered a strong protest. The ambassador refused to accept the protest note, leaving it behind when he left. Hanoi then lodged a counter-protest. Further representations to the Vietnamese government were made in Hanoi. Not long afterwards Hong Kong authorities learned that the ship was no longer in the Saigon River but had moved to a position off the coast of southern Vietnam. On 14 July a report came in that a ship in the same area had been seen repainting its name on the hull. In Hong Kong, the ship's agents received a radio message from the captain: 'No cargo. Forced sailing. We are waiting the order for the next port'. The curt reply was: 'Please contact owner directly. Your agency agreement terminated'. A later message from the ship, signed by the master, gave the freighter's position: it said her last port of call was Vung Tau in southern Vietnam and stated a course and speed that indicated the vessel was heading for Taiwan. A final message was received in Hong Kong confirming Taiwan as the freighter's destination and adding ' 'Nothing on board. Don't worry too much. Have a good time. Master'.

The master was a Hong Kong Chinese. Hong Kong authorities had reason to believe that it was the other officers on the ship, all of them Taiwanese, who actually ran the show on board. When the master eventually returned to Hong Kong, he claimed the freighter was forced to enter Vietnamese waters off Vung Tau and that he was told by a man with 'three stripes and a star on his collar', and a squad of armed militiamen as escorts, to be ready to take 3000

Indo-Chinese to the US island of Guam in the western Pacific. Only on 13 July, when the ship was instructed to move to a new anchorage where there were no guard boats, were they able to escape, he claimed.

On 18 June 1979, the official voice of Vietnam broadcasting from Hanoi said a cargo ship flying the Greek flag, *Nikitas F,* had been detained by Ho Chi Minh City authorities when she was about to leave Saigon harbour on 14 June. She was seized, the broadcaster said, for sheltering and organizing illegal departures for a group of Vietnamese citizens. On searching the ship the authorities had discovered many Vietnamese, including a number of officers and policemen of the old régime and some technicians. The broadcaster added that the security service and the people's inspectorate of Ho Chi Minh City had prosecuted the ship and ordered its detention while inquiries continued.

Eventually the *Nikitas F* was allowed to leave Vietnam. She steamed into Hong Kong on 2 July to bunker and take on stores before going to Shanghai to load Chinese rice for Africa. The Greek skipper told representatives of the Hong Kong marine department that the ship had berthed in Ho Chi Minh City to discharge 1500 tonnes of wheat from India. He had noticed that the Vietnamese dockers doing the unloading were mainly female, but that on 12 June, two days before unloading was due to end, that more males were working. Suspecting that some of the dock labourers intended to stow away, he ordered the crew, on 13 June, to search the ship. A number of Vietnamese were found hidden on board, mainly in the engine room and shaft tunnel. Those in the shaft had immersed themselves almost completely in bilge water to avoid detection; only their mouths and noses were above the surface. The captain said he made a full report on the stowaways to the port police later in the day and asked for police assistance to take them ashore. The next day, 14 June, a squad of about seventy police marched on the *Nikitas F* and rounded up thirty-four stowaways. Despite the captain's argument that he had reported the stowaways and could hardly be held responsible for them since there were four armed Vietnamese guards posted on his ship at all times, the *Nikitas F* and her crew were held captive. Over the next four days, police made frequent visits to the ship and took a total of sixty-nine stowaways ashore.

The vessel remained under arrest until 21 June, when the chief engineer agreed to sign a confession. He, the assistant cook and one sailor were then summoned to appear in court on 22 June. The captain attended on behalf of the owner. The four accused were fined a total of $10 000 and, in addition, the captain was ordered to pay $300 court costs and $1500 for police expenses. He informed the court that neither he nor the crew had the money to pay the fines. On 23 June, although the fines remained unpaid, he was told he could sail.

*   *   *

The accounts in this chapter of how the refugee traffic was organized provide only a glimpse of what actually happened. It is, however, a revealing glimpse. It shows, as might be expected, that when the needs of large numbers of people become desperate, there will be some who profit from their plight. The price the market will bear becomes in these circumstances heavy in human terms, as well as high in terms of money. Were it not for the fact that the Vietnamese refugees believed themselves to be escaping from persecution (or the threat of it) or to a new freedom (or the promise of it), the way in which they were herded into ships, the appalling conditions they suffered, and the way money was made out of them, would be reminiscent of the infamous slave trade.

The accounts show that the export of people from southern Vietnam on seagoing freighters was organized largely by ethnic Chinese inside and outside Vietnam. Those inside wanted to leave; those outside were prepared to help – for a profit. The outsiders were among the more than 26 million Chinese living in the various countries of non-communist South-East Asia – Hong Kong, Macao and Taiwan. The refugee trade was organized through the tightly knit webs of commercial clan, through personal contacts established between Chinese in southern Vietnam and Chinese in other regional countries long before the communists captured Saigon in 1975. It was this network that the Vietnamese government chose to exploit. How deeply and at what level it became involved may be open to argument but the witness of thousands of refugees to the fact of its involvement and the evidence of the big ships is too strong to be denied. However shadowy the connections between the traffickers and the Vietnamese may be – and at times they appear clear and precise – it is hard to believe that Hanoi could not have stopped the human traffic had it wished to do so. How much money Hanoi made from the traffic is a matter of controversy: the estimates vary enormously and run into hundreds of millions of dollars. But it is perhaps not so important to work out by how much Hanoi profited as to note that it did, while denying to the world that it had.

The issues are admittedly complex and difficult to raise in a manner that is acceptable or even understandable by all the individuals, groups and nations caught up in the refugee crisis. The endless list of questions can be endlessly refined. Was the trafficking legal? (According to whose laws?) Was it moral? (Morality is difficult to apply in the market place.) Was it humane? (Certainly not, but the free-market forces that came into operation once it was known that a lot of people had to leave Vietnam created a buyer's market.) Should Hanoi have profited from this human predicament? (A government is entitled to impose an exit tax.) But are these the right questions and answers? Before a judgement can be made, the background needs to be expanded. The crisis did not occur in a vacuum of national prejudices and human passions; to understand its complexities more fully, it is also necessary to examine closely the political and strategic factors that influenced the many parties concerned.

Chapter 6

Stability

The flood of refugees into South-East Asia exposed an unstable situation. They reflected it by their flight; but they also contributed to it, especially by arousing fears that their arrival in such large numbers (particularly of ethnic Chinese) would be a threat to economic well-being and racial harmony.

The word 'stability', like the word 'security', is sometimes used in support of policies that are opposed to social and political change. That is not the intention here. It is true that social change in Vietnam after 1975 caused some Vietnamese to leave, but that was to be expected. Indeed, the flow of refugees from Vietnam in the first years of communist rule reflected a more stable situation than in Kampuchea, where few were able to flee for the simple reason that they were killed before they could. The complaints of the thousands who escaped from Vietnam because they did not want to go to a 'new economic zone' or be 're-educated', or because they did not like the policies of the new government or some of the people in it, were mild compared with the unheard cries of many more Kampucheans – perhaps half a million, perhaps one million, perhaps more – who were murdered in their own land. 'Stability' can mean the peace of the grave.

What the refugee flow has shown, however, is that neither within South-East Asia nor among the major powers is there agreement on what is required to give governments and people in the region a reasonable expectation of stability and security.

Although Vietnam was ravaged by war for thirty years – with France, with the United States and, in a sense, with itself – few people fled the area; there was no large movement of people out of it until 1975. Although many did not like the régimes of Diem and Thieu in what was South Vietnam, they did not leave because, even if they could get away, they had nowhere to go – unless they were prepared to go over to the communist side. They could not flee into the arms of the Americans or their allies, who were supporters of the South Vietnam régimes. In the north, if people were to have considered fleeing to China to escape the bombing, they would soon have been dissuaded by Peking, which was at that time an ally of their government. So, despite war and deprivation, the people of Vietnam stuck it out because they had no alternative.

The situation now is different. Vietnamese and ethnic Chinese in the south believe that the non-communist countries of South-East Asia, as well as the United States, France, Australia and other western democracies, do offer them an alternative. The Chinese in the north now see China as an alternative (forced upon them, perhaps, but nevertheless real). Both these new factors are part of a wider framework of uncertainty in relations between the major powers and the countries in the region.

Unlike Europe, where there is a balance of military power, and unlike Africa and Latin America, where the major powers do not have a determining military presence, in Asia each of the major powers is present, without a balance having been reached. Only in Asia is China militarily significant. The old security system in Asia, which was based after the second world war on Anglo-American military superiority, has crumbled away. Japan, a global economic power, is still unsure what political – and certainly military – role it should play. The relationship between the United States, the USSR and China is fluid, although Peking-Moscow antagonism has hardened. No one living in Asia today can be sure what kind of security system will develop there.

* * *

Washington was traumatized by the fall of Saigon in 1975. For months, even years, policy-makers could not bring themselves to analyse the failures of the past or to focus on the future strategic problems of a victorious Vietnam. 'There was a numbness and a great deal of hand-wringing,' recalls Douglas Pike, himself an influential if troubled adviser to successive American administrations during the Vietnam misadventure.

It was the *Gone with the Wind* syndrome. Remember Scarlett O'Hara, sitting there in her ornate antebellum southern mansion and being told that her estate was in chaos and the old life over and saying 'I don't want to think about that today, I'll think about that tomorrow'? Well, that's how it was then, in the state department and the Pentagon.

As late as September 1979, senior officials in Washington were prepared to concede, at least privately, that the administration's strategic thinking about Vietnam's future role in South-East Asia, and its consequences for both the United States and the region as a whole, was still, in the words of one of them, 'relatively elementary'. Long-term policy remained hostage to America's uncertainty about how long Vietnam intended to maintain its forces in Kampuchea, whether China was planning to teach Vietnam another lesson, and the new instability of great-power relations in the region since Vietnam's friendship treaty with the Soviet Union and China's invasion of Vietnam. The immediate issue was the question of 'normalization': whether, and when, the United States should recognize the Socialist Republic of Vietnam, exchange diplomatic representatives with it, and lift its trade embargo. On that issue, American policy was frozen. On four separate occasions during June and July 1979, senior officials of the Carter administration had told Vietnamese representatives in New York and Geneva that the United States was not prepared to resume negotiations for normalization in the prevailing circumstances.

Soon after taking office in January 1977, President Carter declared his intention to move, if possible, to normal diplomatic relations with Vietnam. By October 1978 Washington and Hanoi seemed halfway to an agreement. The United States, with some reservations, seemed satisfied that Hanoi would provide a full account of the fate of American servicemen still listed as missing in action in the Vietnam war, and help recover their remains. The Carter administration had abandoned its inherited opposition to Vietnam's admission to the United Nations; Hanoi no longer claimed that the United States was bound by the Paris accords of 1973 to provide economic assistance as a precondition to resuming normal relations. But in November 1978 the United States had taken the initiative and suspended negotiations in circumstances that fed each side's suspicion of the other and hardened public and congressional opinion in America. The official explanation blamed the breakdown on

Vietnam's recalcitrance: its determination to invade Kampuchea, the dramatic increase in the flow of Indo-Chinese refugees, and Vietnam's new and disturbing relationship with the Soviet Union. All this, Richard Holbrooke, assistant secretary for East Asia and the Pacific, told the House of Representatives subcommittee on Asian and Pacific affairs on 13 June 1979, had compelled the United States to draw back.

Early in the negotiations, Mr Holbrooke said, the US had told Vietnam that normalization depended on Vietnam's willingness 'to follow policies supportive of peace and stability in the region'. Even before Vietnam's invasion of Kampuchea, the US had warned Hanoi that the Pol Pot régime's 'unparalleled crimes' would not justify a Vietnamese violation of Kampuchea's sovereignity. Hanoi had claimed its military build-up on the Kampuchean border was 'purely defensive' and had given assurances that it had 'no aggressive plans towards that country' – but it had still gone ahead and invaded Kampuchea.

The US had also asked for assurances that Vietnam would follow an 'independent' foreign policy. It had been told that the treaty with the Soviet Union was 'not directed at any third nation'. But Soviet destroyers, submarines and TU-95 long-range reconnaissance aircraft were now using Vietnam's port and base facilities in Da Nang and Cam Rahn Bay, and that was 'a source of serious concern to us and to most Asian countries, not only militarily, but because of the dangers to the region of increased great-power rivalry and the consequent risk of increasing tensions'.

Also, the US had concluded that Vietnam had 'embarked on a deliberate effort to rid itself of those elements of society it considers undesirable'. Americans did not wish to see Vietnam force an end to emigration, but the growing refugee exodus had caused unacceptable human suffering and 'massive burdens' on the other South-East Asian countries. Hanoi had simply claimed it was 'powerless to control the flight of malcontents who were not willing to work to build a new Vietnam'.

The counter-theory, promoted by the critics of the Carter administration's Vietnam policy (and by Hanoi itself), is that the US deliberately stalled the negotiations with Hanoi even before Vietnam invaded Kampuchea or the flow of refugees reached intolerable levels because it wanted to 'play the China card'. Proponents of this thesis argue that, as early as December 1977, the Carter administration had concluded that normalization of relations with Vietnam and China were 'either/or propositions', and that if the US pressed ahead with the Vietnam negotiations it would antagonize Peking and frustrate efforts to reach agreement with China on the exchange of diplomatic representatives and the resumption of normal trade.

An elaboration of this thesis proposed that Vietnam was in effect driven into a closer alliance with the Soviet Union by the antagonism of China and its support for the Pol Pot régime, and by fears that the US, in its enthusiasm for normal relations and trade with China to counterbalance the Soviet's regional influence, deliberately slowed down negotiations with Vietnam. Senior state department officials agreed that US recognition of Vietnam had been a sensitive issue for the Chinese in 1978, and an even more sensitive one in 1979, when China and the US had resumed normal relations and China and Vietnam had fought a limited border war. But they claimed that the issue had never been directly raised with the Chinese during negotiations for normalization in 1978, and that 'there was no particular reaction from the Chinese' when American negotiations had referred to it by hint or inference.

On August 12 1979, Mr Holbrooke restated the American position that 'present circumstances made it impossible and undesirable to resume progress towards normalization of relations' with Vietnam. Some future movement was not impossible, he said, but it depended on 'Vietnam's actions'. The US had already given its conditions for a resumption of negotiations during the abortive talks with Vietnamese representatives in New York and Geneva in June and July: an independent government in Kampuchea, control of the refugee exodus, and assurances about Vietnam's new relationship with the Soviet Union.

While they had no firm formula for a settlement in Kampuchea, US officials could see no possibility of stability in the region unless there was a government in Phnom Penh that represented all three contending forces: the deposed Pol Pot faction, still fighting in the jungles with the support of Peking and claiming representation at the United Nations; the Heng Samrin régime, installed by Vietnamese force and sustained and apparently controlled by Hanoi; and the 'third force' of nationalists, rallying uneasily around the exiled former prince, Norodom Sihanouk. Such an improbable coalition was, they agreed, unlikely in the foreseeable future.

Although Americans had been encouraged by the apparent change of Vietnam's policy at the Geneva refugee conference in July, and by Hanoi's formal but still unfulfilled agreement to admit American consular officials to process applicants for family reunion in the US, the administration was reserving judgement on Vietnam's intentions and its ability to administer a humane refugee policy. The US demand for reassurances about Vietnam's Russian connection was a grey area – less a formal precondition than a warning that growing Soviet influence in Vietnam would inevitably impede progress towards normalization. In Hanoi, on 9 August, the Vietnamese secretary of state for foreign affairs, Nguyen Co Thach, bluntly told a visiting American congressional delegation: 'The US established relations with China with no conditions . . . this is a double standard. This is the China card . . . All over the world, no country has used relations with a third country as a condition for normalization.'

Of the three American conditions, the future of Kampuchea was the most critical and the most intractable. But it was widely acknowledged in Washington that there was little chance that Vietnam would quickly or easily change its position on any of them, certainly not on Kampuchea or the Soviet connection. Some analysts predicted there would be no change in Vietnam's policies until Hanoi's present leaders, still inspired by the 'curse-the-enemy' values they had applied so successfully during more than thirty years of war, had been replaced by a generation more susceptible to compromise and more attuned to economic reconstruction and social reform. Although the average age of the seventeen-member politburo in Hanoi was sixty-nine, there was little confidence in Washington that a new leadership was about to emerge.

There was general agreement among US officials that the issue of normalization was dead – at least until after the presidential elections in 1980. There was no effective constituency pushing for a resumption of negotiations: Americans, for the most part, preferred to avert their attention from Vietnam. There were no clear and compelling economic incentives for the resumption of economic, much less political, relations with Vietnam. The American chamber of commerce, which had earlier supported moves for normalization in the expectation of trade and investment opportunities, was now more interested in developing trade relations with the large and more promising China market. Recent reports of dry wells off Vietnam's coast had dampened the enthusiasm of Houston and Wall Street.

In congress, criticism of Vietnam's policies had hardened significantly since 1975. On 5 September 1979, the House of Representatives voted an additional $207 million for assistance for Indo-Chinese refugees but, by 281 votes to 117, added an amendment forbidding any direct or indirect aid to Vietnam itself. In part, the stiffening of congressional attitudes was the result of electoral pressure, especially from those constituencies (for example, southern California, Colorado and Louisiana) where the influx of Vietnamese refugees had created some social tensions and economic pressures. But it also reflected growing hostility to the Soviet Union, fed by the controversy over the presence of Soviet troops in Cuba and by the claims of conservative congressmen that the Soviet Union was out-distancing the US in the strategic arms race.

Later in 1979 there was some further debate on the resumption of negotiations with Vietnam. A nine-man congressional study mission, appointed by the speaker of the House of Representatives and led by congressman Benjamin Rosenthal of New York, had spent ten days in South-East Asia, including two in Hanoi, during August 1979. In a report published on September 16, it recommended that the US resume negotiations 'at the highest feasible level' to 'explore practical avenues towards establishment of diplomatic relations'. In the meantime, the US and Vietnam should consider immediately opening liaison offices in Washington and Hanoi. It also recommended that the president consider lifting the US trade embargo against Vietnam and providing aid, in order to alleviate the economic conditions that contribute to the refugee flow. But the House sub-committee on Asian and Pacific affairs also sent a delegation to South-East Asia, and its chairman, Congressman Lester Wolff of New York, challenged the main Rosenthal recommendations and warned against a precipitate reconciliation with Vietnam.

We recognize that we should explore possible grounds for agreement with

Vietnam, and that trade, if not aid, would be desirable on mutually beneficial grounds. However, let us not fall into the trap of permitting our attention to be shifted from the goals of the Geneva UNHCR conference to a debate over normalization. To do this would be to allow the Vietnamese argument, that the US is responsible for the refugee flow, to prevail, and that is simply untrue.

Senator Edward Kennedy of Massachusetts was probably the single most influential voice in congress in favour of a rapprochement with Vietnam. Although not on this issue a critic of the Carter administration, he had earlier recommended a new American initiative in Indo-China. In a speech to the council on foreign relations in New York on 2 April 1979, he had urged the US, Japan and the ASEAN states to call a new international conference on Indo-China in an attempt to obtain a Vietnamese military withdrawal from Kampuchea and the eventual neutralization of Kampuchea and Laos. Using 'incentives for co-operation as well as penalties for the failure to co-operate', the US should offer Vietnam 'a positive alternative to deeper dependence on the Soviet Union and unabated confrontation with China', he said. And it should 'clearly state that it is prepared to normalize diplomatic and trade relations with Vietnam in the context of movement towards restraint and co-operation.' He believed that, 'Had we moved to normalize relations last year, it is at least possible that Vietnam would not have concluded its new alliance with the Soviet Union and would have limited its objectives in Cambodia, as did China in Vietnam'. By September 1979, Senator Kennedy's speech was still being hailed by opponents of the Carter administration's Vietnam policy as a clear alternative to the government's tactic of 'conditional negotiation', although, in substance, it was only a more active version.

The White House had abandoned the cause of resuming normal relations with Vietnam as a political liability that a weakened and struggling president could not afford. During the melodramatic reorganization of his government in July 1979, when his standing had fallen to an historic low, President Carter had created a special committee to review the political and electoral implications of the administration's foreign policy. The committee concluded that nothing that could, or would, happen in Indo-China in the foreseeable future would be to the political advantage of Jimmy Carter.

According to one authoritative source, the committee's conclusion, 'amounted to a recommendation not to do anything about Vietnam, but not to be seen to be doing nothing'.

If America's immediate Vietnam policy was effectively in limbo, paralysed by political inhibitions and Hanoi's perceived intransigence, its long-term strategy was equally uncertain. There was, however, broad agreement among policy-makers in the state department, the Pentagon and the national security council that two options were available. The first was co-option: to entice Vietnam into the South-East Asian community by a combination of incentives and penalties comparable to those proposed by Edward Kennedy: 'In response to positive steps by Vietnam, Japan could resume its suspended assistance and the US could make exceptions to our current trade embargo. In the event of continued confrontation [with China] and conflict [in Indo-China] we could increase our economic and military assistance to key ASEAN states and they could cut political and other relations with Hanoi.' This meant, effectively, that unless the US or one of its allies (Japan or ASEAN) took the initiative (and that was improbable, perhaps impermissible, until after the 1980 presidential election), America would be confined to a policy of reaction. It could only wait for a hint of compromise or a sign of repentance from Hanoi.

The second option was coercion: a deliberate strategy of 'squeezing' Vietnam by every means available to compel it to take a more co-operative position on Kampuchea and the refugee problem and to back away from the Soviet Union. It might even be possible to create the conditions for a change of leadership in Hanoi. Vietnam was thought, especially by defence and national security analysts, to be susceptible to such a strategy. Its economy was in a steady decline. Domestic production was dropping, the country was importing 20 per cent of its rice and the transport system seemed on the point of collapse. The danger was that coercion might consolidate the present leadership and drive it closer to Moscow.

To a degree the US was already engaged in a strategy of coercion, simply by withholding recognition and maintaining its trade embargo. Moreover, urged on by some of the ASEAN states (especially Thailand, the country most immediately vulnerable to Vietnamese pressure), it had actively encouraged other governments to cut their aid to Vietnam (Japan and Australia were among those who had responded) and had led the campaign to choke off funds for Vietnam from international lending institutions like the World Bank and the International Development Association.

But, as more than one defence security official was quick to point out, it was China that was doing the serious squeezing – by maintaining the threat of another military intervention. The general expectation in Washington was that if China did go into Vietnam again, its intentions would be, as one defence official said, 'therapeutic not pedagogic – not to teach Vietnam another lesson, but to get rid of Le Duan [secretary general of the Vietnamese communist party] and the Russians'. The possibility of another Chinese military action in Vietnam was the cause of considerable strategic ambivalence in Washington. In the state department, in particular, there was serious concern that it would prompt Russian intervention and develop into a major regional conflict. But there were some officials, especially in the Pentagon, who were willing to contemplate that risk and positively welcomed the prospect of the Chinese 'hammering' the Vietnamese, even if (especially if, in the case of the more forthright) the Russians became involved.

*   *   *

The view from Moscow was that the refugee problem reflected the refusal of the US and China to accept the 'reality' of the new Vietnam. In the Soviet view, the refugee problem was simply a continuation of the Vietnam war, started by the French, taken over by the Americans and now being carried on by the Chinese. The US and China carried the primary responsibility for what had happened and was happening and the solution lay with these two countries rather than with Vietnam. The boat people as such did not greatly concern Moscow, as they were unlikely to seek shelter in the Soviet Union. The political effect of the exodus from Vietnam, however, was of great interest to Soviet policy-makers. Some such exodus over a long period was inevitable, given the fact that nearly two decades of American occupation of south Vietnam had created an artificially consumer-oriented society: those who had become accustomed to it were unlikely to feel happy or secure in an austerely communist Vietnamese society. Beset with a severe economic crisis, the

Vietnamese authorities perhaps did little to discourage the leavers and may even have found this exodus a relief. But the situation was made worse by Chinese agitation among the ethnic minority in Vietnam, and by the eagerness with which the west used the refugee issue to discredit Vietnam – even to the extent, the Russians argued, of allowing thousands of refugees to perish at sea before opening its doors to them. The well-orchestrated outcry about the plight of the refugees made it appear that a racist, doctrinaire Vietnam was cruelly pushing out a sector of the population. When Vietnam was able to provide assurances that it would control the flow, the Americans sent in warships, allegedly to save drowning refugees, but really to encourage another wild, panicky exit from Vietnam.

The Russians argue that a new exodus may start, especially if China again attacked Vietnam. Minorities and disaffected Vietnamese could feel secure only if war tension in and around Vietnam subsides. This cannot happen as long as Hanoi is made a constant object of threats and boycotts. The solution lies in Washington and Peking accepting the reality of Vietnam's emergence as a unified nation with its own security needs and independent outlook. The partial success of Peking's and Washington's propaganda war against Hanoi should not lead to the illusion that Vietnam can be overcome by the Chinese. It can be made to suffer; it cannot be made to bow.

The primary motive of the US, according to Moscow, is to avenge its defeat in Vietnam, and the Chinese have become an excellent proxy. The secondary motive is to regain influence in South-East Asia by presenting Vietnam as a threat to the security of its neighbours. Vietnam has to be portrayed as a monster that threatens the security even of China, an absurd proposition which, however, the disquiet caused by the influx of the Vietnamese refugees in neighbouring countries has made to seem plausible. Lastly, it is in America's interest to encourage the antagonism between China and Vietnam, fulfilling Washington's desire to keep Asians fighting Asians.

China's primary motive, according to Moscow, is to deny Vietnam any opportunity to consolidate itself. The Chinese fear Vietnam, not because it is a threat to their security, as they allege, but because Vietnam is an obstacle to China's expansion in South-East Asia. Their attempt to 'destabilize' Vietnam began even before Saigon had fallen, and continued through the use of the Pol Pot régime in

Kampuchea until, in desperation, Hanoi intervened. Peking's campaign against Hanoi reached a peak with the invasion of Vietnam. As a consequence, the exodus from Vietnam of ethnic Chinese became an uncontrollable flood. It may be that Hanoi did not try too hard to stop it, but who can really blame Hanoi, after thirty years of suffering imposed upon it by one power after another?

The Russians dismiss the Kampuchean question as a red herring: Kampuchea is much more relevant to Vietnamese security than it is to Chinese security. China does not have a common border with Kampuchea, so China's only interest there must be to perpetuate a régime hostile to Vietnam. Given time and restraint by China, a neutral government might emerge in Kampuchea which would keep the balance, but it cannot happen so long as the Chinese back the discredited Pol Pot régime. The Russians feel that the attitude of ASEAN countries, apart from Thailand and Singapore, is far from being as hostile to Vietnam as appears, and if Sino-American attitudes were to change, reconciliation with Hanoi would be possible. As for the allegations that the Soviet Union is establishing hegemony over Vietnam, Russians ask if the Vietnamese would have fought for thirty years only to surrender themselves to Moscow.

*　　*　　*

Within South-East Asia itself, uncertainty has been the keynote since the fall of governments in Cambodia, South Vietnam and Laos in 1975. In 1967, at the height of the Vietnam war, Indonesia, Malaysia, the Philippines, Singapore and Thailand had formed the association known as ASEAN. Although this association's charter excluded military co-operation, its five members could not disguise the fact that as individual states they had been inclined to support the non-communist side in the Indo-China conflict. This was most evident in Thailand and the Philippines, which had sent contingents of troops to serve in Vietnam alongside soldiers from the US, South Korea and Australia. Thai mercenaries, trained, armed and paid by the US, were sent to Laos to fight the pro-communist Pathet Lao and their Vietnamese allies. Military bases in Thailand were used extensively by American forces to bomb suspected communist targets in northern and southern Vietnam, Cambodia and Laos. Bases in Thailand were also established to monitor communist

145

communications in Indo-China and to train special forces for operations in Cambodia and Laos. In the Philippines, American air and naval bases provided vital support for the US war effort.

The reality ASEAN members faced in 1975 was that the balance of power in South-East Asia had been irreversibly altered by the communist victories and the US defeat. ASEAN's immediate response showed a readiness to adjust. It welcomed the end of war and said the five countries were ready to enter into friendly and harmonious relationship with each nation in Indo-China. However, Vietnam had emerged from the war as the region's biggest military power and was seen as potentially expansionist. ASEAN also feared that Hanoi would start exporting revolution, as all five ASEAN countries were troubled in varying degrees by home-grown, communist-led insurgencies. Hanoi's initial statements did little to allay their fears. Flushed with success, it asserted its role as a revolutionary force in South-East Asia and described ASEAN as a prop of American policy. However, by the end of 1977 there was a change. Vietnam's deputy premier and foreign minister, Nguyen Duy Trinh, who had been outspoken in his criticism of ASEAN, became the first of a succession of high-ranking emissaries from Hanoi to visit regional capitals. By mid-1978 it had become clear that Vietnam had launched a diplomatic offensive to improve its relations not only with ASEAN but also with Japan and the west, including the US. In July Hanoi sent one of its most accomplished diplomats, Deputy Foreign Minister Phan Hien, to Thailand, Japan, Australia, Singapore, New Zealand and Malaysia: Hanoi, he announced, was prepared to talk to ASEAN. In the space of less than eighteen months, Vietnam's attitude to ASEAN had done a somersault: the question its five members asked themselves was Why?

It could be partly explained by a natural easing of post-war tensions. Also, ASEAN had proved it was a united front that had to be taken into account in regional affairs. But the main reason was probably the profound shift in alignments among the communist states of Indo-China, the Soviet Union and China. The former allies in the war against America had fallen out with each other. In the absence of a common external threat, conflicting national interests and old enmities had reasserted themselves. It was logical for Vietnam to try to secure its flanks by ensuring the friendship, or at least the neutrality, of ASEAN countries, who were also being wooed by China and Kampuchea. Even the Soviet Union had changed its hostile tune and joined the line of communist suitors.

The chief concern of ASEAN was to avoid being drawn into any of the new disputes. But to avoid entanglements while improving relations with the antagonists was never easy and became impossible at the end of 1978. One reason was Vietnam's invasion of Kampuchea; the other was the exodus of refugees from Indo-China. Thailand was especially alarmed. It was getting the bulk of the refugees from Laos and Kampuchea and was confronted by the spectre of having, along the entire length of its 1600-kilometre eastern frontier, a trio of like-minded communist states dominated by Vietnam. Bangkok had attached high importance to the preservation of Kampuchea as an independent buffer state between itself and Vietnam. The ousted Khmer Rouge régime, although a troublesome neighbour, played this role because it was hostile to Vietnam. With the buffer removed and Vietnamese forces approaching Thailand through western Kampuchea, the Bangkok government felt exposed and vulnerable.

After a meeting in Bangkok in January 1979, ASEAN foreign ministers 'strongly deplored the armed intervention against the independence, sovereignty and territorial integrity of Kampuchea'. They stopped short of using the word 'aggression', nor did they name any country. But they directly implicated Vietnam by 'recalling the Vietnamese pledge to ASEAN member countries to respect scrupulously each other's sovereignty and territorial integrity, and to co-operate in the maintenance and strengthening of peace and stability in the region'.

The foreign ministers also took up the question 'of refugees and displaced persons or illegal immigrants from Indo-China'. The use of the phrases 'displaced persons' or 'illegal immigrants', rather than 'refugees', was a device employed by ASEAN members – particularly Thailand and Malaysia – to placate elements at home that were hostile to the influx of aliens from Indo-China, and to leave open the option of denying them entry. But the choice of these words also reflected ASEAN suspicions that the mass movement of Indo-Chinese across international borders might be essentially for economic reasons.

The refugee and Kampuchean issues exposed within the ASEAN group fundamentally different perceptions of Vietnam and China. These differences occurred not just between ASEAN member states, but also within individual ASEAN governments. Indonesia, Malaysia and the Philippines had all been inclined – at least at the start of the Vietnamese invasion of Kampuchea – to welcome the prospect of a united communist Indo-China at peace with itself and strongly influenced by Vietnam, as a bulwark against the southern extension of Chinese influence. This thinking was especially common in Indonesia, where anti-China feeling ran deep, particularly among conservative leaders in the Muslim community and the military hierarchy. By the end of 1978, all five ASEAN members had diplomatic relations of varying degrees of warmth with Vietnam, while relations with China were more tentative. Malaysia, Thailand and the Philippines had exchanged ambassadors with Peking. Singapore was waiting for Indonesia, which had suspended diplomatic ties with China in 1967 after an attempted coup, in which Djakarta believed China to have been involved. At the end of 1978, Indonesia felt far less suspicious about Vietnam than about China. Peking's senior vice-premier, Deng Xiaoping, had just finished a tour of three ASEAN countries – Thailand, Malaysia and Singapore – during which he had refused to withdraw Chinese support (admittedly token but capable of being stepped up) for communist insurgents in South-East Asia. In contrast, Vietnam's premier, Pham Van Dong, on a similar tour a few weeks earlier, had disowned the insurgents (although, since the communist movements were predominantly Peking-oriented, Vietnam had few links to break). China's Deng had also failed to reassure those ASEAN countries with worries about the allegiance of their substantial Chinese minorities that China would not intervene to protect their rights or influence their behaviour.

Mistrust of China reinforced another trend in official Indonesian thinking. This was that the sprawling archipelago republic – the fifth most populous country in the world, overlooking the crossroads of the Indian and Pacific Oceans, rich in resources, influential in international affairs, and with sizable armed forces – was the natural leader of the ASEAN nations. From there it was only a short step to the view that there were two logical poles of mutually balancing influence in South-East Asia – Vietnam and Indonesia.

Indonesia's foreign minister, Dr Mochtar Kusumaatmaja, in an interview in the *Far Eastern Economic Review* of 15 December 1978, said in reply to a question about Soviet influence in Vietnam:

I prefer not to use any term that denotes subservience of Vietnam to any country or intimates that Vietnam is the proxy of any country. I have had many conversations with their leaders, and I am aware of their pride and their fears since independence. So the fact that they have signed a treaty and have been obliged to receive aid, is, I think, a result of circumstances. They have tried to obtain assistance from other sources. They have encouraged investment and trade [from the west], but not much was forthcoming.

The view from Bangkok was quite different. Hostility between Thailand and Vietnam stretched back for centuries. Without a buffer between them, Thailand felt exposed and therefore turned to its ASEAN partners for support. Thailand had recently broken off a protracted and frustrating series of negotiations with Hanoi over repatriation of an estimated 60 000–70 000 Vietnamese refugees who had come to Thailand before 1975, most of them in the late 1940s and early 1950s to escape the fighting between the French and the Vietminh. They were concentrated in north-eastern Thailand near the border with Laos. Having continually had to deal with communist insurgents in the north-east, some of whom were thought to lean towards Hanoi, Thai authorities saw the Vietnamese refugees in their midst as potential fifth columnists. Bangkok was also worried that Vietnam might be tempted to push across the border into Thailand from western Kampuchea or Laos to settle a number of old scores – one of them being Thai support for the American war in Vietnam. Thailand had fewer inhibitions about moving closer to Peking. Of all the ASEAN states with Chinese minorities, it had been by far the most successful in absorbing them into its national life. Indeed, Peking was seen in Bangkok as a potential protector against the Vietnamese, and Thai leaders greeted the news of China's military incursion into Vietnam, early in 1979, with relief.

In January 1979 ASEAN finally came out with a joint statement naming Vietnam as a source of the refugee problem. This was due to pressure not only from its two most seriously affected members, Thailand and Malaysia, but also from its least affected member, Singapore. Singapore's attitude towards both Vietnam and the refugee problem was tough-minded. It consistently turned away boat people from Vietnam unless they were guaranteed rapid resettlement, on the grounds that Singapore was overcrowded already and would become a magnet for refugees if it relaxed its ban. 'You've got to grow callouses on your heart or you just bleed to death,' Prime Minister Lee Kuan Yew said. In a speech on 17 February 1979, the foreign minister, Sinnathamby Rajaratnam, put forward an argument which other ASEAN governments were to take increasingly seriously as the year advanced and the numbers of boat people arriving in South-East Asian waters reached torrential proportions:

The flow of boat people poses the non-communist world, including the ASEAN countries, with a moral dilemma. We could respond on humanitarian and moral grounds by accepting and resettling these desperate people. But by doing so we would not only be encouraging those responsible to force even more refugees to flee but also unwittingly demonstrate that a policy of inhumanity [the Vietnamese government's] does pay dividends. Not only that, but those countries which give way to their humanitarian instincts would saddle themselves with unmanageable political, social and economic problems that the sudden absorption of hundreds of thousands of alien peoples must inevitably bring in its wake.

While suspecting China's long-term intentions towards South-East Asia, Singapore was equally wary of Vietnam and Russia. Singapore wanted ASEAN to give Thailand assurances of support in the face of the Indo-China crisis; otherwise, it feared, Thailand might become excessively dependent on China. Singapore also wanted ASEAN to speak out and put pressure on Vietnam to change its policies so that people would not feel impelled to leave by the back-door sea route. In his New Year message for 1979, Prime Minister Lee called for an international campaign to prevent the exodus. Past suffering in Indo-China had been the result of acts committed in the heat of war:

This latest exodus of 'boat people' and 'ship people' is the result of acts of cold calculation, measured in gold, and long after the heat of battle has cooled. What is ominous is that unless world leaders and leader-writers register their outrage at this cynical disposal of unwanted citizens, many more victims will be sent off on packed boats and ships.

The ASEAN country most seriously affected by the deluge of boat people from Vietnam was Malaysia. Until late 1978, refugees wanting to land there pending resettlement overseas could usually do so without too much difficulty. Malaysian fishermen and villagers often helped the newcomers, sometimes for a fee but also from spontaneous compassion. However, the tidal-wave dimensions of the refugee inflow changed Malaysia's mood. The influx generated undercurrents of political and communal tension in Malaysia. In 1969 the country's multi-racial, multi-religious fabric had been stitched together again with care after the delicate balance between Chinese of immigrant stock and indigenous Malays had been shattered by race riots in Kuala Lumpur. The population was now about 14 million, the overwhelming majority living in peninsular Malaysia (as distinct from the eastern states of Sabah and Sarawak) where Muslim Malays (53 per cent) barely outnumber non-Muslim races – mainly the Chinese (35 per cent) and Indians (11 per cent) – the forebears of whom had arrived to work in mines, plantations and towns over the past 150 years. As in other parts of South-East Asia, the Chinese became influential in the country's commerce, trade and finance. This caused resentment from Malays whose traditional occupations were farming and fishing.

The refugees from Vietnam, more than half of whom were of Chinese descent, could hardly have chosen a more sensitive place to land than the north-east coast of peninsular Malaysia. The three states there – Kelantan, Trengganu and Pahang – which face the Gulf of Thailand and the South China Sea, are all overwhelmingly Malay in composition and strictly Islamic in character. Malaysia (whose state religion is Islam) had accepted more than 1500 Muslim refugees from Kampuchea after 1975, and allowed an estimated 100 000 Filipino Muslims escaping civil war in the southern Philippines to take refuge in the east Malaysian state of Sabah. But the flood of so many non-Muslim aliens from Vietnam created a backlash in conservative Malay communities along the north-east coast. By late 1978 some Malay villagers were stoning incoming boats and the men, women and children on them. There were rumours in the *kampongs* (villages) that Malaysia would never be able to get rid of the refugees. The government was accused of allowing a form of backdoor immigration (it had encouraged this kind of alarmism by referring to the boat people as 'illegal immigrants'). Critics within the ruling Malay party, as well as the opposition, accused the government of not taking firm enough action to stem the refugee tide.

Foreign journalists on visits to the north-east coast in late 1978 and early 1979 were handed an official note at their hotel: 'For your own safety, you are advised not to go to the coast where any illegal immigrants are landing. If you do so, you are doing it at your own risk. The government will not take any responsibility if anything happens to you by [sic] the Kampong people'. In December 1978, a senior Malaysian police officer in Kuala Trengganu was put in hospital with a jagged gash in his head after being hit by a rock while helping supervise the landing of a boatload of more than 200 Indo-Chinese who had beached their craft near the harbour. A crowd of several thousands gathered and stones were thrown at Vietnamese as they huddled on the sand under police guard. Malaysian soldiers and police – most of them Malays – found themselves in the invidious position of having to protect Indo-Chinese from Malay villagers.

Malays claimed that the refugees were being given privileged treatment; that their presence in such large numbers was forcing up the cost of living; that they had a corrupting influence on fishermen, villagers, merchants and officials, who were being tempted by black-marketeering; that they occupied scarce hospital beds that should have been available to Malaysians. While many of these claims were either exaggerated or untrue, they were widely believed.

Malaysian authorities reacted by locating the main UNHCR-run camps for displaced Indo-Chinese well away from the local population, on uninhabited offshore islands. A task force under the command of an army general was formed to co-ordinate military and civilian efforts to control the refugee problem. At about the same time, navy ships began regular patrols in offshore waters, a chain of refugee watchtowers manned by soldiers was established in areas where boats often landed, and an increasing number of boats were turned away or towed out to sea. In June 1979 Malaysia's deputy prime minister, Dr Mahathir bin Mohamad, was quoted as saying that 'shoot-on-sight' legislation would be enacted so that security force patrols could drive off all boats attempting to land.

Malaysian authorities were also concerned at the security implications of the refugee inflow. The home affairs minister, Tan Sri Ghazali Shafie, said in November 1978: 'One could well suspect that the ejection of overseas Chinese and even Vietnam citizens of Chinese origin from Ho Chi Minh City might be motivated by the desire of Hanoi to remove the "Wooden Dragon", not just Chinese merchants of Cholon, but Peking-oriented communists'. Like its ASEAN partners, Malaysia was troubled by a pro-Peking communist guerilla movement, with a membership and basic support that was almost exclusively ethnic Chinese. Malaysia had no difficulty identifying the source of the refugee problem and its effects but it could not make up its mind whom to blame: Vietnam, China or the United States. As late as July 1979, Mr Ghazali said that every time China 'rattles its sword or swings its cane', the ethnic Chinese in Vietnam panicked and fled the country.

*   *   *

Early in 1978 China had revived suspicions that it might manipulate for subversive purposes some of the 13 million Chinese residents in ASEAN countries. Following a 'preparatory conference' in Peking on overseas Chinese affairs, an article on 4 January 1979 in the *People's Daily* by Liao Cheng-Chi, a member of the Chinese communist party's central committee and former chairman of the overseas Chinese affairs commission (abolished during the cultural revolution in the late 1960s), made an assessment of Peking's policies towards ethnic Chinese in other countries in what amounted to a major restatement of policy. Overseas Chinese were encouraged to adopt the nationality of the country in which they were living, and surrender their Chinese nationality, but should not be compelled to do so. Ethnic Chinese could be permitted to remain Chinese nationals while living outside China, although they should abide by the laws of the host country. Liao's article went to some lengths to discredit the dogma that 'overseas relatives' were 'reactionary political connections'; on the contrary, overseas Chinese were traditionally patriotic and revolutionary, and he praised the contribution to China's development made by them, especially that of doctors, teachers, scientists and intellectuals. Relatives in China of overseas Chinese, and overseas Chinese who had returned to China, were entitled to receive cash remittances from abroad. Communications between overseas

Chinese and their families in China, as well as family reunions, were to be encouraged.

Liao's article may have been aimed mainly at a domestic audience and was probably intended to reassure those Chinese with relatives overseas that the discrimination they had suffered during the cultural revolution and at the hands of the 'Gang of Four' had ended. It may also have been designed to encourage skilled Chinese abroad to come home to assist with the program of modernization and economic growth. However, if its intention was also to reassure the countries of South-East Asia about Peking's policy on the sensitive issues of dual nationality and allegiance, it had precisely the opposite effect in Indonesia, Malaysia and Singapore. Singapore authorities thought Liao's phrasing sounded like 'communist liberation' jargon. One key passage worried them:

Most of the overseas Chinese are working people, who are the masses forming the base of the patriotic united front among overseas Chinese and are a force we should rely on . . . the majority of the bourgeois class are patriotic. They have also made contributions to the economic and cultural development in the countries where they live and are part of the motive force for combating imperialism, hegemonism and colonialism and winning national and economic independence in these countries . . . we should work energetically among them and strive to form the broadest patriotic united front among the overseas Chinese.

Four months later, in April 1978, China made a stand against Vietnam by seeking to protect the rights of tens of thousands of ethnic Chinese it was claimed were being persecuted and driven into southern China by Vietnamese authorities. Vietnam's recent 'socialization' measures had especially affected ethnic Chinese with private-enterprise interests and Liao's statement was to prove an embarrassment when Hanoi parried with the charge that China was 'throwing a life-belt to Vietnamese capitalists of Chinese stock'. Then, in early June 1978, Hanoi twisted the blade: 'If those Hoa capitalists lived in China, they would surely have to go through a similar transformation'. The point was valid. Peking had not protested at the 'socialist transformation' of North Vietnam in the 1950s; neither, more recently, had China done anything to defend ethnic Chinese from the excesses of the Khmer Rouge régime, its ally in Kampuchea.

Later in the year, Indonesia's foreign minister, Dr Mochtar, made the point that the 'big question mark' about Peking's contentious policy was that overseas Chinese, while told to remain law-abiding residents of their host country, were expected also to maintain social and economic links with China – links that Liao had referred to as those between 'kinsmen'. Dr Mochtar said Indonesia – with four million ethnic Chinese, one million of whom were theoretically Chinese citizens and 800 000 stateless – wanted to see how Peking applied its professed policy on overseas Chinese. He added, referring to the flight of ethnic Chinese from Vietnam: 'When developments occurred in Vietnam we were of course interested, because that was the proof of the very question which we were so curious about. And to say the least, what happened in Vietnam with regard to the overseas Chinese did not reassure us.'

When ASEAN foreign ministers held their regular annual meeting for 1979 on the Indonesian island of Bali, their mood was sombre. Late on 30 June, they issued a joint communiqué which dealt again with the two related issues that dominated the gathering: the Indo-Chinese refugee crisis and the armed conflicts centred on Indo-China. This time they put Vietnam in the dock. There were a number of reasons for the hardening of ASEAN's position. The five member governments were still divided in their diagnoses of the root causes of the outflow from Vietnam (whether it was due to policies of the Vietnamese, Chinese or American governments, or a combination of factors). But they had become convinced that Vietnamese authorities had the power to control the rate of exodus, and could only be prevailed upon to do so through pressure from international opinion. As they knew from the attitude of the US, British and Australian governments, international action was now possible.

Singapore, as before, led the attack. In a dramatic speech to the opening session, Foreign Minister Rajaratnam proposed that the five ASEAN governments should side with anti-Vietnamese forces in Kampuchea. (He later told the press he believed ASEAN and friendly non-communist governments should provide arms and material support to the resistance movement in Kampuchea, just as the Soviet Union was giving aid to Vietnam.) In his speech, he branded Vietnam as an expansionist power with ambitions to dominate the whole of South-East Asia. He claimed that Hanoi was deliberately expelling hundreds of thousands of refugees from Vietnam and Kampuchea to 'destabilize, disrupt and cause turmoil and dissension in ASEAN states . . . only a deliberate policy can achieve an exodus on so monumental a scale. This is not spontaneous combustion but organized arson to set alight the rest of South-East Asia.' Vietnam had 'picked on' the Chinese

because they know that almost all ASEAN countries have delicate problems with their Chinese minorities. The massive unloading of Chinese refugees onto these countries can only exacerbate racial sensitivities and, if the flow is sustained long enough, lead to racial warfare which could tear these societies apart quicker and far more effectively than any invading Vietnamese army. In no time ASEAN prosperity, stability and cohesion would vanish into thin air and conditions of life would soon be on par with those now prevailing in Indo-China.

*　　*　　*

This was the picture in late 1979, when the Geneva conference gave everyone a breathing space. It was not reassuring. The United States seemed no closer to a sound policy. The Soviet Union, although cautious, was locked into a relationship with Vietnam that would continue to antagonize China, and China was locked into a conflict with Vietnam over Kampuchea that would continue to antagonize the Soviet Union. There were other neuralgic points. Conflict between China and Vietnam over islands in the South China Sea, such as Spratly and the Paracels, had been brought to the surface by the voyages of the boat people. Thailand worried as Vietnam's influence in Laos and Kampuchea increased. Most ominous of all were reports of fresh horrors in Kampuchea - that after years of war and civil strife, the economy had collapsed and the people, prevented from fleeing into Thailand, were starving to death.

Also, there was Hong Kong. The British colony had long been assimilating refugees from mainland China and was expected to work miracles in absorbing boat people. But they were straining its resources to breaking point and the territory's government came under local fire for being too generous. Hong Kong officials were also bitter about what they saw as discrimination in favour of the

ASEAN states, especially Malaysia, for resettlement places. The chief secretary, Sir Jack Cater, said in July 1979 that, while Hong Kong had received 35 per cent of the boat refugees during 1979, it had received only 13 per cent of the resettlement places. Hong Kong had taken strong measures against the seagoing freighters but had always given sanctuary to small boats. It did seem that it was now being penalized for not having adopted a harsher policy.

Chapter 7

Resettlement

On 20 June 1979, which was also his 74th birthday, the French philosopher Jean-Paul Sartre launched an appeal for French aid for the boat people. Making a rare public appearance, Sartre said of the Indo-Chinese refugees: 'Some of them have not always been on our side, but for the moment we are not interested in their politics, but in saving their lives. It's a moral issue, a question of morality between human beings.'

After his speech, Sartre sat down beside an old political enemy, writer Raymond Aron and, for the first time since the Algerian war, Sartre smiled at Aron and shook his hand. Also associated with the appeal were actress Simone Signoret, her actor husband Yves Montand, and one of the most prominent of the 'new philosophers', André Glucksmann, who had gone to the beaches of Malaysia as a correspondent for the Italian daily *Corriere della Sera*. Later, in a discussion with Daniel Cohn-Bendit, the leader of the French students' revolt in 1968, in the left-wing daily *Liberation*, Glucksmann said: 'Yesterday the Americans killed babies when they bombarded a civilian population with napalm. Today the communist authorities drown other babies. Yesterday we protested. Today we are silent.' Glucksmann and Cohn-Bendit recalled how the left had preferred to close its eyes to communist atrocities in Vietnam – Ho Chi Minh's brutal purge of the peasants and the Hue massacre during the war with Saigon. As it appeared to Glucksmann, whose latest book *The Discourse of War* is a study of the ideological pressures behind warfare, 'The Vietnamese refugees are the fall-out of two lines of warlike discourse . . . Both stem from Hegel – the communist thesis and the anti-communist thesis. They come to the same thing in the end.'

However, the immediate scandal for those who demanded a massive rescue of the Indo-Chinese outcasts was that the west was refusing to face up to its responsibilities. Glucksmann pressed home the same charge as had his friend Sartre: 'The French and Americans who spend so much money for their wars can't find the money to save those who are the victims of their policies.'

Unlike the intellectuals of France, America's intellectuals have been uncommonly, perhaps uncomfortably, silent in the search for a new Vietnam policy. None of those who passionately defended or denounced America's intervention in Vietnam in the sixties has emerged to pronounce on the issue. Even those among the more articulate critics of America's Vietnam tragedy have elected to ignore or avoid the new Indo-China crisis: Noam Chomsky and David Halberstam, Frances Fitzgerald and Susan Sontag, are still writing and teaching, but none of them has said a public word on Vietnam for more than two years, and I. F. Stone has retired, taught himself Greek and is happily translating Homer. Only among the remnants of the old peace movement has the new Vietnam issue stirred any passion. It began with the apostasy of anti-war folk-singer Joan Baez, who took full-page newspaper advertisements in May 1979 to publish an 'Open letter to the Socialist Republic of Vietnam' (co-signed by eighty-three other former peace campaigners) to denounce Hanoi's human rights record. 'Thousands of innocent Vietnamese, many whose only crimes are those of conscience, are being arrested, detained and tortured in prisons and re-education camps,' Baez wrote. 'Instead of bringing hope and reconciliation to war-torn Vietnam, your government has created a painful nightmare that overshadows significant progress achieved in many areas of Vietnam society.'

The letter split the old peace movement. The peace council replied with its own full-page advertisement – 'The truth about Vietnam' – accusing Baez of ignorance and implying hypocrisy. Actress Jane Fonda, who had refused to sign the Baez letter, released her own reply to it: 'Such rhetoric only aligns you with the most narrow and negative elements in our country who continue to believe that communism is worse than death.' William Kunstler, the communist lawyer who had defended many of the peace-movement radicals, called Baez a 'CIA agent'. The peace council published a second advertisement in which the Australian journalist Wilfred Burchett, who had travelled extensively in Vietnam both during and after the war, claimed that Baez's charges revealed 'complete ignorance of the realities of today's Vietnam'. Burchett claimed that the Vietnam government's re-education program had been singularly benign. He knew, he said, 'dozens of generals, colonels, captains, ministers and other top cadres of the various Saigon régimes, some still under detention, who had unanimously praised the humane attitude of those who have tried – and still try – to point the way to a useful role in society'.

The intellectual-political debate continued in most countries, as resettlement proceeded after the UNHCR Geneva meeting in July 1979. As the following reports show, the factors influencing acceptance of refugees were no less complex than those behind their flight and their initial reception in the countries of South-East Asia.

United States

Each day they arrive by the dozen at airports across the country: brown-skinned statistics who, after struggling through war and its aftermath, must struggle again for a foothold in a strange new land. The adjustments are painful and the culture shock extreme. But both are confronted quietly: these people are not noisy sufferers.

So far, about 228 000 Indo-Chinese refugees have made the trip, one-third of them between 1977 and 1979. The majority, perhaps 75 per cent, are Vietnamese; Laotians and the proud mountain tribe known as the Hmong make up 20 per cent and Kampucheans 5 per cent. Once in America, they all face common problems. On one level they must learn the rudiments of subways, supermarkets and suburban living. On another, they must find jobs in a time of high unemployment, houses in a time of deepening recession, and acceptance from communities that feel threatened by strangers.

The early arrivals – 130 000 Vietnamese who fled to the United States after the communists marched into Saigon in 1975 – are already well established. They were by and large South Vietnam's skilled and better educated. Many spoke English and were westernized to some degree. By conventional indicators – employment rate, salaries, adequate accommodation – those of this first wave have done well. By December 1978, 94.9 per cent of the 1975 arrivals included in the labour force (working or looking for work) had jobs.

About one-third of the workers earned $200 or more per week, compared with just 14 per cent eighteen months earlier. A substantial proportion, 33 per cent, were still receiving some form of welfare payment, but this was explained as mainly to supplement low wages. Generally, they were hailed as model refugees: hard-working, well motivated and eager for self-sufficiency.

But behind the statistics there was, and is, another picture. Many, perhaps most, of those with jobs, were working at levels considerably below those they had held or were trained for in their homelands: generals were washing dishes and teachers were working in garment factories. Few, except the children, were assimilating into the American mainstream and there were indications of widespread emotional problems, especially mental depression, sometimes leading to suicide. Vietnamese notions of social class, the extended family and morality were all challenged by American ways. There was also the guilt of having left friends and relatives behind in Vietnam and of having abandoned one's own country.

This was the picture of outward success and inward dislocation around mid-1977, when the second exodus got underway. After two quiet years, during which a total of 16 000 refugees had come to America, thousands suddenly started to stream into the country. The congressional limit on the number of immigrants from communist countries or the Middle East was 17 400 a year. But President Carter used his executive authority to clear the way for the refugees, pushing up the quotas from 4000 a month to 7000 a month until, in June 1979, a figure of 14 000 a month was reached.

While the government organizes admission of the refugees, the actual resettlement is handled for the most part by one of nine private voluntary agencies, church and charitable organizations. The agencies are paid $350 for each refugee by the state department, to cover all initial resettlement costs including rent, food and clothing. The refugees are then allocated to sponsoring groups, which are morally (but not legally) responsible for their welfare.

Although the refugees are dispersed across the country, they have tended to move around with a rapidity that has bewildered most people responsible for their resettlement. By far the largest number, almost 71 000, have ended up in California, mostly in the south around Los Angeles and San Diego. Texas has at least 22 000, drawn

161

by the climate and the thriving economies of Houston and Dallas-Fort Worth. Washington DC has somewhere between 8000 and 20 000 (the figures are unclear, because many come to Washington for official reasons but do not stay), Louisiana 8300, Illinois 7600 and New York 6300.

The more recent refugees have in some ways gained, and in some ways been disadvantaged, by their later place in the arrival line. As a group, they tend to be less educated and trained than the first-comers, so they are easier to place in low-level jobs. They may have friends or relatives already in the country who will help them settle. Also, because they have deliberately escaped and have usually spent months, even years, in camps, they tend to expect less from resettlement services than the first wave. Yet they are sicker as well as poorer than those who came before. Many suffer from malnutrition, skin infections, intestinal parasites and tuberculosis. California health officials have reported isolated cases of leprosy and diphtheria among new refugees. Since their arrival, cases of typhoid fever have increased 92 per cent in Los Angeles and 58 per cent statewide.

Also, America's ailing economy, tight housing market and rising unemployment rate all work against the refugees' resettlement attempts. Linked to this is the growing antagonism from America's own poor and displaced: the old cry that immigrants take local jobs and services is to be heard again. In Seadrift, a tiny fishing port in Texas, four years of simmering distrust between residents and resettled refugees over alleged poaching by Vietnamese of crab-trapping sites erupted in July 1979 into open racial warfare. A second serious incident occurred a month later, when a riot broke out in a Spanish-speaking quarter in Denver, Colorado, which had been occupied in parts by Vietnamese refugees. Other anti-Vietnamese outbursts around the country had the same ingredients: economic competition, and the belief, partly true, that the Vietnamese were getting special welfare treatment from the government.

Blacks, who were among the first Americans to urge national action on behalf of the refugees, have begun to show resentment. 'A lot of blacks are uptight,' said Mr John Robinson, director of the Martin Luther King community centre in the Washington suburb of South Arlington. 'It's the threat over jobs and housing. These people are the new niggers – they are doing the work blacks don't want and getting their own shops, which a lot of blacks who've been here all their lives can't get. They could have stayed in their own country and fought the system like we did, but they chose to leave.'

It is something of a double-bind for the bewildered refugees. If they fail to adjust, they are lambasted as a burden on the taxpayer. When they succeed, they are accused of taking jobs or businesses away from native Americans.

One Vietnamese who has been in America long enough to assess the resettlement experience is Colonel Nguyen Be, a former south Vietnamese infantry officer who fled in 1975, the day after the US evacuation of Saigon. He had waited until the last minute, then boarded a sampan and floated out to sea alone, leaving behind his wife and seven children. Now aged fifty, he was well known to Americans in Vietnam as the inventor of Saigon's answer to the Vietcong – the black-pyjama-wearing 'rural development cadre', which was intended to counter colonialism on the one hand, and communism on the other, by practising a 'revolutionary' form of Vietnamese nationalism. Shirtless, literally, when he left Vietnam, Colonel Be today wears button-down collars, thin-striped suits and carries a samsonite suitcase. During his four years in America he has worked for various government refugee programs, first in New York and now in Washington DC, as a consultant for the department of housing, education and welfare's Indo-China refugee task force.

'The problem of so-called adjusting to the new society is not really that difficult for Vietnamese people,' Colonel Be said recently. 'We can accept. The problem for us, almost always, is being accepted. And many of the local communities have found that hard.' He spoke of the deep cultural gaps which caused confusion on first arrival.

America is a new orientation for the Vietnamese – a country run by laws, not by men . . . In Vietnam, you feel secure and proud if you have your family around you and money in your pocket. Here, it is a new concept of security. There is no family. You have to put the money in the bank. The security of your survival is the welfare benefit, the unemployment and all the social services. Until you realize that, it can be very frightening.

Colonel Be explained that American and Vietnamese notions of property were different.

At home, you go out and get a bit of land, perhaps a cow, which will provide you with enough to eat. The lesson is to look after yourself and your own. There is no sharing, no idea of community protection. That is very different here. Car insurance is a good example. In Vietnam, only the rich took out insurance and only because they wanted to protect their own property from damage. Here, insurance is a protection for the poor, so that they can pay for the damage they may cause other people. That is a big mental adjustment for the Vietnamese to make.

While humbler Vietnamese often did better in America than they had in Vietnam, responding enthusiastically to the new opportunities, many from the former upper class were depressed by their inability to find correspondingly high-status employment.

Therefore, psychologically, they must carve out a new position of superiority by disdaining to work ... this of course means staying on welfare ... The blacks have had to struggle for so long, since they were slaves. Now they see a new group coming in, getting much better care than they did. It looks so much easier for us. The illegal immigrant, too. In areas where the illegal Mexicans do jobs for $1 or $2 an hour – the refugee will go to the same area, go after the same jobs and alienate the worker and all his family.

White Americans compounded the situation by favouring the refugees. They were non-violent, not likely to vandalize property, more respectful to whites than those who had had to fight for their rights. The refugees could be safely patronized, letting whites feel humanitarian at the same time. As Colonel Be explained: 'When there is a new housing project going up, or services being handed out, the white community will often support the Vietnamese as a way of getting rid of the blacks. Of couse, that is good for us. But it creates conflicts with the other minorities – it is the human way.'

Colonel Be himself felt that, while he did not regret leaving Vietnam, neither was he entirely satisfied with his new life. 'I'm a runaway boy,' he said sadly. His wife and children were still in Vietnam. He hated to see communists running his country. He had no vote or leverage in America. But even though he would be eligible for full American citizenship next year, he doubted that he would apply. 'To accept a new nationality means acceptance that we have already been defeated by the communists. As it is, I can believe that we've lost that battle but not yet the war, that Vietnam will be free again one day and I can go back. The struggle is always going on.'

China

The drama of the boat people has inevitably overshadowed a mass emigration and resettlement of a different nature: the exodus from northern Vietnam to the southern provinces of China of a quarter of a million ethnic Chinese. The view from Peking of the refugee crisis (and the view generally of those who sought refuge in China) is understandably markedly different from those of Hanoi and of refugees interviewed in non-communist Asia.

To leave or to stay is a bewildering choice for people who, though they cherish their Chinese heritage, regard Vietnam as their home. Some are from families that have lived in Vietnam for as many as fourteen generations. Some had fought for Vietnam in wars against the French and the Americans. Some had become local officials or members of the Vietnamese communist party.

According to some of the refugees who have crossed into China, there was a change of mood in Vietnam in about the mid-1960s, a growing coolness towards China and a corresponding consolidation of the relationship with the Soviet Union. Small, almost trivial examples of anti-Chinese discrimination insinuated a tension into communities in northern Vietnam. People of Chinese descent found themselves awarded inferior rations and deprived of job opportunities. Limits were subtly applied to the use of the Chinese language. The Hoa were confused – they had been raised on a diet of propaganda that had always emphasized the solidarity and friendship of the peoples of Vietnam and China.

From the perspective of China, the real purge began in the early months of 1978, when Vietnamese public security officials and soldiers moved through the provinces of northern Vietnam with orders to clear the Chinese out. Chinese urban-dwellers were fired from their jobs and their rations were stopped. Chinese villagers' homes were knocked down, their possessions confiscated. Truckloads of them were driven to the Chinese border and herded out of Vietnam at gunpoint. The expulsion went almost unnoticed by the rest of the world until Chinese photographers scooped it with television film which was screened round the world. It showed scores of peasant families slithering down the Vietnamese bank of the Hong River, opposite the Chinese town of Kekou, terror in their faces as they waded to safety carrying the pitiful parcels that were all they owned. Behind them Vietnamese soldiers brandished rifles and jeered. At Pingxiang, a Sino-Vietnamese border pass, hundreds of refugees were straggling across the frontier into China each day.

Most of the refugees were peasant farmers from northern Vietnam who told of a gradual intensification of abuse at the hands of Vietnamese officials. Police and soldiers had warned them that all 'undesirable elements' – people whose loyalty to Vietnam might be questioned in the event of hostilities between Vietnam and China – were unwelcome. Their choice was either to renounce their Chineseness and take Vietnamese nationality, accepting resettlement in the 'new economic zones' away from the sensitive frontier with China, or to be expelled from Vietnam. The first was an unacceptable option for most of these simple farmers who discovered in themselves an ineradicable cultural loyalty to their ancestry. There was almost no resistance as they were dispossessed of homes and goods and crowded into trucks and trains for the journey into China.

Up to 4000 refugees a day crossed the Friendship Bridge at Dongxing, a border checkpoint that had been best known as the route for Chinese military aid to Vietnam during the conflict with South Vietnam and the Americans. In 1960 Ho Chi Minh had walked over the bridge in a gesture of friendship towards China. In 1978 those walking across the bridge were confused by the decay of that friendship. One refugee told of a meeting in his village at which a Vietnamese official had said no person of Chinese descent would be allowed to stay in northern Vietnam. A Hoa engineer was fired from his job and ordered onto the road to China with his two small children but his Vietnamese wife was forbidden to accompany him. An old Chinese man, who wanted only to be able to end his years with his Vietnamese wife in the village that had always been their home, was packed off alone across the border, where he sat in a makeshift shelter at Dongxing trying to make sense of his loneliness.

As it was quick to point out, China also had its invasion of boat people – fisherfolk of Chinese descent who had worked for generations alongside the Vietnamese boatmen among the islands of the Gulf of Tonkin. In April and May 1978, more than 1250 of their fragile sail-boats streamed into the south Chinese port of Peihai. Most of the 10 000 people they carried came from the Vietnamese island of Jipo, 290 kilometres and ten days to the south. These were not boat people like those of southern Vietnam, who were often urban, middle-class people so unable to adapt to the economic rigours of socialism that they would buy their way out of the country in boats they barely know how to sail. The Jipo islanders are the peasants of the fishing grounds. They did not want to leave their homes or the simple living they made from the Vietnamese state fish markets but, as Chinese, they were targets for the many forms of intolerance that had inexorably pervaded all levels of northern Vietnamese officialdom. Vietnamese officials extracted impossibly high quotas from their catches, leaving the Hoa fishermen with insufficient food for their families. Their supplementary grain rations were reduced and what they did get was rotten. Vietnamese patrols applied capricious regulations and arbitrary taxes; when arguments broke out with Vietnamese fishermen, who were not similarly harassed, police invariably decided in favour of the Vietnamese. The move towards the sanctuary of China began, the Hoa boats being harried, sometimes shot at, by Vietnamese patrols.

According to Peking sources, about 150 000 Hoa were pushed northward from Vietnam in the four months between April and July 1978. A further 100 000 made the journey on foot or by sea in the following year. It became harder to get through after the Sino-Vietnamese border war in February 1979, when the frontier was transformed into a military zone with heavily armed encampments lining both sides. The February war was the climax of a rapidly deteriorating relationship between Peking and Hanoi, exacerbated by the Vietnamese policy of displacing Chinese nationals from its northern provinces. When the first surge of refugees arrived, imposing economic strain on China's southern provinces, Peking retaliated by terminating aid projects in Vietnam. The money would be diverted to the care of the refugees, said the Chinese government. Then, as the Hoa influx continued, China ordered Vietnamese consular offices in Canton, Nanning and Kumming to close. Finally, after protracted bickering about territorial intrusions across the tense border, China carried out its threat to 'teach Vietnam a lesson'. A hundred thousand Chinese troops swept across the border, destroyed Vietnamese fortifications and returned to China with a promise to do it again if Vietnamese provocations continued.

Meanwhile, China's population had increased suddenly by 250 000 people who, no matter how Chinese they might be, were formerly residents of Vietnam. When the influx was at its peak, newcomers were housed for several weeks in staging camps quickly erected in towns near the border. Their accommodation was often primitive: tar-paper or raffia lean-tos propped above footpaths. With an average of ten square metres of space for each family there was little privacy and less comfort. Others were billeted in railway-yard warehouses or taken in by resident families. Local governments provided the refugees with rice, meat, vegetables, sugar and oil, clothing and basic household necessities.

Representatives of the office of overseas Chinese affairs screened the refugees and started on the enormous task of finding them homes and jobs. Where possible, they were sent somewhere close to their ancestral origins, where they might find remnant family ties, and given work to which they were accustomed. The fishermen who had fled to Peihai were accommodated in the local fishing fleet and promised a new harbour, to be financed by the central government; farmers were posted to state farms especially set up in southern provinces; urban workers, of whom China already had too many, would be retrained in 'suitable' rural jobs. Around Canton alone, more than 30 000 refugees from Vietnam were installed in four months in 1978 on tea and vegetable farms. At Fa Shen, a state farm sixty kilometres north of Canton, a group of young women learning to pick high-grade tea were described as former office-workers, pedlars and transport workers from northern Vietnamese towns. Massive housing schemes have been undertaken by municipalities and individual farms to provide accommodation of normal Chinese standards.

The cost is high. In the first half of 1978 the Chinese government estimated that it was spending 1700 yuan ($1110) a head on the refugees. At that rate, China's bill for temporary shelter and urgent relief reached more than $276 million by mid-1979, and Peking was then making tentative inquiries about United Nations aid for its resettlement program.

Some of the Hoa who found life in Vietnam intolerable will like China little better. Among those who took the northern route to escape are a minority from southern Vietnam, some of them from the former small-capitalist class whose businesses were seized and who decided that flight was a better risk than a new economic zone. Some believed that southern China was near enough to Hong Kong, Taiwan and the Philippines to offer them a chance of joining more affluent relatives in those countries eventually. They were easily distinguishable as they crossed the Chinese border among the majority of roughly clad peasants and small-town northern Vietnamese Hoa: an urban suavity, an eagerness to claim the ear of foreigners who might know someone influential, and property that could only have come from the south – television sets, radios, sometimes small motor-cycles – gave them away. They are unlikely to make rice-farmers and the Chinese realize this. An official in Canton, asked whether such people would be helped to reach other countries to rejoin relatives, implied that China would not stand in their way. But at the time China was too busy to deal with that problem. As the time passes, those other countries too are finding themselves too busy – dealing with the tragic flotsam of the South China Sea.

France

When the refugee planes fly into Paris, a crowd of immigrants gathers at the airport, and later at the transit centres, to scan the faces of the new arrivals. The stoic calm of these waiting people and their automatic smile when addressed give them a deceptive air of uniformity; in fact, they are frequently of disparate origin – Vietnamese, Chinese Vietnamese, Kampucheans, Laotian Hmong hill tribesmen. But the hazards of exile give them a common bond, and a common hope: pieces of shattered Indo-China look for other pieces. There are parents who were parted from their children, children who were sent on the journey alone, families who are reassembled except for a grandparent, and lonely men or women who had to leave everyone behind. Some have an outside chance of a joyful reconciliation: they have applied for a stranded member of the family to join them. But others know that the most they can expect is to find someone who remembers a face or a name.

The French feel they have a special duty towards the outcasts of their former colony, especially as French diplomacy has been moving back into the area over the wreckage of American influence. Moreover, France shares with the United States a time-honoured reputation as a haven for the persecuted. There are now 4 200 000 foreigners living in France, among them 150 000 registered refugees. After the United States and Australia, France is the third host country to refugees, with Britain close behind in fourth place. The victims of political persecution have come to France in waves – the White Russians after the first world war, the Spanish republicans in 1938, a million French Algerians after Algeria won its independence, and now the Indo-Chinese.

Since the collapse of the Saigon régime in 1975, France had been accepting the immigrants at the rate of 1000 a month. But the boat people began arriving at a time when the French welcome was a shade less bright than it had been in the past. Faced with high unemployment, the French government had recently decided it would reduce its total foreign population by one million before 1985. Nevertheless, President Giscard d'Estaing met the new demand for asylum by finding room for an additional 5000 and it is estimated that, by the end of the year, France will have an Indo-Chinese immigrant population of 61 000.

The 5000 quota came as a bitter disappointment to those who had hoped Paris would make a generous gesture that would jolt the conscience of the world. Jean-Paul Sartre said it was tantamount to an out-of-court dismissal of the demand for action. At a demonstration in the streets of Paris in favour of a much larger quota, a young Vietnamese girl read a line from a poem by her father: 'Open your city as one opens one's door at dawn'. To many Frenchmen their door seemed only just ajar. Pierre Mendes-France, who as prime minister had terminated French rule in Vietnam, said:

Five thousand people is nothing. It even falls well short of the total offered by individuals and mayors. The least the government could have done was offer the local authorities the number of refugees they had declared themselves ready to accept. If Valery Giscard d'Estaing had announced 'France accepts 50 000 refugees', he would have given our country an enormous moral advantage over its allies and, what is most important, might have compelled them to make similar efforts.

French diplomatic activity during the worst months of the boat people emergency was governed by the notion that nothing was to be gained by driving Hanoi into a corner. France urged Hanoi to impose a moratorium on the departure of refugees, even to establish camps where the exodus would be controlled so as not to swamp the reception facilities of the host countries. 'The moratorium is better than death at sea,' said the French foreign minister, Jean François-Poncet, in a comment on Hanoi's promise, at the UNHCR meeting at Geneva in July 1979, to halt the flow of refugees.

This did not go unchallenged. Olivier Todd, of the Paris weekly magazine *L'Express*, described the Geneva call for a moratorium 'a moral and juridical scandal'. He pointed out that it was the first time that an international organization had been encouraged to urge one of its member nations to limit the right of its citizens the freedom of movement. Todd charged that the United Nations would be giving the politburo and police of Hanoi the implicit right to say who should be allowed to leave the country and when they should go.

For those who succeed in reaching France, the first stop is one of the three transit centres of an organization called France Terre d'Asile. These are crowded but comfortable hostels where new arrivals are put through medical examinations and interviews to assess how much help they will need in making a new start. Considering what many of them have gone through, their physical condition is surprisingly good. But psychological damage is another matter. Those who make the first contacts with the refugees feel they are dealing with people who have been stunned. 'One must never conclude from their smiles that all is well,' says an official of France Terre d'Asile. 'There are all sorts of anxieties at work underneath.'

For the most fortunate, the new life can start straight away. They have relatives, friends and accommodation waiting for them, and their knowledge of the French language means that acclimatization is easier. The less fortunate move on to centres in the provinces where they spend up to six months – sometimes longer in difficult cases – learning French and being instructed in the customs and formalities of life in their new country. The French imprint on Vietnam faded more than one might expect: two-thirds of the refugees speak no French.

Somewhere along the process of rehabilitation many of the exiles encounter a formidable anxiety barrier. During the ordeal of the escape they were sustained by a vague idea of the future as a rescue from all that made their past lives unbearable. Now the future narrows to a choice between a few small lodgings and a few probably not very inviting jobs. For many an immigrant what matters is less the respective merits of the jobs that are offered than the need to ensure that they are well placed to catch the ideal opportunity when it presents itself. 'They are afraid of the future,' says a France Terre d'Asile organizer. 'One of the signs is that they all want to stay in Paris. The idea of being sent to the provinces frightens them. They will tell you they have friends in Paris even if it isn't true.' Perhaps in the back of some minds the provinces are associated with re-education camps, enforced agricultural labour, the brutal evacuation of Phnom Penh by the Khmer Rouge. But Paris is preferred chiefly because there it is possible to lead an indefinitely provisional life, where new identities do not become fixed for lack of choice.

Waiting in line for the cafétéria in the transit centres at Creteil, a southern suburb of Paris, is a 24-year-old chemistry student. His family paid for him to make the journey alone by boat. 'I want to continue my studies,' he says. 'I had the addresses of friends here in Paris who would help me. But the pirates took everything. Now I am trying to find my friends. Perhaps in a few days I shall succeed.' A true story, or another ploy to stay on in the capital?

The prevailing feeling among the refugees is that they will not see their homeland again. They are eager to adapt themselves to French ways, but their ethnic ties remain strong. Their experience may have brought them resignation, patience and tolerance, but it has not levelled differences of origin and class. There is no strife between the different national groups in the transit centres, but they pass one another without a sign of recognition. A French official at Creteil says: 'If you can't understand a Cambodian and ask a Vietnamese to translate for you, he won't even answer; he'll just turn his back.'

So far, France has assimilated 61 000 South-East Asians with remarkably few outward signs of tension. It is not a large enough minority to stir the racist resentment that surrounds the 1 400 000 north African immigrants. The plight of the boat people brought offers of help flooding in from all parts of the country. But many a generous impulse was found to be impractical when it was sounded out. French families could offer a roof for a time, but not language classes and help in finding a job. Some rural communes that have been working hard for months to prepare a home and a livelihood for a boat family may be disappointed when the project gets properly under way. The refugees are frightened of isolation and, however kind their French hosts are, they want to be in a community of their own people.

Every variation of fortune is to be found among France's Indo-Chinese population. Some are happily integrated shopkeepers, restaurant-owners and workers, with children doing well at lycées and universities. Others drift miserably in a world too busy or uncaring to make room for them.

A 33-year-old Cambodian woman, Bun Vandy, whose husband was killed by the Khmer Rouge, told the magazine *Paris-Match*: 'Paris is admirable. But in certain ways it is a city of loneliness and ghosts. It is not very easy to make contact with people. There is a distance between the whites and the yellows. It is not very easy for you to understand us. You know us so little.' Bun Vandy escaped without her family and is now involved in the long process of getting them over to join her. She has moved through a long series of jobs and lives with her 11-year-old son in one tiny room where he has to sleep on a windowsill.

She has met both great generosity and sharp hostility and describes her experience of exile up to now as alternately frightening and farcical. 'Put an average Frenchwoman in a Charlie Chaplin film and add Auschwitz and you would have some idea of our situation,' she says. She still yearns for her country. 'If South-East Asia was at peace, if there were no hatred, if there were something to eat, not a single person would have wanted to leave. And it is you who would come to us and you would not leave.' Of France, she says:

When you come down to it there are very few real racists. There are just people whose habits have been disturbed. We are a disturbance. That's the word. Because we show you in a terrible way how fragile the world we live in is . . . You didn't really know this, in your skin, in your life, in every second of your life. You knew it, but in a theoretical way. The massacre of the Jews was your first warning. We are your second warning. I think it is the last . . .

Canada
'A haven for the homeless' is how government literature describes

Canada. Since 1945 it has welcomed more than 350 000 of the world's refugees: from Hungarians and Czechoslovakians to, more recently, Ugandans, Chileans and Lebanese. In character with this tradition, the Canadian government announced in July 1979 that it would increase its quota of Indo-Chinese refugees to 50 000 by the end of 1980. This meant a trebling in the country's monthly intake, from 1000 to 3000.

Unfortunately, it has also meant the creation of a backlash which, by late August 1979, was taking the form of full-page newspaper advertisements condemning the refugee program, fiery radio attacks on 'do-gooders' and isolated reports of active job and housing discrimination. But this reaction is said not to be typical, and judging by community response to the government's private sponsorship scheme and various fund-raising efforts (one newspaper raised $60 000 within six weeks), there is certainly a public commitment to provide aid. Yet the backlash is undeniable, and divisive. During a coast-to-coast radio 'phone-in' show run by the Canadian Broadcasting Company, for example, eleven people rang to express support for the high quota, while thirteen callers urged a lower inflow, or none at all. A Nova Scotia man objected that 'over the years, Canada has become the dumping ground for foreigners', and a Halifax woman suggested that 50 000 refugees would put Canada in the 'poorhouse' because 'they multiply'.

It is the volume of refugees rather than their origin that seems to be the issue. Until January 1979, more than 9000 Indo-Chinese refugees had settled in Canada. Most arrived within a few months of the fall of Saigon. The bulk of them chose to live either in French-speaking Quebec (65 per cent went to Montreal) or in the province of Ontario. In November 1978 the *Hai Hong* incident in Malaysia was given dramatic coverage by the news media and Canada offered to take 600 of the 2500 refugees crammed on the rusting freighter. The quota ceiling was raised progressively in the following months, as reports of the intense suffering of the boat people drifted in. The public rallied, wrote letters and lobbied; the government finally responded with a scheme whereby it would match, one for one, the number of refugees sponsored privately, up to the 50 000 limit.

To obtain permission for private sponsorship, Canadians must form into groups of at least five and sign an agreement with the government to provide 'material assistance and moral support' for an immigrant family for at least a year. This could cost up to $10 000, the government estimates. It is also a considerable personal responsibility. The idea is to make the number of refugees entering the country conditional on public sentiment: if the current refugee fervour fades, the upper limit will not be reached.

The latest figures show that 7270 refugees arrived between January and mid-August 1979, bringing the Canadian total to roughly 15 000. Of the latest arrivals, about one-third have settled in Ontario, another third in Quebec, 12 per cent in British Columbia and 9 per cent in oil-rich Alberta. The remainder are sprinkled lightly around the other provinces. The new refugees represented 'the whole gamut of occupations, from pilots to factory workers', according to an official, but most were white-collar workers or had run some kind of small business, and were ethnic Chinese. The poor, the illiterate and the peasant-farmer were not reaching Canada. 'There has been some sniping about Canadian officials skimming the cream from the refugee camps,' the official said. 'But the prime consideration, for us, is whether they will fit into the life here, whether they can adjust. And obviously that's going to be easier for someone who's educated, who can speak English and has some sort of training, than for an illiterate rice-farmer.'

Just how well the Vietnamese have adjusted is a moot point. Some get jobs within two weeks of arrival; for others, it might take six months. Very few, however, spent any length of time on welfare. Some of the more practical, less weighty problems, as described by John Chu of the Toronto Vietnamese association, were: learning to walk on ice, mastering elevators and escalators, learning wristwatch-type punctuality and understanding that it was not permissible to wander around hotels or the street in pyjamas. Another more serious assessment came from Nguyen Van Khan, a 27-year-old former civil engineer from Vietnam. He arrived in Canada with his wife in April 1979. He had paid $2500 in gold for the boat trip, then spent five months moving between three Malaysian camps. Mr Nguyen's mother and three sisters are still in Vietnam.

I came to Canada with no money. The government brought me and I was paid at first $49 a week [unemployment benefit] . . . It was very hard, I found my house by walking the streets and seeing a board 'For rent'. For two months I studied English at night and looked for a job, and now I work in a mercantile re-insurance company. My pay is $8700 a year. I think this is enough for my family which is small now.

The cold, he said, was bothersome, as was the language barrier. But his main problem was his work:

I am a builder, not an insurance worker. I spent many years in university learning my business, but here I have not the qualifications. I would have to take an examination in Toronto, but my English is not good enough and it's not possible to learn quickly when I have to work every day.

Mr Nguyen said he was aware of some resentment towards the refugees, but he had not encountered it personally.

The people at work, they seem to like me very much; I have received mercy from them. I think that I love the Canadians very much. But I am not happy. How can I be? I always miss my family. I think all the time of Vietnam. Canada is my country for a time. But I will go back immediately if Vietnam has another revolution. I will not want to stay here then.

It is still early days for Canada. If the country ends up accepting the full 50 000 to which it is committed, this would represent the largest movement of refugees to Canada since the end of the second world war. An opinion poll taken in July 1979, just before the quota was boosted, showed that, nationally, about 50 per cent of Canadian adults favoured the admission of more refugees from South-East Asia, while 38 per cent disapproved. By contrast, a poll taken five months earlier had indicated that 52 per cent of adults felt that too many refugees were being admitted – and the figure at that time was a meagre 5000 a year. Which is the real opinion?

United Kingdom

Although Britain was co-chairman with the Soviet Union of the Geneva agreements and, before that, played a role in occupying southern Vietnam after the second world war, it was not directly involved there as a colonial power and was not a military ally of the United States during the Vietnam war. The sense of guilt and responsibility that Britain feels about many of its former colonies therefore does not extend to Vietnam. The relief, now that Vietnam has become an international issue again, is shared by politicians from all parties and the British people in general.

Prime Minister Margaret Thatcher said what many voters wanted to hear before the elections in May 1979: her government would introduce strict controls on immigration because many Britons felt they were being swamped by 'alien culture'. She drew loud protests from human rights and race relations organizations, but observers believe her stance contributed to her election victory. Mrs Thatcher was later asked if she had modified her attitude: she was adamant that she had not.

Some people have felt swamped by immigrants. They've seen the whole character of their neighbourhood change. I stood by that statement 100 per cent and continue to stand by it. Of course ... some minorities can be absorbed – they can be assets to the majority of the community – but once a minority in a neighbourhood gets very large, people do feel swamped. They feel their whole way of life has been changed.

Against this background, the Indo-Chinese refugee crisis reached its climax. Mrs Thatcher at first stuck firmly to her election strategy of restricting 'black' immigration. (All Asians, Afro-Caribbeans and other non-whites are officially 'black' in British statistics.) She relented only after the foreign secretary, Lord Carrington, toured the refugee centres of Hong Kong and South-East Asia and expressed his concern at the tragedy of the boat people. Urged by him and the UN secretary-general, Kurt Waldheim, Mrs Thatcher moved from opposing any significant intake of refugees to a commitment to resettle 10 000 – all from the British territory of Hong Kong. Before that commitment, the Labour government had agreed to settle 1500 from South-East Asian camps. Another 1033 have been accepted on humanitarian grounds, many of them rescued by British ships.

The British press has been more enthusiastic about accepting refugees than have the British politicians or the British people. Despite opposition to entry of Indo-Chinese refugees expressed in the letters columns of the daily newspapers, editorialists and columnists responded positively, arguing that the boat people especially should be allowed in to Britain. The *Guardian* said: 'Mrs Thatcher's niggardly attitude towards accepting more Indo-Chinese into Britain derives from the same awareness felt in South-East-Asian capitals, that the refugees are a hot potato and not worth risking one's skin to help.' The weeklies, especially the *Economist* and the *Spectator*, also urged a more positive British response.

The Thatcher government's cautious attitude undoubtedly reflects concern about its responsibilities in Zimbabwe-Rhodesia, which is a potential source of thousands of refugees, both black and white. Many of the whites in Zimbabwe-Rhodesia will qualify for automatic residence as patrials – having a parent or parents born in the United Kingdom. Whites with a British grandparent will qualify for indefinite residence. But the blacks will qualify for neither: British policy is that Rhodesians, unless they qualify through patriality or ancestry, have to meet standard immigration requirements, which means that Britain would be effectively closed to blacks seeking residence. In other words, while Britain would be prepared to let neighbourhood African states take refugees from Zimbabwe-Rhodesia, it would itself refuse them refugee status and treat them as normal – and therefore usually ineligible – immigrants to Britain.

To justify its limited intake of refugees, Britain falls back on its experience in settling about 2 million Africans, Asians, Pakistanis and Indians. It argues that if Britain is to contain racial tensions, it must stop coloured immigration. Every official survey shows that the non-whites, who now comprise 3.3 per cent of Britain's population, are distrusted or feared by whites and fear or distrust whites in return.

The extent to which Vietnamese will be confronted by the same racial reactions is still unknown. There have been mild protests at the provision of council housing for them, as housing is short throughout the country. But generally, Britons feel sympathy with the boat people, as a result of dramatic press and television coverage of their escapes and extraordinary voyages. Britain's Vietnamese resettlement program is run through the British council for aid to refugees. The council's projects officer, Jeanne Townsend, believes the Vietnamese may more easily be accepted than Britain's other coloured citizens.

They have endeared themselves to the British people. They are not nearly as inscrutable as Asians are believed to be and they do not have the same religious and social taboos as Indians and many Africans. They like a drink, love parties and are an outgoing people. The English are dotty about anyone who rides a horse or sails a boat and they have admired the courage of the Vietnamese boat people. It has been an emotional reaction. The Vietnamese are proving to be remarkable gardeners, buying plants and trees wherever they settle, and this endears them to the British people. I don't say they are angels. They have their problems: their expectations are rather high. Long-term, we just cannot know what it is going to be like. There is always a tendency later towards depression and anxiety with refugees.

The most immediate problems, however, are finding housing for the refugees and teaching them English. Miss Townsend said the refugee council did not want to house the Vietnamese in those areas that were already subject to racial pressures. It preferred to settle them in groups of three or four families out of London, unless jobs or welfare needs prevented this. Councils and communities had co-operated in providing housing, welfare and work. The indications so far are that the government's policy is working in one sense: with so few Vietnamese coming into Britain they have a better chance of being absorbed harmoniously and sympathetically.

Australia

If evidence were needed that Australia's future depends on how it adapts to developments in Asia, the boat people, drifting through the seas and straits of South-East Asia and actually landing on Australian shores, provided it. Since the second world war, a carefully managed immigration policy has brought to Australia 3.5 million people, mostly of European stock, so that one in every three Australians today is an immigrant or has immigrant parents. The aim of the policy, while not racially exclusive, was to increase the population without changing its dominantly European composition, or at least to change it slowly. The boat people were not part of the policy. They had not been processed thousands of kilometres away by skilful immigration officials. Reflecting population pressures and political turmoil near at hand, they simply turned up, uninvited, asking for refuge. For Australia, history and geography had merged, causing a shiver of apprehension.

Fifty-one vessels, carrying 2011 boat people, landed in Australia. The total number of Indo-Chinese refugees settled in Australia by September 1979, however, was 25 000 (21 000 Vietnamese, 3000 Laotians and 1000 Kampucheans); by the middle of 1980 Australia will have redeemed its pledge at the UNHCR Geneva conference and settled 37 000. Most are flown at government expense from camps in South-East Asia. Those with relatives in Australia are given first priority. Selection is then made on the basis of past associations with Australia and integration prospects, including job skills and ability to speak English. However, as a reminder that this is a humanitarian program, a number of 'hard to settle' cases (unskilled people without English) are deliberately chosen. Most of the resettlement expenses are borne by the government, although charitable bodies also play a role. The cost in public funds is about $2500 for each refugee.

A national poll conducted by the *Age* in June 1979 (before the promise to UNHCR to take more refugees) showed that Australians had mixed feelings about the new arrivals. While 23 per cent thought Australia should continue to accept refugees from Indo-China, only 7 per cent thought more should be taken. Against this, 30 per cent thought fewer should come, while 37 per cent went further and said no more should be accepted.

The poll's negative finding could be partly explained by reservations on the political left and among trade unions. They had opposed the commitment of Australian troops to Vietnam and now argued that the refugees were a continuing consequence of that war. With increasing unemployment, Australian workers also tended to see refugees as a threat to their livelihood. Immigration to Australia has traditionally served the political interests of the conservatives (who favour a competitive labour market and anti-communist immigrants) and the Vietnamese seemed to fit that tradition. Another factor was that two of the three communist parties in Australia were aligned with Moscow and Peking, and bitterly opposed over Vietnam, giving the refugee issue a high profile in trade-union politics. In the state of Queensland, a riot broke out and arrests were made when resettled Vietnamese gathered to protest against two visiting unionists from Hanoi. Some antagonism to the refugees has also been shown by Australians who are themselves immigrants, or of immigrant parents.

Australia's conservative Liberal/Country-party coalition government was also, however, in a quandary, because racial politics in Australia had always been active on the extreme right, especially in country electorates. The Australian League of Rights distributed a pamphlet which asked: 'Why should loyal Australians, including many who risked their lives to defend the nation, be smeared as racist and undesirable because they protest against an immigration policy which, if continued, must ruin Australia as it is ruining other countries?' Some Australian conservatives used the arrival of the boat people to advocate the acceptance of white Rhodesian refugees, when their time comes. However, as both the Liberal/Country party government and the Labor party opposition evidently have problems about the refugee question within their own ranks, the boat people have not become an issue between the two main parties and have been able to settle in with considerable success.

When the refugees first arrive in Australia they are sent to migrant centres; employment opportunities determine where they go from there. It is difficult to measure the exact number of refugees in each Australian state because interstate movement is common: families and individuals move to join relatives and friends; single young men (who are 57 per cent of the total resettled) are also highly mobile. At present, 10 000 are in New South Wales, Victoria has 7500 and South Australia, Western Australia and Queensland each has 2500.

Despite local unemployment, difficulties with English and lack of recognized qualifications, in Victoria about 3000 Indo-Chinese refugees (or nearly half) have found jobs, especially in manufacturing, which is the most competitive sector of the labour market, and in the automotive industry. It is not uncommon to find academics and professionals on a production line or taking fares on Melbourne's public transport. Some refugees find the housing centres inadequate because there are no cooking facilities and the food there does not suit them. There have also been incidents of violence in these centres. In 1979 fighting among rival factions of Vietnamese refugees was reported, involving about a hundred Vietnamese men in the grounds of a centre in Adelaide and resulting in the stabbing of a 23-year-old man. But, until they have learned English and become employed, it is difficult for them to move from the centres.

Through church groups and community agencies, the federal

government has evolved a scheme to help Vietnamese cope with housing, schools, shopping, and welfare entitlements. A spokesman for the department of immigration and ethnic affairs, which is organizing the project, said there had been fewer problems than expected with assimilating refugees. He described them as quiet, law-abiding people, like those refugees who came immediately after the second world war. They had settled in very well.

Nguyen Van Dong is twenty-nine and a bachelor. 'The main problem for Vietnamese in Australia is that there are not enough Vietnamese women,' he says with a soft smile. He sits in his small Sydney room – a student's room, with a bed and books and an electric jug – and talks about Vietnam. He is grateful to Australia but he wants to talk about Vietnam. 'Australia is your country,' he says, 'Vietnam is mine.' He is ruefully honest about his people: 'Vietnamese are stubborn, stubborn and arrogant. Vietnamese cannot live happily anywhere except in Vietnam. They are the most nationalistic people in the world.' He was in the army and left Saigon a few days after it fell in 1975. He does not like the communist régime, but supports it against China. 'The Chinese in south Vietnam made a lot of money when the French and the Americans were there. They looked down on us.' He is amused that some formerly rich Chinese who had arrived in Australia without any money had come to him for help. 'I gave them something. In a year or two they will probably be rich again.' He laughs. 'The Chinese will be just as happy in Australia as in Vietnam, Singapore or Hong Kong. All they want to do is make money. Where they make it does not matter.'

Prompted to talk about his life in Australia, he remarks on the spacious countryside and the wide streets, which frightened him when he arrived. Vietnamese like to cluster together. 'We spend hours arguing about what is happening in our country. Some hotheads want to stir up public opinion in the west, so that the régime in Hanoi will be overthrown.' He smiles at the fantasy. 'But most of us want to keep out of politics in Australia. We are grateful. Australia has been good to us. We do not want to be a nuisance.' Despite all the talk about politics, he believes most Vietnamese left because of food shortages. He keeps in touch by letter with members of his family in Vietnam (the mail, though slow, seems regular).

Some Vietnamese in Australia, he said, have had 'bad experiences' (of racial prejudice) in Queensland and Western Australia, but those who have settled in Sydney, Melbourne and Adelaide have been made welcome. Could he marry an Australian girl? 'It is possible,' he says thoughtfully. 'But there would be cultural problems. We Vietnamese are difficult to live with ... very intense and self-centred.' In any case, he is not thinking about marriage. When he has completed his course (in engineering) he intends to work hard in Australia, to establish himself and also to repay his adopted country, and then, perhaps in ten or fifteen years, he would like to return to Vietnam – 'to help my people'.

Scandinavia
What they lose in the way of climate, the boat people who come to Scandinavia make up in the highly organized welfare-state operation to assimilate them into Nordic society. Apartments are found for them, they are given free tuition in their host country's language and get the same social benefits as a native. Scandinavia has a liberal attitude on racial questions: protests at the influx of Vietnamese have been so rare as to be virtually non-existent.

In Sweden, where 1250 refugees will eventually be settled, the operation to assimilate them into Swedish society proceeds with all the precision of a Volvo production line. When the refugees step ashore at Ahus in the southern province of Skane, they are given a medical examination and for the next two to three weeks live collectively in a resettlement centre. They then move out to other towns in the south where they are given apartments where they shop, cook and look after themselves. There are intensive courses in Swedish for adults, and children are looked after in special day centres. All children over the age of seven start school in the ordinary Swedish educational system, one of the best in the world. Even when the boat people leave their protected environment, the social welfare authorities will maintain contact with them and they will continue to be given free language tuition.

As the refugees come into Sweden, they will be spread fairly evenly around the southern provinces. As to how they feel about their new homeland, it is difficult to say. Most of them are still so pathetically grateful to have left the camps that they are unable to formulate any opinion beyond 'we are so happy to be here'. Sweden has a good record with immigrants, who enjoy most of the rights Swedes have, including, after three years, voting rights in local elections.

The first intimation that Sweden would take in boat people came from the king, Carl XVI Gustaf, when he paid a two-day visit to Geneva, on 5 December 1978. He told a press conference that the Swedish parliament was considering the refugee problem and might agree to take some 2000 refugees – but he hastened to add that he had no authority to make a decision himself. By the beginning of 1979 there was still no decision by the parliament. But by now Sweden was under mounting international pressure to take her quota of boat people. Foreign Minister Hans Blix admitted the Vietnamese refugee situation was difficult and said every nation must contribute in its own way to a solution.

There was speculation that Sweden's delay was caused by her special relationship with Vietnam. During the Vietnam war Sweden was one of the few western nations that recognized Hanoi and broke off diplomatic relations with Saigon. Then, when the war ended, Vietnam became one of the largest recipients of Swedish foreign aid. Aid in 1978-79 stood at 380 million kronor ($88.3 million) and in 1979-80 it will rise to 400 million kronor ($93 million). By 12 January 1979, international pressure and the worsening situation in South-East Asia proved too much. In a special extra session of the cabinet, just before Prime Minister Ola Ullsten was due to leave for a two-week visit to the United States, the government agreed to accept 250 boat people. Immigration Minister Eva Winther admitted that this was largely a token gesture, designed to encourage other countries to accept their humanitarian responsibilities for the refugee problem in South-East Asia.

On 21 June Sweden announced it was doubling its refugee intake for 1979, as a direct result of the worsening situation in South-East Asia. The refugee quota was increased to 2500, with an estimated 1250 refugees from Vietnam. It was also announced that Sweden would give 15 million kronor ($3.4 million) to the United Nations campaign to aid refugees in South-East Asia. Blix emphasized that Swedish aid to Vietnam would continue. The aid was for long-term projects like hospitals and a lumber mill and should not be used to influence the short-term decisions of the Vietnamese government.

However, with reports that Vietnam was openly encouraging ethnic Chinese to leave the country, criticism of the aid program mounted. In the parliament the discontent was voiced by Bertil Fiskesjö, of the Centre Party, who said all new aid to Vietnam should be stopped. 'It is completely fantastic that, when a régime is casting out a large part of its population to possible death and an uncertain fate, Sweden should continue to give large sums in aid to the country in question,' he said. Meanwhile Prime Minister Ullsten revealed that he had made repeated appeals to Vietnam's premier, Pham Van Dong, to take steps to ease the situation. Opposition leader Olof Palme, who in 1968 marched alongside Hanoi's ambassador in a Stockholm street demonstration against American involvement in Vietnam, revealed that he too had made appeals to Pham Van Dong.

Of the other Scandinavian countries, Norway has agreed to take 3000 boat people but by late 1979 only 200 had arrived. They were being housed in apartments in three main centres: Oslo, the capital, Bergen and Hamar. There they are given free language tuition, full social help and assistance in obtaining work. Finland has taken a hundred boat people. They have been accommodated in apartments in Korso, near Helsinki, and there they also get all social benefits, free language tuition and help in getting a job. Finland took refugees regardless of their professional status and qualifications. When the first refugees arrived they were a bit alarmed to learn that Russia was so close, and even more surprised to learn that there were communists in Finland.

New Zealand

Far from the world's trouble spots, New Zealand has never had to face the problem of refugees arriving empty-handed on its shores. Although New Zealanders have often showed a high degree of compassion, relatively few refugees have sought a haven there. Since 1944, when a first group of 840 Poles arrived in New Zealand, fewer than 10 000 refugees have been taken in by a population that now numbers 3.1 million. The largest group was 4500 European refugees after the second world war, followed by 1100 Hungarians after the abortive 1956 uprising. However, there has been a surge of public demand, particularly from church groups and specially formed interest groups, to take more Indo-Chinese refugees, a demand the government is finding increasingly difficult to resist. New Zealanders seem to appreciate that, in this case, as a near neighbour, their country has special responsibilities.

Until mid-1977 most of the Vietnamese settled in New Zealand had been associated with the country during the Vietnam war, such as embassy staff or students granted asylum. But in May 1977, the UNHCR appealed to New Zealand to take some boat people and the government agreed, provided they held UN status as refugees and had 'occupation qualifications useful to New Zealand'.

By January 1978, 535 Indo-Chinese had entered New Zealand, mainly in two big airlifts. They were settled largely through the efforts of the inter-church commission on immigration, the traditional agent for refugee resettlement. The government declined to take more until it had seen how the first groups had settled. By October, the inter-church commission had compiled a report outlining the success of resettlement and recommending an increase. In December, the government announced it would take 600 during 1979. Early in July 1979, two brothers, Hugo and Bill Manson, both experienced television journalists, wrote to all the country's 230 local authorities asking them to indicate the willingness of their communities to support a refugee family. The Mansons suggested a ratio of one refugee for every thousand citizens, or a total of about 3200 Indo-Chinese. Within two months, with more than half the councils' replies returned, 80 per cent had indicated support.

Pressure on the government came from other sources, including the ASEAN states and New Zealand's ANZUS colleagues, the United States and Australia. By the time the Geneva conference was held in July 1979, the government had agreed to take 3235 refugees (or one for every 927 of the population), but spread over two years. 'The government is being cautious to the point of cruelty,' said Hugo Manson. Officials defended government policy, arguing that the quality of sponsors, not just the quantity, had to be taken into account. One official asked: 'What about the African nations? Why have they not taken any?' The government argued further that its selection policies were humanitarian: age or youth of refugees was not a barrier to acceptance and not only skilled people were sought.

A cautious approach would create the necessary favourable public climate.

The only refugee reception area in New Zealand is at Mangere in South Auckland, where the newcomers spend their first month in medical checks, cultural orientation and language courses. An experimental community-based resettlement program in Rotorua, on North Island, is planned. But there appears to be growing opinion that more refugees should be taken and that another reception camp should be opened. The Manson brothers may yet have their way.

Nguyen Phi, forty-two, with his wife and six children, was part of New Zealand's first intake of boat people. On arrival his only possessions were the clothes he wore. He had taken a Leica camera and lenses with him from Vietnam but had sold them in a Malaysian refugee camp to buy food. This was his second time as a refugee. He had already fled from Hanoi to the south in 1955, after the Geneva agreements. This time he was leaving behind the results of his successful settlement in the south: a house, a car, and two ice-cream factories, employing eighteen people. The main reason for fleeing was what the Phi family describe as 'pressure' – such as having to attend daily meetings organized by the communists, and having to do 'voluntary' work.

Other refugees described how their businesses and property were confiscated. A Saigon man said he had lost a family bakery, a cattle farm and an orchard in May 1978. He had been sent to a 'new economic zone' where it was too barren to make a living. A 37-year-old former lieutenant commander in the south Vietnamese navy went through a 're-education' camp 150 kilometres north of Saigon, where work occupied the days, and meetings the evenings. 'The hardest thing was that we had to denounce our sins and the sins of our parents and grandparents. We had to denounce them as members of the capitalist classes.'

While New Zealand has taken fewer Indo-Chinese refugees than, according to some of its citizens, it could, all those who have come have been settled successfully. The government says it knows no examples of failure: this in itself is a success in human terms.

Japan

Since the fall of Saigon, 2860 Indo-Chinese refugees have made

187

their way uninvited to Japan. Of these, only three have been accepted for what, with the Japanese genius for obfuscation, is miscalled 'permanent residence'.

Japan, the rich man of Asia, has survived both the actual arrival on its shores of boat people – picked up usually not by the Japanese vessels that are most numerous in the South China Sea, but ships of other flags – and the scorn of many western nations. Japan the unique, the pure, the homogeneous, has preserved itself from contamination yet again, as it did in the nervous days after its long seclusion was broken by Commodore Perry in 1854 and again, in equally uncertain times, when it was occupied after defeat in 1945.

It has succeeded this time by the deft combination of firmness, the illusion of accepting some refugees under the specious 'permanent residence' category, and generous contributions to the UNHCR that have deflected unfavourable world opinion. Japan has already given $35 million and, in accordance with its promise at the Geneva conference in July to pay half the total spent by the UNHCR worldwide on the refugees in 1979, it has budgeted another $15 million, making a total of about $50 million for 1979.

The three boat people accepted as 'permanent residents' were Huu Loi Mai, a former south Vietnamese army officer, and his wife and small daughter. By late September 1979, 1685 of the 2860 who had reached Japan had already left, accepted for resettlement in other countries. The United States accepted 1223, Canada 152, Norway 88, Belgium 61, Britain 46, Switzerland 42, Paraguay 31, France 22, Holland 11, and Australia 9. This third-country resettlement scheme of Japan's is unusual. France and Australia, both very active in resettling boat people, began refusing to accept refugees passed on by Japan, in an effort to make it change its exclusionary policies. But almost certainly Japan will not change, and the losers, the pawns in this game of international moral one-upmanship, will be the refugees themselves, including several who already have close relatives in France or Australia – a condition that, in other circumstances, would ensure their acceptance for resettlement. Few of the 1172 refugees who remain will settle down like Mr Loi Mai and his small family.

Shortly before the seven-member economic summit of industrialized nations in Tokyo on 28-29 June 1979, Japan announced that it proposed to accept up to 500 boat people for settlement. The Japanese have begun processing several hundred applicants abroad under this proposal, but the nature of so-called 'permanent residence' in Japan makes it a hollow affair. Japan already has a minority population of about 600 000 people of Korean descent. Most are born in Japan but are not Japanese, just 'permanent residents'. These Koreans and their children, as well as about 75 000 Chinese, are the legacy of Japanese colonialism in Korea, Taiwan and China.

To apply for 'permanent residence' within the 500 quota, two basic and highly particular conditions have to be satisfied. First, the refugee must have some previous association with Japan – either a relative already living in Japan, experience of working for the Japanese embassy or a Japanese company in Vietnam, or experience of living in Japan as a student or technical trainee. Second, the applicant should have a job to go to in Japan, and a Japanese sponsor. Ninety-nine families, a total of 357 people, have applied for entry under these conditions. By late September, twenty-two families, or 69 people, had been approved; the remaining seventy-seven families, 288 people, will probably make their way to Japan in due course. The Japanese government says that no applicant under this scheme has been rejected. This is somewhat disingenuous. Besides the select ninety-nine families, a great many refugees in camps in the Philippines and South-East Asia (how many, the Japanese will not disclose) expressed their desire to go to Japan, but were saved the pain of refusal: they were simply not given the opportunity to apply. In most cases they lacked previous connections with Japan; their chances of finding a job and a Japanese sponsor were therefore nil.

Refugees who have been accepted for 'permanent residence' seem to have no illusion about the impermanence of their situation. They are grateful for the breathing space that, by chance association with Japan, they have been allowed. Most see their long-term future not in Japan but in resettlement in a third country or, perhaps in the very long term, in their return to Vietnam.

Japan's exclusionary policies, whatever gloss is applied to them, leave little room for humanitarian criteria. The appearance of heartlessness this gives is a cause of much anguish among western-influenced Japanese, but even such Japanese insist their country is not racist. Their refusal to accept refugees is based simply on their inability to conceive of a person who abandons his country. Of all people, the Japanese have shown least enthusiasm for emigration themselves. Their attachment to their own country, however unkindly it treats them, is so absolute that they regard leaving its shores as a denial of self, a kind of suicide.

Professor Michio Royama, professor of international politics at Sophia university in Tokyo, says that despite appearances, Japan was not truly internationalized.

It's all been one-way traffic. We send people out to foreign countries, and they return with useful ideas. But we still do not accept foreigners into our society in any real sense. The proof of this is in the Japanese universities, which should know better, but which exclude foreigners from their teaching staff, except as teachers of foreign languages.

Professor Kei Wakaizumi, professor of international politics at Kyoto Sangyo university, says Japanese should not be criticized.

We are only human beings, who understand human behaviour from our own experience. Japan is a country of consensus. It is homogeneous, if not in the strict racial sense, then certainly culturally, to a degree unique among nations. We cannot imagine a conflict where, at the end of it, a person becomes a refugee. For that reason we find it difficult to accept a person who is a refugee.

This is not sophistry, but an honestly held view common among intelligent Japanese who know very well how the rest of the world thinks. Such views sound arrogant: but the Japanese make no such show when they advance them, rather the contrary. Japanese strongly believe that the Vietnamese should not export their problems: the Japanese would not drive out their own people in the way Vietnam has. Holding such a view, the exclusionary policy of the Japanese is arguably their most realistic solution. And, in view of the casualty rate among desperate boat people, who is to say that the toll would have been higher if the Vietnamese had been obliged from the start to sort out their differences, as the Japanese suggest they would do in similar circumstances?

At the personal level the Japanese view looks crude and selfish. One Japanese confided:

We blame the refugees as much as we blame the Vietnamese government. Either they're criminals, or they're weak-willed people. Whatever they are, we do not understand why they can't remain in their own society to help rebuild it after all their fighting. Some of the refugees may be good people, unfairly treated by their government. But how are we to know them from the rest. And how do such problems become our responsibility in the first place?

Professor Wakaizumi says he understands such feelings of ordinary Japanese and even partly shares them himself.

I am ambivalent in my attitude. It is clear that as reasonable human beings we should open doors and welcome refugees from wherever they come. There is no question about that on humanist grounds. And at the same time we must make every effort to urge the Vietnamese government to stop those atrocities and unacceptable policies that give rise to the problem. But when it comes down to the question of realistic action we should take here in Japan, this rather inexplicable emotion, this psychology of ours, comes to the fore and dictates our policy. I would not say it is a racist attitude, because as you know as individuals we're hospitable and ready to welcome others, irrespective of race. But to have refugees settle down in Japan and treat them just like our friends and neighbours, without prejudice or preconceptions – well, we have difficulty.

Professor Wakaizumi sees the problem as one of human relations, and the fear held by Japanese that they will simply fail to get along with the Vietnamese if they come in substantial numbers. This personal fear weighs more than any abstract idea of humanity, and far more than any remote consideration of international politics, such as taking China's side against Vietnam. It comes back to Japan's Korean minority, a case of the most vicious of vicious circles. The Chinese minority, once about 100 000, has melted fairly thoroughly. Many thousands have taken Republic of China (Taiwan) nationality; far fewer have taken People's Republic of China nationality; about 50 000 have sought and have gained, or are in the process of gaining, Japanese nationality. The Koreans are different. ('They are more homogeneous, more nationalistic, more like us,' says Professor Royama.) Few Japanese-born Koreans have chosen to take either North or South Korean passports, and only a few have applied for Japanese nationality. They say that the procedures are long and uncertain and that Japanese prejudices are so deeply ingrained that even if they took Japanese nationality they would still not be equal in Japanese society. There is evidence that there is some truth in this, but the Koreans' attitude must also be counted as part of the reason why, in the way of vicious circles, their lot is not likely to improve quickly.

'For us, the Korean story is a story of failure,' Professor Wakaizumi said. 'Because of it, we do not have confidence in ourselves. We are really afraid that if we welcome the boat people in large numbers, we cannot be happy living with them and they will not be happy living with us.' That attitude, so artlessly put, expresses a defeatism that sets up its own vicious circle. However, Kei Wakaizumi concluded by saying that, whatever the difficulties, Japan should try to change: it should accept, say, 10 000 refugees. 'The boat people represent a challenge. If we are to be really good members of the international community, we ought to run the risk of failing as we failed with the Koreans. We should try again.' But he was speaking to a foreigner: in Japan, among Japanese, that kind of view is not popular and therefore is hardly heard, let alone discussed.

India

New Delhi's attitude to the unfortunate boat people was shown in July 1979, when the British foreign and commonwealth secretary, Lord Carrington, drew a blank trying to persuade Prime Minister Morarji Desai to use his influence with Premier Pham Van Dong. Prime Minister Charan Singh's coalition ministry, which took office at the end of July, was too busy trying to survive to attend to world issues.

The horror stories of Vietnamese privation that made headlines in the western media seem far less gruesome to a people who have lived with refugee suffering ever since India became independent thirty-two years ago. The 9 million Bangladesh refugees who were given sanctuary in 1971 have gone back, while the 80 000 Tibetans who fled with the Dalai Lama are adequately provided for. But India has not yet solved the problem of about 12 million Hindus who were uprooted when the country was partitioned in 1947. The steady flow of dispossessed families – many of them still languishing in the squalor of temporary camps – may have dulled India's response to similar tragedies elsewhere.

Historical experience and the inherited perspectives of the British Raj also explain India's indifference to events in South-East Asia; rather, Indians react more readily to developments in the west. Even at the height of the Vietnam war there were no demonstrations in Delhi, Bombay and Calcutta to match the massive rallies in European and American cities. The relatively mild protest of radical politicians and left-wing intellectuals was not so much inspired by Vietnam's plight as an expression of hostility to the United States.

Recently, however, the Indian government has tried to rationalize its lack of interest by indirectly accusing the western powers, notably Britain and the United States of conspiring with China to politicize the hapless boat people. The conspiracy theory is buttressed with the charge that the west, now brimming over with sympathy, remained unmoved when 2 million Palestinian Arabs were displaced, or by the continued exodus of people from mainland China to Hong Kong, or by more recent displacements of humanity in Somalia, Sudan and Ethiopia. Peking's aggressive policy in relation to the overseas Chinese is blamed for the plight of the boat people. According to a Bengali journalist, Khagen De Sarkar, writing in the pro-Soviet newspaper *Patriot*, China withdrew all capable Hoa personnel engaged in trade, production and engineering, weakening Vietnam. Above all, it managed to give a bad name to Vietnam, the only country capable of standing up to Chinese hegemony and expansionism in South-East Asia.

This point of view is most forcefully presented by the articulate and influential left lobby which includes Marxists, communists, Mrs Indira Gandhi's Congress faction, as well as a fair sprinkling of politicians in the opposition Janata party. It seems also to underlie the decisions of the Charan Singh government which, at the summit conference of non-aligned nations, in Havana in September 1979, moved perceptibly closer to the school of thought that regards the boat people if not as a figment of the Sino-western imagination, at least as the product of its wicked stratagems.

Abandoning its earlier implicit, if lukewarm, support for the Pol Pot régime, New Delhi voted at Havana to keep the Kampuchean seat at the conference vacant. The earlier disposition of Desai to support Pol Pot was explained by his deep misgivings about Moscow's role in India. During the 1977 election campaign Desai had promised to scrap the Indo-Soviet treaty of peace and friendship, a pledge discreetly shelved when civil servants in New Delhi explained to him the extent of India's military and industrial dependence on the USSR. But he remained reluctant to extend ties or overtly to support Moscow's position in world affairs. Desai's options were closed, however, when his attempts to win back Indian territory seized by China during the 1962 border war came to nothing; a failure that was compounded when the sudden outbreak of the Sino-Vietnamese war – China's aggression in Indian eyes – forced his external affairs minister, Atal Behari Vajpayee, to cut short a visit to China and return home.

Charan Singh was similarly in a dilemma. The logical course after the Havana conference would have been to withdraw all semblance of support from Pol Pot – whom Indians believe guilty of liquidating two or three million Kampucheans – and to recognize the Heng Samrin régime. This would not only have placated Moscow but would also have pleased its ally in Hanoi. But to do so might have confirmed the Soviet connection and put an end to Indian hopes of a rapprochement with Peking and of recovering lost territory. Until a government is established in New Delhi with a working majority in parliament, India will continue to talk non-committally of Vietnam's 'intervention' in Kampuchea, to blame the United States for egging on China to 'punish' Vietnam and to avoid explicitly taking sides, while despatching medical supplies to Kampuchea. However, not even a firmly established ministry in New Delhi can afford to take any step that might be construed as pandering to China until the disputed Himalayan border question, hanging fire since the 1950s, has been resolved. Knowing this, Hanoi will continue to play astutely on New Delhi's inherent suspicion of Peking's aims.

Chapter 8

Prospect

The story of the boat people exposes power politics in its most primitive form. While men and women of goodwill hopefully discuss the prospect in the last quarter of the twentieth century of a 'new world order' or a 'common heritage of mankind', the boat people have revealed another side – the ruthlessness of major powers, the brutality of nation-states, the avarice and prejudice of people. At times, when telling the story of the boat people, it seemed that Indo-China had become the vortex of all that is wrong with mankind.

Vietnam gained sympathy with its long struggle for independence but, in the period investigated in this book, its passionate nationalism and understandable suspicion of China turned sour, allowing racism and *realpolitik* to come to the surface. Vietnam has profited financially from the exodus of refugees, has embroiled itself in Kampuchea, and has become increasingly dependent on the Soviet Union for aid and military support. A moment of reflection should be enough to convince Hanoi that something has gone wrong. When Peking says that Hanoi has become 'swell-headed' and has 'reached the heights of rabidity and insolence', the world is forced to listen.

The Pol Pot régime in Kampuchea must rank with the most brutally senseless ever known. A small country with few resources, relying on the gifts of its people, was almost destroyed after 1975 by an army of single-minded ideologues and rampant children. Two brawling communist factions, one backed by Hanoi and the other by Peking, have lately brought the country to a standstill, facing famine and disease, with hundreds, perhaps thousands, dying every day, while the world's governments argue bitterly, or cleverly, about which faction to support.

China, for its part, has deliberately harassed Hanoi, armed Pol Pot, roused the ethnic Chinese in Vietnam, withdrawn its aid, and then, finally, invaded Vietnam, killing and destroying in order to 'teach a lesson'. The lesson it has taught the world is that it is just another great power, determined to bring Vietnam to heel.

Such is the behaviour of three of the main protagonists. These are not, it must be noted, states in historical decline. Their wars are not the last twitches of colonialism or the result of imperialism's crude appetites. These are brothers and sisters in communism, representing the future. From their own standpoint, it is a dismal prospect.

The fourth communist state, the Soviet Union, has been more cautious. While also playing power politics, it has behaved as if it appreciated the responsibilities and dangers. China thought its support for Kampuchea would deter Vietnam, but it did not. Vietnam thought its treaty with the Soviet Union would deter China. It did not. China thought that the USSR's strategic relationship with the US would restrain it from retaliation, when China invaded Vietnam – and at least that rational assumption held. The Soviet Union is slightly detached, by virtue of distance from the events, which has perhaps helped it to remain cool. But it may be tempting fate to press temperance too far.

The United States must also bear responsibility for what is happening in Indo-China. It refused to help Vietnam after 1975, withdrawing, perhaps understandably, to lick its wounds. But four years later it had still done little to repair relations with the country it had weakened so savagely during years of war, nor to use its influence with the ASEAN states and its new relationship with Peking to counsel restraint. Rather – as shown by the visit of vice-president Walter Mondale to Peking in August 1979, when he denounced Vietnam with ringing phrases – Washington seemed intent on encouraging Peking in its conflict with Hanoi. Supported by allies such as Australia, which closed down its small but symbolic aid program in Vietnam, Washington's campaign against Hanoi, while at the same time deliberately cultivating Peking, could only create fears among the Vietnamese people, including many potential refugees, of another war.

The non-communist states of South-East Asia have also been exposed, only slightly less seriously, by the boat people story. Their prosperity has been shown to be fragile, their humanity to be thin and their rhetoric to be shrill, and they are also undecided, even divided, on the reasons for the embarrassing exodus of refugees in their region. In the countries of resettlement, the boat people have uncovered economic and social uneasiness, as well as racial tension, and national psyches have been stimulated to surprising self-revelation. The ability of governments of the industrialized democracies to weep crocodile tears over the boat people, while doing little about the root causes of the exodus, has been notable. The boat people have indeed made us all look again at ourselves and at the state of our world.

The boat people, like other Indo-Chinese refugees, left their country for a variety of reasons which have been documented in earlier chapters: internal factors, including the politics of Vietnam's rulers and the country's threadbare economy; and external pressures on Vietnam, among them hostilities with China and its ally in Kampuchea. There were also other forces, like magnets, attracting people abroad: the strongest of these was the belief that life in the main resettlement countries – northern America, Australasia and western Europe – offered a sharp contrast with their bleak existence at home. Dozens of refugees in interviews said they had gained favourable impressions of life in these countries from letters they had received (or heard about) and from foreign radio broadcasts, particularly by the BBC, Voice of America and Radio Australia. Certain items of news were avidly received and remembered: news of increased intakes of displaced Indo-Chinese, especially to the United States; news of the two conferences on refugees in Geneva in December 1978 and July 1979; news of foreign ships, including the US Seventh Fleet, picking up refugees in the South China Sea. Most refugees were also influenced by a countervailing fear of what could happen to them at sea, or when they reached countries of first asylum in South-East Asia and tried to land. But while they were aware before they left of some of the terrors that could befall them, few had any real idea of what the sea passage might be like, for the simple reason that they had never experienced it. Most refugees had never been to sea before.

The 'pull' factors must be acknowledged with the 'push' factors in the complex of causes that turn people into refugees. Generosity in resettling refugees, and foreign broadcasts that invite comparison between a free and materially pleasant life and the deprivations of life under communism, may help to enlarge the outflow and increase the problem. Some ASEAN governments may have had this in mind when they set out to flaunt their inhumanity, hoping that word would get back that their receptiveness could not be taken for granted. However, when the main issues brought to a head by the story of the boat people are considered, the room for decision in influencing the 'pull' factors appears severely limited.

The first of these issues is stability. The link between the flow of refugees from Indo-China and the instability of the region is clear. The cause of this instability is also clear, although there are several layers: it is the conflict between Vietnam and China. If this conflict continues, as it shows every likelihood of doing, the result will be more destruction in Kampuchea, and possibly Laos, anxiety in the ASEAN states, especially Thailand, and increasing military support by the USSR for Vietnam. So when it is sometimes suggested that the flow of refugees can only be stopped at the *source*, namely Vietnam, the assertion is only half true, unless it is meant to suggest that Vietnam is responsible for its conflict with China and should resolve it single-handed. The evidence, rather, is that the responsibility is shared and, in particular, that each bears responsibility for the flight of the ethnic Chinese from Vietnam.

The prospect of reconciling Hanoi and Peking is depressingly slight. The intensity of their history, their rivalry in Kampuchea, China's deep suspicion of the Soviet Union and the reluctance of the United States to normalize relations with Hanoi make a sharpening of the conflict a more likely prospect. It is just possible, however, that the refugees, by embarrassing everyone, have caused second thoughts about what appeared to be - at the height of the crisis in mid-1979 - a concerted policy on the part of the United States, its allies, the ASEAN states and China to isolate Vietnam. The ASEAN states in particular, being on the scene and touchy (some of them) about China's role in their region, might discover that their interests lie in trying to reassure Vietnam, although how, in the present dire circumstances of the show-down in Kampuchea, this can be done, is not easily evident. There is an urgent need of statesmanship for South-East Asia. What we witness instead is a merciless kind of statecraft that is both callous and precarious.

Can nothing be done? One possibility that has not been explored is for a conference, on the lines of the Geneva conference of 1954, with Kampuchea as the main item on the agenda. Kampuchea appeared, in late 1979, to be almost at last gasp. Apart from terrible human suffering, civil administration had almost disappeared; there was a real prospect that the nation-state itself would be destroyed, or just disappear. While Vietnam and China are each intent on creating a government in Phnom Penh that is responsive to them, other states in the region and, for that matter, in the world, would more likely be happy with a deliberately neutral Kampuchea. Why should not a neutral Kampuchea also appeal to the two superpowers, the USSR and the US?

If the Soviet Union's calculation is that it can back Vietnam successfully in the war with China, as it did in Vietnam's war with the United States, it may be mistaken. While it is abundantly true that Vietnam is a defiant nation and is unlikely to capitulate to China, it is also true that China is a more difficult adversary than the United States – it is near at hand, patient and has the means (one of them being the Chinese inside Vietnam) to keep Hanoi on the boil. Also, it is hard to see what interest the Soviet Union has in a pro-Vietnamese régime in Phnom Penh, except to deny China. If Hanoi is successful in Kampuchea, the border with Thailand will harden, creating tensions within ASEAN. As a global power, with an interest in moving its ships through the straits of South-East Asia (all of them controllable by Indonesia, with assistance from Malaysia and Singapore), the USSR needs good relations with the ASEAN states.

It is obvious that some cushioning is needed between Vietnam and Thailand: the answer could be to take Kampuchea out of the hands of both or either Peking or Hanoi. Another possibility, of course, is that Thailand could become passive, assuming its historical buffer role, not now between France and Britain but between a Vietnamese Indo-China and a non-communist South-East Asia. But while this could happen, it would only be after much more blood has been shed – after, indeed, Vietnam has won out in Kampuchea. The case for a neutral Kampuchea is much more striking on humanitarian grounds, indeed on every ground. In a sense that is almost literal, it is a case for the preservation of an endangered species.

Hanoi might find some unpleasant resonances in the revival of the 1954 Geneva conference, which became for it an instrument of deceit. Let the conference be held elsewhere and a fresh start made: the instrumentalities of that Geneva conference, such as its control and supervisory bodies, are in any case dead. Its co-chairmen were Britain and the Soviet Union: would they again be elected? The need is not to retain the Geneva lineage – although a sense of continuity is not amiss when dealing with Indo-China – but to bring together those major powers and regional states who must be aware by now that what is happening in Indo-China is so destructive that no one can expect to gain from it, and is so dangerous that its effect upon the balance of war and peace cannot be calculated. The boat people story puts in another perspective the duty of statesmen, whatever their politics, to act. Political leaders must act because people are needlessly suffering.

What of America? Throughout this book there has been a vein of criticism of the United States, intended and justified. A blind spot sometimes enters one country's vision of another: this has happened with America's view of Vietnam. It has led since 1945 to one mistake after another: the decision, after Roosevelt's death, to back the French; the refusal to accept elections after the Geneva agreements; the military onslaught during the Johnson presidency; the widening of the war into Cambodia during the Nixon-Kissinger rule; the dishonouring of the pledge in 1973 to provide aid of $3.25 billion over five years to Hanoi. Now, under another president, the United States is again following a policy that gives Hanoi no quarter, apparently designed to allow China a free hand in dealing with its troublesome neighbour. It is difficult to avoid an impression that deep within the strategic mind of Washington is a plan of hostility to Vietnam which, except for a moment when the madness became intolerable, the American people have not questioned. The madness is again mounting.

America's responsibility for what happened in Indo-China was considerable. Today, by omission and contrivance, it remains considerable. It would be a giant step for the United States – and for the region – if it would change policy on Vietnam, discarding notions of revenge and recognizing that the present conflict is too serious to be allowed to find its own, tragic level.

On balance, a realistic prospect is that the conditions that gave rise to the Indo-Chinese refugees will continue, which leads to a second consideration: What is the potential pool of refugees still in Vietnam? Clearly, it is not a static figure. It will rise and fall according to several factors, including the success of Hanoi's measures of security (or connivance) and economic and social conditions in Vietnam. However, an estimate can be made. The Chinese community in Vietnam must be considered a potential source. In northern Vietnam, there are probably no more than 30 000 ethnic Chinese left, but in the south there would still be about one million. Interviews in this book with refugees have shown how sensitive the Chinese community is to pressure and how many of them, now that their businesses have been closed down, are living on diminishing savings. Not all the Chinese wheeler-dealers who organized the exodus of the Hoa in 1978 and 1979 would have left and, however directly or indirectly Hanoi was involved officially in the exodus, corrupt security officials undoubtedly remain (and the local Chinese would know who they are).

The hard core of Vietnamese anti-communists, like many of those who left Vietnam when security arrangements were tight and before Hanoi became engaged in the subterfuge of assisting departure, will not be deterred from leaving by tighter security measures. These, probably numbering about 1.5 million, include those with close connections with the previous régime in Saigon, especially its armed forces and administration, and political and religious groups who gave it support and are now strongly anti-communist. Among these are the 800 000, including many Catholics, who left northern Vietnam for the south after partition in 1954 and who have shown an implacable hostility to the present régime. They are unlikely to be encouraged to stay even by an improvement in political, social or economic conditions.

These two sets of figures - one million ethnic Chinese and one and a half million counter-revolutionaries - account for most of the figure of three million that Vietnam's secretary of state for foreign affairs, Nguyen Co Thach, suggested to American newsmen in Vietnam in August 1979, as the number of Vietnamese who might want to leave Vietnam, depending, as he put it, on the political situation. This figure was first aired in conversation with the Swedish delegation at the UNHCR Geneva meeting in July 1979 by the deputy foreign minister, Phan Hien, and, when word got around, the unease was discernible, especially in Hong Kong and the ASEAN capitals. This would be ten times the flow of boat people between 1975 and 1979; although the figure is only a guess – and fails to take account of those who might be caught or lost at sea – it nevertheless should give everyone pause. Perhaps, indeed, that is why Vietnamese officials use it.

It is possible that Hanoi could be persuaded to 'scatter' this group of potential refugees, by pushing some into China, some to Thailand through Kampuchea, some into re-education camps, NEZs and preventive detention, as well as ejecting some onto the high seas. Even so, the prospect is daunting from the vantage point of the countries of first asylum in Asia.

By late September 1979, the reduction in the number of boat people leaving Vietnam had provided a welcome breathing space for countries of first asylum and for resettlement countries outside the region. The UNHCR conference in July achieved its aim of doubling the number of resettlement places on offer for refugees seeking permanent asylum in third countries, from 125 000 to 260 000. In the weeks following the meeting the pace of resettlement from the congested and insanitary camps in Asia was accelerated, easing the pressures on most ASEAN countries a little. In Malaysia, for example, the Indo-Chinese refugee population fell from 74 817 on 30 June to 63 343 on 15 August. In Hong Kong there was little change, partly because the slow-moving sailing junks that left northern Vietnam continued to arrive after the clamp was applied, and partly because some hundreds, perhaps thousands, of Hoa who left Vietnam for China in 1978 were unhappy there and were moving on to Hong Kong.

In January 1979 Vietnam suggested an expanded, legal emigration system, particularly for those wishing to rejoin relatives abroad, who would fly direct to their chosen destinations, bypassing overcrowded camps in the ASEAN nations and Hong Kong and avoiding the dangerous sea voyage across the South China Sea. The proposal seemed plausible: once the legal channel was expanded, the illegal exodus would dry up and eventually stop. At a conference in Djakarta in May 1979, Vu Hoang, head of the consular affairs office in the foreign ministry in Hanoi, said he 'hoped' people could start leaving Vietnam at a rate of up to 10 000 a month from the end of

June. However, by 11 September, there had been only eight flights out of Vietnam, carrying a total of 879 family reunion cases to Europe, Australia and north America.

Hanoi blames lack of air transport and insufficient co-operation from the west, especially the United States, for the scheme's slow start. However, there is evidence that the Vietnamese selection procedures are causing difficulties. When Vietnam had first announced its plan, it excluded from leaving all those liable to compulsory military service (virtually all males between the ages of sixteen and forty), but was reported to have dropped this exclusion in negotiations with the UNHCR in May: only those whose jobs involved access to state secrets, workers for whom replacements were not yet available, and criminals and accomplices were to be debarred. Yet in guidelines announced later, Hanoi said the scheme would be limited to 'family reunion and other humanitarian cases', and that the number of such people and the speed of their departure would depend on the volume of applications for exit from Vietnam and on the readiness of receiving countries to issue visas. The final say on who was to go and who was to stay would rest with Vietnam. Would many of those wanting to leave be prepared to wait for a plane instead of taking a boat, especially if they thought they had little hope of being approved, mistrusted the authorities controlling the scheme, and realized they might have to wait a long time? ASEAN countries were sceptical that the scheme would work, although it appeared to be trying to take their interests into account. In any case, the scheme was not of sufficient scope to deal with the potential number of refugees in Vietnam that could at any time be released. And, of course, it does not touch the other refugees in Indo-China, especially those in Kampuchea.

Legal exit arrangements, such as those proposed by Hanoi, raise another issue that simmers beneath the story of the boat people. Are the beneficiaries migrants or refugees and what are the obligations of others? The issue here involves a vital principle – a refugee has a 'well-founded fear of being persecuted for reasons of race, religion, nationality, membership of a particular social group or political opinion'. Officially approved exodus is also a cause of political concern in the rich countries of the world. The prospect of poor countries exporting population to rich countries is not one that politicians in the western democracies view with equanimity. If people were prepared to risk hardship or even death - as the boat people did by escaping by sea - they were accepted as being refugees, even if their reasons for fleeing were mainly economic ones. But for a government itself to decide which of its citizens should leave, expecting them to be given the rights of resettlement somewhere abroad, was another matter.

In practice, in dealing with displaced Indo-Chinese after 1975, the UNHCR - established by the United Nations general assembly in 1950 to protect refugees, give them material assistance and help them to find permanent homes - granted blanket refugee status to virtually all people leaving Vietnam by sea, whether on small boats or big ships, whether they left secretly or with official sanction, and whether they paid or not. The UNHCR adopted this approach believing it had a firm mandate to do so.

Persecution, although a prominent feature of the 1951 UN convention on the status of refugees, is not defined. It clearly includes a threat of life and liberty, so that execution, arbitrary detention, torture and other forms of extreme maltreatment are readily included. In interpreting 'persecution' in the case of the boat people the UNHCR took the view that it was not necessary for persecution actually to have occurred: it might simply have been anticipated. For this fear to be 'well-founded' meant that there should be sufficient facts to support a finding that the applicant for refugee status, if returned to his country of origin, would face a serious possibility of punishment. Since there were well-documented cases of people from Vietnam being caught and gaoled for months for trying to escape by boat, and since the Hanoi government refused to give safe-repatriation guarantees, the UNHCR could hardly justify withholding protection. Refugees are obviously created by conditions - political in the broadest sense - that make continued residence intolerable. Persecution can include measures such as serious economic disadvantage, and denial of access to employment, to the professions or to education, which, coupled with other restrictions, may well be intolerable.

The legal adviser in the UNHCR office in Sydney, Australia, Dr Guy S. Goodwin-Gill, in a speech in July 1979, drew attention to allegations that boat people from Vietnam were not refugees but economic migrants, or that they were not genuine refugees because in some cases they paid to leave. He commented:

The fact that an asylum-seeker has paid for his passage out does not prejudice his status as a refugee; people have been paying to escape oppression for centuries and others have profited thereby for as long. Again, the fact that an asylum-seeker has 'economic motives' will not of itself prejudice his claim to be a refugee. Such motives are often revealed in practice to mean that the individual has been denied the right in his own land to earn his living in peace, or in the occupation, skill or profession in which he is qualified. Secondly, important as the traditional legal definition of refugees is, it does not constitute the final word on who is worthy of humanitarian assistance by the international community. This has been recognized by the UN general assembly which has time and again widened the [UNHCR's] terms of reference, even to the point of authorizing assistance to persons displaced within their own country. It has also been recognized by countries of resettlement, in their immigration legislation, and by other countries, in their practice on asylum.

If the definition of refugee is to continue to be broadly applied, suggesting that the number of refugees internationally will increase, where are they to be resettled? The boat people provoked some ingenious responses. The camp on Bidong Island has become a model, in some minds, of enterprise and organization, so that a little Singapore or Hong Kong is seen rising from its present squalor. Put the boat people on an uninhabited island, it is said, and within no time they will make a city-state of it. Another suggestion is for 'holding centres', such as is now being prepared on Indonesia's Galang Island, to which refugees would move from camps in first-asylum countries for a specified period, during which they must be found a place of resettlement. Locations for these have been suggested on China's Hainan Island, Japan's Okinawa, America's Guam and in Australia's north, so far without a positive response. Another proposal was that a camp for refugees should be established *within* Vietnam, run by the UNHCR, to which unauthorized escapers would be sent and from which they would be resettled. All these proposals have some merit as exercises in crisis-management, and variations of them may well turn out to be useful if another outflow of Indo-Chinese refugees has to be accommodated. But they do not touch the central issue, which is that refugees from one nation should not be left stateless by the refusal of other nations to accept them. It is this issue which goes to the heart of the problem of the refugee in the twentieth century.

The rise of the nation-state in the nineteenth century changed the way peoples saw themselves and this tendency has strengthened in the twentieth century. The great religions of the world have long resigned themselves to accepting parity, even inferiority, with the power of the nation-state. Communism has challenged nationalism – and lost. The arbitrary power of the nation-state over human beings can be frightening; and it behaves, more often than not, towards other nation-states irrationally, refusing to allow the slightest interference with itself yet demanding the right to interfere with others. But its authority to protect its citizens from outside attack and, within the nation itself, to protect the weak, or the majority, make it a formidable fact of modern life. Weak nation-states are prey to great powers, ideologies and commercial and cultural tyrannies, all of which, especially in the so-called 'third world' of developing nations, have given the state ample justification for increasing its power.

A person who is forced to live outside the authority of the nation-state becomes, in the modern world, a person without the rights and duties of a citizen. The idea of an 'international citizenship' is attractive in principle, as is the idea of living in isolation in a utopian community. But each is a way of opting out of the issues posed by the boat people who, like the Indo-Chinese refugees generally, are too intensely connected with the forces of history and politics that have erupted to displace them, for them to become citizens in limbo, sanitized against time and place. If kept in anonymous camps or processing centres indefinitely, they are more likely to become disaffected than to become citizens of the world. It is from the interplay of people and nations in the real world that solutions to the real problems of refugees are likely to come.

It is imperative, therefore, for nation-states to become more inclusive, less exclusive, if it is to be within the nation-state itself that the problems of the twentieth century are to be solved. This is not to deny the need for international organizations, such as the United Nations, which is valuable, indeed indispensable, as an instrument of conciliation and, sometimes, effective organization.

The UNHCR is a case in point. But without a growth of civilizing values within states, the United Nations is no more than decoration, a vine that covers hard stone. As remarked earlier, the number of refugees in the world is growing and they are now predominantly from Africa, the Middle East, Latin America and Asia. If they are to be resettled, there will need to be major changes in the attitudes of all nations, especially in racial and cultural tolerance, as the backgrounds of the refugees are likely to be very different from those of people in the probable countries of resettlement.

Both the fierce nationalism of Vietnam and the nationalism of affluence of the industrial democracies have been shown by the story of the boat people to be inadequate. Vietnam's nationalism, which is one of its strengths, causes tension within itself and uneasiness without: it is not a model for developing countries in South-East Asia, which generally have a more pragmatic attitude to international influences and currents of life in the wider world. One of the several tragic consequences of Vietnam's conflict with China is that its nationalism, which needs to be moderated, has been inflamed.

The nationalism of the western democracies, which makes them loath to share their wealth and social organization with people from poor countries – so that they will accept refugees with racial or cultural backgrounds similar to their own, but not from Africa or Asia – is no model for the rest of this century, either. Communist states have perhaps the poorest record of all, although, as the traffic is away from them rather than towards them, they have not yet been seriously tested. Communist states have played politics with refugees, admitting only those whose ideological credentials are acceptable and ignoring the international problem as such. One of the interesting effects of the exodus of refugees from Indo-China is that, because its causes are complex, and praise and blame is not easily apportionable, and because also its political and strategic implications are sensitive and serious, the communist states, including the USSR, have been drawn into discussions. This, at least, is hopeful because it is unlikely that Vietnam will be the last country in which a refugee crisis follows revolution.

During the writing of the story of the boat people, analogies and metaphors kept coming to mind – and being discarded. The Nazi analogy did not fit. The Gulag archipelago did not fit. The similarity between Chinese refugees and Jewish refugees did not hold. In the end, only one possible parallel remained and, as it is a hopeful one, it can bring the book to a close.

In 1945, millions of refugees left the new communist countries of Europe, after decades of political and social turmoil and the devastation of the second world war, in a dramatic exodus that seemed painfully endless at the time. Some of them, now citizens of other countries, return occasionally for holidays and to visit relatives in the lands of their birth. Many of them have enriched the life of their adopted country. When they visit their homeland, they are protected by the authority of their adopted state and their new citizenship is protected by international law. Despite the tumultuous events that made them refugees, civilization and humanity have crept back.

It is the hope of this book that the boat people have the same prospect, and may be able to return to Vietnam one day. And Kampucheans too – if their country still exists.

Maps

South-East Asia
Resettlement

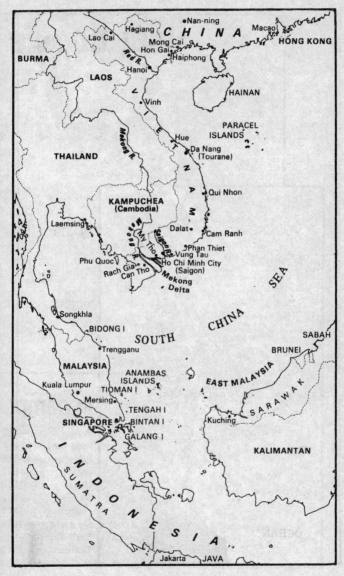

Boat people

5

22

SOUTH
KOREA

JAPAN

4

18

MACAU
HONG
KONG

THAILAND

PHILIPPINES

BRUNEI

MALAYSIA

SINGAPORE

INDONESIA

In camps

Brunei	—20
Hong Kong	—66,419
Indonesia	—46,189
Japan	—531
Macau	—3256
Malaysia	—66,222
Philippines	—5540
Singapore	—1098
South Korea	—42
Thailand	—9112
TOTAL	—198,537

around the world

Resettled

#	Country		#	Country	
1	Australia	— 17,571	14	Malaysia	— 8
2	Austria	— 134	15	Netherlands	— 290
3	Belgium	— 230	16	New Zealand	— 735
4	Brazil	— 37	17	Norway	— 799
5	Canada	— 7429	18	Paraguay	— 31
6	Denmark	— 270	19	Sweden	—267
7	France	— 5527	20	Switzerland	— 876
8	Germany	— 2595	21	UK	— 2505
9	Greece	— 44	22	US	— 53,815
10	Hong Kong	— 149		Others	— 73
11	Israel	— 168		Repat. and	
12	Italy	— 100		Deaths	— 81
13	Luxembourg	— 45		Total	— 93,778

Based on UNHCR figures as on 31 July, 1979

Chronology

1975

April — Phnom Penh, capital of Cambodia, captured by Khmer Rouge forces, who later rename the country Democratic Kampuchea.
Saigon falls to Vietnam people's army. About 130 000 Vietnamese leave with Americans. Provisional revolutionary government of the republic of South Vietnam established.

June — 'Re-education' begins of members of defeated armed forces and former administration. 'New economic zones' announced; partial ban on private trade.

August — United States vetoes application by the two Vietnamese governments to join the United Nations.

December — Coldest winter in Vietnam for twenty years, followed by drought.
The number of boat people in 1975 was 377.

1976

April — Elections to new national assembly (249 deputies from north, 243 from south).

July — Vietnam formally reunified and named Socialist Republic of Vietnam.

December — Fourth congress of Vietnam communist party. Policy of 'gradualism' in south is confirmed.
The number of boat people at the end of 1976 was 5619.

1977

January to March — Severe cold followed by drought heavily reduces grain yields.

July	Vietnam and Laos sign 25-year treaty of friendship and co-operation.
	Border disagreements between Vietnam and Kampuchea.
August	Worst typhoon season for thirty years.
	Rice deficit of over 1 300 000 tonnes.
October	Vietnam appeals for emergency food aid, and alleges China is supplying military aid to Kampuchea.
December	Heavy fighting along Vietnam-Kampuchea border.
	Vietnamese troops advance on Phnom Penh, then withdraw; Hanoi calls for talks.
	The number of boat people at the end of 1977 was 21 276.

1978

January	Peking issues statement of policy on 'overseas Chinese', calling for 'the broadest patriotic united front' among them.
March	Hanoi nationalizes remaining businesses (mostly ethnic Chinese) in south.
	Amalgamation of dual (north and south) currencies.
April	Ethnic Chinese in northern Vietnam enter China because of rumours of war between Vietnam and China over Kampuchea.
May	China accuses Vietnam of persecuting Chinese residents; terminates seventy-two aid projects in northern Vietnam.
June	Vietnam applies to join Communist Council for Mutual Economic Assistance (COMECON) whose members are Soviet Union, east European countries, Cuba, Mongolia.
July	China cancels all remaining aid to Vietnam, withdraws technicians; seals border to refugees from Vietnam, claiming has accepted 160 000.
August	Japan and China sign treaty of peace and friendship.
September	First seagoing freighter, the *Southern Cross*, with about 1200 refugees, leaves southern Vietnam; beaches on Indonesian island.

Stalemate between China and Vietnam on whether 1.7 million ethnic Chinese in Vietnam should be considered citizens of Vietnam or China.

October   Most severe flooding in Vietnamese history; 1978 rice crop is 7.5 million tonnes short.

November   Vietnam and Soviet Union sign a 25-year treaty of friendship and co-operation.

December   United States and China agree to establish diplomatic relations.
Vietnam invades Kampuchea.
The number of boat people at the end of 1978 was 106 489.

1979

January   Vietnamese forces occupy Phnom Penh; China-supported Pol Pot régime replaced by the Heng Samrin government, friendly to Hanoi.

February   China invades Vietnam.

March   China announces phased withdrawal from Vietnamese border provinces. Vietnam announces general mobilization.

April to   Number of boat refugee arrivals in neighbouring countries
June   rises from 26 602 in April to 51 139 in May and 56 941 in June. Chinese refugees from Vietnam entering China reach 250 000.

July   United Nations conference in Geneva considers problem of Indo-Chinese refugees; Hanoi promises to halt flow.
By 31 July 1979 the number of boat people was 292 315.

Index

Index

Index